The
High-Country
Backpacker

The
High-Country
Backpacker

DONA AGOSTI

WINCHESTER PRESS
TULSA, OKLAHOMA

Library of Congress Cataloging in Publication Data
Agosti, Dona.
The high-country backpacker.

Bibliography: p. 241
Includes index.
1. Backpacking.   2. Mountaineering. I. Title.
GV199.6.A35   796.5'1   81-24082
ISBN 0-87691-366-4   AACR2

Published by Winchester Press
1421 South Sheridan
P.O. Box 1260
Tulsa, Oklahoma 74101

Book design by Janice L. Merz

Printed in United States of America

1 2 3 4 5   86 85 84 83 82

This book is gratefully dedicated to Lino, long suffering husband; and to Jan, Ann, Tam, Jon, Tim, Tom, and Dave, who shared the trail with their Mom.

ACKNOWLEDGMENTS

Sincere thanks go to my brother, Joe Wolking, whose big idea started it all; Father Dick Tero for encouragement and help in the beginning; Rodman Wilson, M.D., who helped with the chapter on health and the high-country; Paul Denkewalter, owner of Alaska Mountaineering and Hiking, who read the manuscript and made many good suggestions; Ted Fathauer and Elliott Barske, of the National Weather Service, who advised me on the weather chapter; and John Nevin, Emile and Pierce McIntosh, Kay Bielawski, Pat Klouda, Jean McDowell and countless other Mountaineering Club of Alaska members who have backpacked with me. These MCA folks not only put up with the rigors of the terrain—they put up with me!

CONTENTS

FOREWORD

When Dona asked me to write the foreword to her book, I wanted to know why she didn't ask someone important to write it. She said, "That's why I asked you."

She's right, you know. In Alaska there isn't anyone more important to you than a good friend. On the trail, that importance is magnified in direct proportion to the problems and perils one encounters. Heaven only knows, Dona and I have been through a few of those in our six years of backpacking together. Of course, the delights and joys of backcountry travel are magnified by sharing with a good friend.

I hope this book will not be one of the myriad of hiking books that you pick up, glance through, and toss aside. This one is different because its author is different. Dona isn't a young person trying to "find herself" in the wilderness or a macho type opting for wilderness instead of work-a-day responsibilities. She is, rather, a mother of seven in her early fifties who didn't start backpacking until she was forty-four years old. Dona had "found herself" long before then, and she knew there was no use hiding out in the wilds. With seven kids at home, one of them was bound to find her.

There is a message in *The High-Country Backpacker* for the "just folks" population—those people pushing forty or fifty (or who have quit counting) whose cocktail circuit just isn't cutting it. That message is, You can make your life better if you really want to. Among Dona's amusing anecdotes you will find good down-to-earth advice on beginning backpacking, alpine hiking, climbing, and skiing. But more than that, reading this book can give you encouragement to open the door to a world you might have thought was out of reach; it will show you that the backpacking business is for everyone. Prudent preparation, reliance on nature, and use of your own ingenuity can give you a feeling of self-worth that will spill happiness over into your family life and your work. No matter if the peak you conquer is an 800-foot hill or a 20,000-foot mountain, you'll feel better for having tried it.

Bless you, Dona, for writing this book. Those among us who call you friend can only be thankful you didn't tell all you know about our hiking escapades.

Emile McIntosh
Anchorage, Alaska

PREFACE

Back in the early 1970s, when backpacking and counter-culture shared the same sentence, you could easily attract attention at a cocktail party. Simply tell the other guests you were a backpacker. Even better, if you walked into a restaurant with a pack on your back, the lull in the conversation was deafening. And once, when my hiking group boarded the railroad at Lake Bennett, Yukon Territory, after five days climbing the Chilkoot Trail, we were met by lethal looks from a horde of pant-suited, gray-haired ladies and their husbands, just off the tour boat at Skagway, who had preempted *our* reservations. Mind you, we didn't smell bad; those folks just didn't understand.

I like to contrast these earlier reactions with the present-day backpacking mania. Talk to the outdoor club leaders about numbers. Ask the sporting-goods store owners about gross sales. Read about the industrial chemists scrambling to rearrange molecules into lighter, warmer, inexpensive insulation. Or speak with any of the thousands who have found renewal in a day or week or month in the backcountry.

If you'd like to know *who* is hiking, ask the group who walked seventy-five miles with me through the Arctic Wildlife Range. They were three housewives, three school teachers, five lawyers, one architect, and an engineer. Query the group with whom I explored the mountains of Kodiak Island, Alaska, and you'll find a priest, three doctors, a computer engineer, an interior decorator, an IRS accountant, an engineer, and three teenagers. Though their professions and backgrounds were varied, ask any one of them to describe his feelings about backpacking and you will find unusual unanimity. They'll speak of renewal, therapy, peace. They'll talk about challenges met and self-doubts erased. They will most certainly mention the scares and discomforts, but they'll remember the good times, too.

I can feel uniquely smug and cozy after a cloudburst when I realize that I am still warm and dry in my sleeping bag and tent. I know the sense of accomplishment that comes from crossing miles of trailless mountain and valley and finding the tarn exactly where the map said it is. And there is more. Call it exhilaration, emotionalism, call it spiritual. Log books record the ecstasy of bagging a summit, but I like to think of it not so much as conquering the mountain as achieving a union with it. Life's meanings seem to focus sharply up there. Could it be the symbolism of peaks and valleys, of reaching for new heights and succeeding? Or is it the sudden realization that Somebody's in charge and looking out for His universe?

I find this entry in my log book for August 3, 1976, written after a day trip from base camp to a ridge overlooking the Arrigetch Peaks in the Brooks Range of Alaska:

Today Merrilyn and I climbed on hands and knees up the steep gully to a high point on the ridge overlooking Arrigetch Valley. We could see the complete circle of granite peaks and all the inside ridges which form Aquarius Creek and its feeder stream at valley end. What a stupendously rewarding sight! This was what we had come to see, why we had flown 450 miles and hiked for three days through bush, bog and brownies. The peaks were truly unique granite spires, a rarity in this land of crumbling sandstone and limestone. We traced the unusual shapes and could understand why eastern climbers had chosen names such as The Maidens, the Camel, Turkey Bluff. As Merrilyn and I sat in the hot Arctic sun seeing more and more detail in the mind-boggling facade before us, I realized that my feelings of the moment were why I climbed mountains.

Several years later I was thumbing through old issues of *Scree,* the monthly publication of the Mountaineering Club of Alaska, and I found Dr. Bill Brant's eloquent account of the same trip:

The real memory of Arrigetch is not described in technical details. There is a special aura about the place that eases the mind and body into timelessness and tranquility. Many previous visitors have mentioned it in their writings. It seems to arise from overwhelming quiet, a minuteness of being in a world of massive dimension, the beauty of deep aqua lakes and lush multicolor lichen growth on huge boulders in mystical Aquarius Valley, and the peaks themselves, jagged facades of rock ever-changing in the play of sun and clouds. The aura is far easier experienced than described, but leaves a mellowness unlike any I have experienced before.

Now, perhaps, you can understand why a fifty-five-year-old mother of seven children would spend her waning years in the great outdoors. I began my backcountry experience in search of therapeutic peace and quiet when my youngest child entered kindergarten, eleven years and some two thousand miles ago. As hiking chairman for the Mountaineering Club of Alaska, I led large groups through many wilderness areas and soon realized that my lively experience as a homemaker was most relevant to the trail.

Being prepared on the trail was akin to being prepared at home. Handling a sprained ankle in the Wrangell Mountains was just a tad more complicated than rushing a kid off to the emergency room in Anchorage, but you used the same book. Accurate route finding, city or alpine, drew on a common source of expertise: good research and the right maps. A happy camp and happy home were similarly achieved with strong but diplomatic leadership, care that a group was not pushed beyond the endurance of its weakest member, encouragement of the less experienced, and soothing of ruffled feathers.

And now, you can also understand why I would write a book about mountain backpacking. If you want to backpack, but are hesitant, I hope you will find inspiration in these pages. If you've used up all the flatland and want to step a little higher, this book will give you confidence. After all, look who's talking.

Dona Agosti
Anchorage, Alaska

GETTING READY FOR THE HIGH-COUNTRY

Whatever their reasons, thousands are heading into the great outdoors, carrying their homes on their backs. There are some differences in style of home and destination of owner.

A beginning day hiker carries a daypack, meanders along established trails, and learns all about blisters and the necessities he forgot to include. He sometimes shows up in shorts and sneakers, without windbreaker or parka. His trips are usually in wooded country in lowlands, or at lower elevations in the mountains. If he overcomes his deficiencies, the day hiker graduates to the category of overnighter with framepack, sleeping bag, and tent.

With this additional equipment, the hiker gains weight, but also mobility, and can add both altitude and mileage to his hiking repertoire. He's now ready for above-timberline, or alpine, backpacking—my favorite type and the main subject of this book. There are yet other heights to which one can soar, including technical mountain climbing and winter backpacking, both of which also will be discussed in later chapters.

If you're new at the game, you may learn something in the pages ahead to ease your entry into the great outdoors. If you're an old-timer, there may be a new trick or two for you as well. Whether you're coming from the Appalachians, the Cascades, or the Rockies, I would venture to guess that your feelings will not be too different from your fellow hiker in the Sierras or the Alaska Range. True, the high point may not always require the same amount of heavenward movement, but the rewards seem to be strikingly similar.

CHAPTER ONE

LEARNING ABOUT MOUNTAINS

A mountain is more than just height. Although the highest peak in the Arrigetch in Alaska is only about 7,190 feet, it's true arctic alpine country. But in New Mexico, you would have to climb to around 12,000 feet to find similar conditions. In the San Juans of southwestern Colorado, the timberline occurs at about 11,500 feet, which is higher than is common in the northern Rockies. On the otherhand, you could be above the trees at 5,000 feet in the White Mountains of New Hampshire.

John Jerome in his book *On Mountains: Thinking About Terrain* says that characterizing conditions in the high mountains as "polar" may not be too far-fetched. He uses a unique imagery to describe his theory that in the middle latitudes mountains are very similar. He builds two imaginary mountains with their bases at the equator and their peaks at the poles. While he admits that not all mountains arise from equatorial rain forests, he does believe that starting half way up the hemisphere in the middle latitudes one would encounter very similar conditions everywhere. For instance, he says the vegetation zones that march up a mountainside compare directly to those you would encounter if you traveled from the middle latitudes to the pole. Grassland turns into broad-leafed forest, which in turn gives way to needle-leafed forest, which in turn grows more sparse and filled with miniature trees. Finally, the forest dies out completely and is replaced by tundra, dwarf species of flowers and grasses, mosses and lichens. In the end, only snow and ice remain. I like Jerome's analogy and think it's valid in the middle latitudes, except possibly on volcanic islands.

Jerome also says that timberline is never surgically precise and that cold is more significant than altitude in determining what grows in mountains. Despite extreme winter and summer temperatures in the Brooks Range of Alaska (I've recorded 100 degrees Fahrenheit in the summer and

3

The mountain environment is determined by latitude as well as altitude. Compare the landscape (*left*) in Rocky Mountain National Park (10,000 feet, latitude 40 degrees north) with that (*right*) in the Wrangell Mountains of Alaska (3,500 feet, latitude 60 degrees north). In general, the farther away from the equator, the lower the altitude at which alpine conditions exist. (*Photos by Bill Wakeland.*)

minus 80 degrees in the winter), its flora is strikingly similar to alpine areas in the lower forty-eight states. Moss campion, lowbush cranberries, crowberries, sedge tussocks, dwarf willow and birch, lichen, and labrador tea cover the ground during the three months of summer. Nature seems to have compensated for the arctic blasts by prolonging the hours of sunlight.

No, you won't find a sequoia in the Wrangells of Alaska, but you'll find some good-sized spruce and hemlock in southeastern Alaska. You won't find deer on the arctic plains, but their cousins, the caribou, do roam there. The black bear in the Pecos is as formidable as its brother in the Brooks Range. I'll even wager that the grouse in the Appalachians flushes as noisily as the Alaska spruce hen.

But I won't press the point. There are admittedly a few differences among mountains and high-country trails. Wilderness in Canada and Alaska conjures up images of uncharted trails and cabinless backcountry; in other regions the "wilderness" is rather more settled and subject to regulation. Fortunately, you can learn quite a lot about all the possibilities right in your own home town.

■ Trail Guides and Maps

Today's backpacker can walk into his local library or bookstore and find a how-to or where-to book on any phase of wilderness walking. There

4

is even a bibliography of books called *Outdoor Recreation* by Robert G. Schipf. It lists sources for trail guides for areas throughout the United States, including the Blue Ridge Mountains, the San Gabriels, the Apache Trail, the Potomac Trail, the High Sierras, and others. Your library might also have a copy of *Great Outdoors Guide* by Val Landi. It contains thousands of sources for maps, guides, and trail information for every state and province in North America.

Backpacker Books publishes a catalog with over one hundred titles, including hiking guides for fifteen states, Canada, and foreign locations. To obtain this catalog, write to Wilderness Bookstore, Bedford Hills, New York 10507. Both the Wilderness Press and Signpost Books publish many excellent trail guides. Their addresses are: Wilderness Press, 2400 Bancroft Way, Berkeley, California 94704; Signpost Books, 8912 192nd St., S.W., Edmonds, Washington 98020.

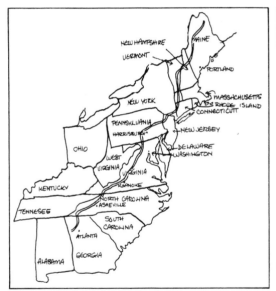

The two longest trail systems in the continental United States are the Appalachian Trail, in the east, and the Pacific Crest Trail, in the west.

The Appalachian Trail Conference (1718 N. Street, N.W., Washington, D.C. 20036) is a source for guides to that 2,000-mile trail from Maine to Georgia. The Appalachian trail is probably the best known of all trails. It's western counterpart, the 2,300-mile Pacific Crest Trail, follows the high ridges of the Cascades in Washington state, passes Mt. Hood in Oregon, reaches the high ridges of the Sierra Nevadas in California, and finally ends at the Mexico border. Information can be obtained from Pacific Crest Trail

THE HIGH-COUNTRY BACKPACKER

System Conference, Hotel Green, Pasadena, California 91109. Another newer route, not yet a trail, is the 3,000-mile Rocky Mountain Route, which follows the Continental Divide from Mexico to Canada. The Colorado Mountain Club (2530 W. Alameda Ave., Denver, Colorado 80219) can give you the latest on it. You can get information on 4,000 miles of Pennsylvania trails from Keystone Trails Association, P.O. Box 144, Concordville, Pennsylvania 19331 (enclose 25 cents).

If I were a beginning backpacker, the very first thing I would do is subscribe to *Backpacker*. Not only is this bimonthly magazine filled with informative articles, but its Weekend Wilderness column keeps the urban hiker up to date on nearby backpacking getaways. The magazine features articles on equipment and techniques for mountaineering, kayaking and canoeing, skiing, and backpacking, along with reviews of new products, which alone is worth the subscription price.

Another source of where-to-hike information is your local mountaineering club. Don't be intimidated by the word mountaineering. Most clubs now have hiking sections. However, the word club can describe groups ranging from the 300-member Mountaineering Club of Alaska, whose volunteers put out a mimeographed newsletter each month, to institutions such as The Colorado Mountain Club which has clubrooms and a paid secretary in Denver, twelve local groups throughout the state, and publishes a very professional and informative schedule of hikes. The Mountaineers (719 Pike St., Seattle, Washington 98101) is another biggy group with some 8,000 members. The Seattle Mountaineers (P.O. Box 122, Seattle, Washington 98111) has 7,000 members and emphasizes climbing and winter sports. The Adirondack Mountain Club (172 Ridge Street, Glen Falls, New York 12801) has 9,000 members. And the granddaddy of them all is the Appalachian Mountain Club (5 Joy Street, Boston, Massachusetts 02108) with a whopping 25,000 members and fifteen state groups.

Unless these clubs maintain a permanent club room, it is not always easy to locate them. For instance, the Alaska group has a post office box only and no listing in the telephone directory. It does publish its monthly meeting date and slide show program in the local papers, which may be true in other communities with smaller clubs. As a last resort, you could ask the local tourist bureau or Chamber of Commerce.

I have learned a lot from the people at our local equipment shops. One even has a coffee and tall-tales corner complete with books. Since most of the salespeople in such stores are mountaineers, they're a good source of information on local clubs and places to hike.

Then there's the United States Government. Lots of it. In the phone book, start with United States Government, Interior, Department of. Then let your fingers walk to National Park Service. Call, write, or visit them if you're interested in guides to trails in national parks or monuments. U.S.

Fish and Wildlife Service handles the ranges and wilderness areas. These government agency folks also write lots of regulations and issue permits and campsite reservations. But more about that later.

While paging through the U. S. Government listings in your telephone directory, you may also see a listing for Agriculture, Department of. Look for the Forest Service recreation listing. Here is another good source for trail guides, wilderness cabins (walk-in or fly-in), and avalanche forecasts. And they issue wilderness permits also.

Then flip to your own state listings and look for the cover name for your state park system. A word of warning: Many state park systems are miniature versions of the regulation-minded national parks, so check to see if permits and reservations are necessary and if there are backcountry camping regulations.

You also need topographic maps of the areas you plan to visit. The "inch to the mile" maps are my choice for areas without trails because of their detail. When only a "four miles to the grid" map is available, aerial photographs or satellite photos may help to supplement the map. Maps and photographs can be obtained from the United States Geological Service

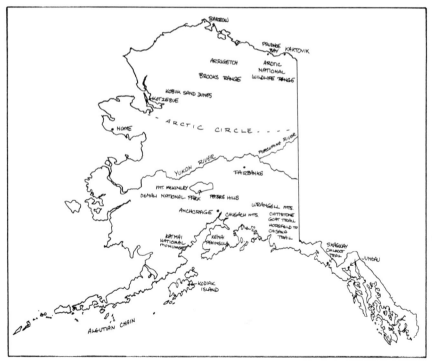

Alaska contains a wide variety of wilderness backpacking terrain. Major geographic features, as well as areas mentioned in the text, are shown on this map.

7

(USGS). If you plan to hike in states east of the Mississippi River, write Distribution Section, USGS, 1200 Eads Street, Arlington, Virginia 22202. If you'll be west of the Mississippi, write Distribution Section, USGS, Box 25286, Federal Center, Denver, Colorado, 80225. For Alaskan maps write Alaskan Distribution Section, USGS, Box 12, Federal Building, 101 12th Avenue, Fairbanks, Alaska 99701. Canadian contour and topo maps are available from Map Distribution Office, Dept. of Mines and Technical Surveys, Ottawa, Ontario, Canada K1A OH3.

If you are not sure of the name (designation) of the map you need, ask for a free index map of the general area. This is an overlay map indicating the topographic maps available for a specific area. For instance, the index map for Alaska covers the entire state and is divided into rectangles or quadrangles, each containing twenty-four subsections labeled with section name, subsection number, and date of survey. Some of the larger quadrangles, such as the Arrigetch Peaks mentioned earlier, have no subsection maps. When you hike in an area with only a quadrangle map, the compass is put to constant use because topographic details are compressed and not as clear as they are on larger-scale maps. Don't be confused by the twenty-four section designation. This has nothing to do with townships which are divided into thirty-six sections. (I only say this because I was confused.)

When you have determined which subsection maps you need, pick them up in person from one of the regional offices (see Appendix II for locations) or order them by mail from the distribution centers. Index maps are free, but the quads and others cost about $1.25. These same maps are sold in some retail stores at a slightly higher price.

When my planned trip covers several maps, I cut off the edges of each and tape them together. I trace the route with a yellow marker (you can see through the yellow line), then fold the map to fit my pack map pocket and place it in a Ziploc bag. To protect the map even more, cover it with clear Contact paper, or with paint-on waterproofing material, which is now available.

More detailed information about reading maps and finding your way will be covered in Chapter 4.

■ Regulations and Permits

If you happen to select a popular wilderness area for your outing, you will quickly learn that the demand greatly exceeds carrying capacity. For instance, your chance of getting a permit in the Grand Canyon is one in twenty. There can be no substitutions, and the rangers make sure you're you by checking your driver's license and birth certificate. You also carry out your sewage! In the Great Smoky Mountains National Park in Tennessee permits are required for all overnight backcountry camping, are issued no more than thirty days in advance, and must be affixed to pack. Camping parties are limited to eight persons. In contrast, no permits are required in Idaho's Selway-Bitterroot wilderness.

In Alaska's 8.9-million-acre Arctic National Wildlife Range, permits are required. Before taking a group into the Range in 1978, I wrote for information and received a list of regulations, which included a ban on campfires and the admonition to carry out used toilet paper. Our seventy-five-mile trip took us up the Hulahula drainage, over the Continental Divide, and through several other drainages to the south slope of the Brooks Range. The rivers usually flowed through wide valleys with broad sandbars. Adjoining flatland often contained boggy tundra and tussocks. The alpine meadows were green. All these conditions made me wonder why campfires were forbidden, especially if one was carrying used toilet paper in his pack. I could only surmise that new blood, fresh from the crowded parks of the lower forty-eight had invaded the management level of the Arctic National Wildlife Range.

Backcountry use permit must be affixed to your pack when hiking on federal lands. Regulations and permit requirements vary, so it's wise to contact the area you wish to visit ahead of time.

I encountered a similar point of view when I arranged for a group of thirty club members to visit the Katmai National Monument one year. I worked out plans with a most accommodating superintendent many months before the trip. All proceeded efficiently through the commercial flight, the charter floatplane flight, and bus to the trailhead. The group soon spread out and was lost in the vastness of this lava desert. Winds erased our sand tracks within hours. We returned to the trailhead several days later and, while waiting for our bus, were confronted by a lady park ranger who proceeded to rake me over the coals for having the colossal temerity to bring so large a group into the monument, thereby spoiling its wilderness value. Bear in mind that only a few hundred people visited the monument that year. The total numbers to visit the Arctic Wildlife Range in 1979 were about six hundred. Compare this with the nearly 2½ million visitors to the 2.2-million-acre Yellowstone National Park in 1978 or the 1½ million people who visited Glacier National Park in Montana, an area one ninth the size of the Range.

While we're on the subject of regulations, one which is almost unknown to many is the common requirement to camp at least one hundred feet away from a water source. Camping is also forbidden within one mile of a paved road or nature trail, or within sight or sound of the trail, or in any meadow in the Crater Lake National Park. In other words, make yourself invisible to passing hikers. This rule becomes somewhat impossible above timberline, but common sense and concern for your fellow hiker should prevail.

Another instance of extreme rules and regulations was reported in *Backpacker* (October / November 1978). The authors of an article about hiking through Baxter State Park in Maine mention an example of ridiculous protection overkill with respect to climbing Katahdin Peak. In 1976 the peak was closed more days than it was open because of cloudy days, no climbing before 7 A.M. or after 10 A.M. etc., etc. Said the authors, "Regulations like these (the list of winter climbing rules is unbelievable) have led many freedom loving hikers and climbers to avoid the park entirely. We've heard people say, 'Baxter Park's as bad as McKinley.' But not even on McKinley does someone tell you when you can and cannot climb."

By now you get the point. Learn the rules of the game and secure the necessary permits in advance, and save yourself the trauma of a shattered vacation.

■ Matching Hike to Hiker

Planning a trip is half the fun, but sometimes advance information is misleading as the following letter from friends of mine in California illustrates:

The climb up Mt. Lassen was such a great experience, we decided to plan a trip south to include a climb up Mt. Whitney. It was really exciting to plan such a trip and we enjoyed that part as much as the trip itself. Unfortunately, the literature we were able to get did not properly prepare us for the climb. It was described as an easy two-day trip. We feel, had we known how steep the first day's climb was to be, we would have divided the

Dense cover like this in the Chitistone flats in the Wrangell Mountains and many other factors affect the difficulty of a trail and the time required to hike it. (*Photo by Bill Wakeland.*)

trip into three days and could then have reached the top. All of us were affected by the altitude, especially Ed, who started having chills. Finally, after piling on extra clothing and getting into his sleeping bag with his heavy jacket, hat and gloves on, he got warmed up enough to get some sleep. None of us slept much that night, the wind was very strong and kept blowing our tent in on us. The other two in our party . . . decided to push on to the top and arrived on the peak about mid-day, the second day. We enjoyed it very much, even though we couldn't help feeling some disappointment in falling short of our objective.

This story is an example of why it is so difficult to evaluate trail difficulty for various skill levels. When I helped research the hiking book *55 Ways to the Wilderness in South Central Alaska*, editor Helen Nienhueser and I spent considerable time trying to calculate hiking time based on trail length and degree of difficulty. We tried to arrive at some figure midway between the speed of a decrepit oldster and a macho teenager. I wore a pedometer but learned it wasn't much use on the ups and downs of Alaska trails. Larger mountaineering clubs tend to use a conservative approach in their evaluations. I find, however, that government trail guides use the word *easy* much too loosely.

When planning your trip, I suggest you consider your degree of experience, the altitude gain, and the map distance before you estimate the time it will take to finish. If you're moving above nine thousand feet, be sure to include acclimatization time. (More on this in Chapter 14.)

Ingenious backpackers will find a long-lost relative or old school chum in the area in which they plan to hike and wangle an invitation to visit along with local trail information. Getting to the trailhead can be a major logistical problem if you're not driving your own car. Which brings us to the subject of how to get there.

CHAPTER TWO

HOW TO GET THERE

Act one, scene one: A kitchen in Brooklyn, Wichita, or Oxnard. Props: Kitchen table, chair, telephone, directory, Rand-McNally, trail guides, maps, backpacking magazines. Open on puzzled backpacker.

So why the puzzlement? You've been hiking for a few years. You went to the Adirondacks, or the Ozarks, or the San Gabriels last summer and came back to brag about it. You drove your car to the trailhead, parked it, remembered where you put the keys, and came back to it a week later. This year you're ready for a little Class D stuff—more than 15 miles, altitude gain up to 3,500 feet, scree, steep grass, other rough terrain. Problem is, that stuff needs a mountain to go with it, and there aren't any in Brooklyn or Wichita or Oxnard.

Enter transportation to trailhead. Fast transportation. A two-week vacation doesn't allow much horsing around with automobile unless you live in Denver or Fresno or Seattle.

Enter airplane. Shopping around for the best airline fare is in these days. Don't depend on your favorite travel agency to do all the research—they've got competitors too. Rising fuel prices have resulted in a new phenomenom: The airlines raise their prices the first of each month. Beat the system by buying your ticket six months ahead (reservations alone won't hold the ticket price). Check out group rates for ten or more; then find nine other people. Ask about tours. These rates are even better, but backpacking tours are not all that plentiful and some have an outrageous price tag.

Guide services are listed in outdoor magazines, as are charter air services. Sometimes, government information brochures will give the names of charter pilots in bush areas. Major airlines can usually direct you to local charters, but drag their feet on arranging reservations because it can't be

13

done by computer. Reaching charter pilots is not always easy because many take a little time off in January or February, about the time you're trying to contact them. As a last resort, look up the area code and ask the information operator for listings under air charters. If the operator can't give you a telephone number, try sending a letter to the pilot with just the village address. Most are very well known in their areas. (The Alaskan bush pilot ranks somewhere between God and the President.)

All of this effort is superfluous if all you need is a bus or taxi ride to the trailhead. Heaven forbid that you might have to walk to the beginning of your hike. Lucky those who can be dropped off on one side of a mountain and be picked up fifty miles away on the opposite side. Shuttling cars from trailhead to trailend can be a big pain.

■ Dealing with Your Bush Pilot

Once you do track down a bush pilot, set a firm date for your arrival. Ask what kind of plane he has, how much he charges per hour, and what he estimates to be your flight time to the drop point. Some pilots quote flat fees; others calculate using tenths of an hour. For example, the fee for six minutes is one tenth of the hourly fee of $160, so six minutes of flying time would cost you $16. Usually only the airborne time—from when the wheels leave the ground to when they touch again—is counted. This eliminates hav-

The Cessna 206 is being loaded for a fly-in trip to a remote trailhead in the Wrangell Mountains. The low-slung belly of the plane holds gear. (*Photo by Bill Wakeland.*)

Good landing sites like this one at Glacier Creek in the Wrangells are not plentiful in many backcountry areas. (*Photo by Bill Wakeland.*)

ing to pay for taxi time. There is one catch: You have to pay for the pilot's return time, so double the one-way cost.

Also ask how many passengers the plane can carry. Some pilots with six-place planes will carry only four passengers and gear because they are severely regulated by law as to weight limits. A wise trip leader will obtain the weights of each hiker in his group beforehand and use the weight total, rather than the number of persons, to calculate the number of charter trips required to fly his group in or out. I was considerably chagrined recently when, because of weight restrictions, our pilot permitted only four passengers and gear rather than the five I had planned. This resulted in an additional flight and added cost for each member of my party.

Remember to talk over landing sites with your pilot. Ask if there is a possibility that a sandbar might be under water on the date you plan to fly in. If you're traveling by floatplane, discuss whether the lake or river might be too low on your scheduled date of arrival. Then discuss alternatives.

I learned about landing sites the hard way on one trip when hot weather had melted the high-country snow, inundating our planned pickup landing strip. Our pilot radioed a pilot friend and had him drop a map to us indicating a new pickup point—this one ten miles upstream. This might not have been so serious had we not been in the vast wilderness of the Arctic Wildlife Range. Not only was it difficult for the pilot to find us—he flew

Carrying enough food for a lengthy backcountry trip may be difficult. One solution is to cache some food near the trailhead drop-off point, as these hikers are doing at Glacier Creek "International Airport." (*Photo by Bill Wakeland.*)

over several times before he spotted our camp—but landing sites are not that plentiful in many wilderness areas. Had there not been an alternate site, we might have had to signal for a helicopter rescue because the nearest villages were many swamps, mountains, and days away.

It is often difficult for a city dweller to comprehend the isolation of a wilderness area. This is why it is so important to give your pilot very specific information about your route. If you can, sketch your route on his navigation map. See that he writes down your pickup time. Have an emergency plan of action if you fail to make the pickup point on time or if weather prevents his landing. Discuss signals. You might agree to use those appearing on the back of a fishing license. Or give him a copy of those illustrated in Chapter 4.

This also is the time to confirm locations where food will be airdropped. Other backpackers may have tricks that I don't know, but I have trouble carrying more than a seven-day food supply on my back. Airdrops really ease the burden. Pilots have instructed me to pack food loosely, possibly in plastic "popcorn," and to tie the cardboard box with an easy-to-grasp rope handle. Anyone who is flying a Super Cub with one hand and throwing boxes out the window with the other wants something that's easy to grab.

16

Remember to discuss what type payment will be accepted. Believe it or not, Mastercharge and Visa or even traveler's checks, have little value in an isolated village with no banking facility. Cash is the name of the game there, and no fifty-dollar bills, please. Change is in short supply at the local grocery store. (I just read a story about a hunting guide who, after six months, was still trying to get a check given to him by a German client through the international money mill.)

■ In and Around the Airport

Before checking in at your airport, be sure all pockets of your pack are securely zipped. Waist straps should be buckled and no loose paraphernalia should dangle from the frame. All fuel should be emptied from your mountain stove and fuel containers. Leave your butane or propane cartridges at home because the airlines will not permit fuel of any type to be carried on passenger flights. This means you will have to buy fuel near the trailhead, so check out the availability of fuel at your charter site when you discuss flight arrangements with the pilot. Most village stores stock white gas or kerosene, but butane or propane cartridges are not always available.

Airlines also ask that guns be broken down and checked as baggage.

Because commercial airlines will not carry flammable products on passenger flights, fuel for camp stoves often must be purchased in villages. In Kaktovik on the Arctic Ocean, bush pilot Walt Audi provides white gas for clients. *(Photo by Chuck Heath.)*

17

Knives also must be checked. If you have packed such items in your carry-on baggage, the security guards will ask that the item be left with the flight attendant, who will return it to you before you leave. Better to check it through with your pack.

Where do you go in a large city if you have an overnight stop? Here's where that long-lost buddy would come in handy for bed, board, and taxi, but he didn't answer your letter. Usually you can't hoist your pack and walk to the nearest motel or campground because backpackers and freeways don't merge too well. So you pop for a six-dollar ride to a nearby hostel, motel, or campground. Only the hostel movement is still in low gear in America and campgrounds in the center of a city are hard to come by. But the situation is improving.

Our daughters backpacked through Europe during their college days and used hostels ninety percent of the time. They were dismayed that U. S. cities offered no equivalent hospitality. One daughter set about to remedy the situation and Anchorage now has its first hostel under the auspices of American Youth Hostel, Inc., which is affiliated with the International Youth Hostel Federation. A booklet listing 250 hostels in the United States is available from American Youth Hostel, 1332 I Street, Washington, D. C. 20005. There is a separate handbook covering hostels in Canada. The Inter-

Floatplanes are another way to get into backcountry. Twin Otter, shown here in Katmai National Monument, carries ten passengers with packs but requires fairly deep water for landing. (*Photo by Chuck Heath.*)

national Handbook lists hostels in North America and Mexico, as well as those in other parts of the world.

Membership cards are a prerequisite for staying at a hostel and may be obtained from the American Youth Hostel office at the above address. Cost is $7 for persons under seventeen and senior citizens; $14 for others. There are special rates for families, non-profit organization groups, and life-time members.

Most hostels contain several bunks and single beds in a dormitory-style room, with separate sections for men and women. Sleeping bags are encouraged, but bedding is available for rental. Showers and limited cooking facilities are provided. Hostels open around 7 P.M. and stop registering guests about 11 P.M. Cost is from $2 to $5 per night per person. This is a saving worth considering if your budget precludes $50 per night for a hotel or motel room.

Campgrounds near major airports are rare. Centennial Park in Anchorage is six miles away on the opposite side of town. Fairbanks offers a mid-city campground, but it is usually filled during tourist season. My kids tell me that Portland has a park about twenty minutes by car from the city center. The Rand-McNally Atlas can give you some help in locating campgrounds near cities where you may have an overnight stop. The following information was gleaned from Rand-McNally for thirteen cities with airports in the mountain areas of the western United States:

Phoenix, Arizona	If you're heading towards the Sierra Ancha Mountains, the Lost Dutchman State Park might be on your way.
Salt Lake City, Utah	Pioneer Trail State Park seems close by.
Denver, Colorado	Somewhat south of Denver are Chatfield Reservation State Recreation Area and Roxborough State Park. Golden Gate Canyon State Park lies northwest.
Sheridan, Wyoming	No campsites are identified near the city.
Cody, Wyoming	Buffalo Bill State Park is a short distance west.
Pocatello, Idaho	Indian Rocks State Park is located south of this Idaho city.
Boise, Idaho	Many parks are named, but no campsites indicated.
Coeur d'Alene, Idaho	Several parks are located in the Coeur d'Alene National Forest, but none within the city.
Spokane, Washington	Riverside State Park is not too far away. If you're heading west, try Lake Sammanish State Park.

19

Seattle, Washington	Salt Water State Park is about six miles south as the crow flies, more as the car drives.
Redding, California	No campsites are shown here, but there is a bus which travels west daily into the Trinity Alps Wilderness. Driving north on Route A-5 will get you into Mt. Shasta country.
Sacramento, California	Several parks are named, but no campsites indicated.
Fresno, California	No campsites are shown.

If you want more detailed information write to the State Park Division in the capital city; to the city Chamber of Commerce or tourist bureau; or to the U.S. Forest Service or National Park Service if either has jurisdiction in the areas in which you are interested.

Once you've successfully reached the end of the commercial airline route, there's still the jog to the trailhead. In some places, surface transportation is available: bus, taxi, or a rental car. Another possibility is helicopter, though it's more expensive than surface transportation. If you're planning to use a charter service, the pilot will sometimes arrange to meet you at the airport and transport you to his hangar office, often at the same field. Solving these problems at your kitchen table saves frayed nerves and gets you on the trail with a minimum of snafu. Besides, you can enjoy the trip twice—in your kitchen and for real.

CHAPTER THREE

CONDITIONING THE BODY

Somebody's been reading my mail. I found these words by Joseph L. Sax in the February/March 1980 issue of *Backpacker*:

> To the uninitiated backpacker, a day in the woods can be, and often is, an experience of unrelieved misery. The pack is overloaded; his tender feet are blistered; he stumbles; he finds that he has climbed when he should have stayed low; or he finds himself in a marshy lowland when he should have taken the high ridge. He is alternately too hot, bundled in heavy clothes, or too cold. If it rains he is miserable. He has the wrong gear, or he has packed what he needs in the wrong place; he puts his tent where it attracts every gust of wind and rivulet of water. He can't get a fire started, or his stove fails him just when he needs it. Such experiences, familiar in one form or another to all beginners, are truly unforgiving; and when things go wrong, they do so in cascading fashion. Yet he looks around and sees others who are suffering no such miseries . . . .

Any similarity to persons living or dead is purely intentional.

Let's talk about ways to ease beginner's pains. A good percentage of hiking's thundering hordes—as many as thirty million regulars (*Newsweek* said it)—stride forth from an office on Friday night, intent on using every hour of the weekend or a two-week vacation to experience an EN-COUNTER WITH NATURE. They begin with physical bodies in varying degrees of fitness. I would like to hope that you—the high-country hopeful—learned early, and possibly painfully, that muscles need a little tender, loving care before giving them the acid test.

21

So how do you train in Brooklyn for a backpacking trip in the high mountains? Easy. Hoist your pack, take the subway to Prospect Park, and walk the trails there. (Would you believe this rural Minnesotan learned to ride a horse in Prospect Park?) Sure you'll get some funny looks, but those looks are a lot less penetrating than the ones you'll get if you poop out two miles up the trail during the big hike. Start at home running up and down stairs with a pack on your back. If the only stairs available are those in your apartment house, do it while everyone's still asleep. Try some plain old jogging around your neighborhood. Muggers should have learned by now that joggers don't carry billfolds. In my own suburban Anchorage neighborhood one sunny day in April, I counted six joggers by the house before 6 A.M. In case you haven't read one of the ten million books on the subject, start jogging slowly and work up to that New York marathon.

Fire stairs in an office or apartment building are ideal spots for pre-trip conditioning.

CONDITIONING THE BODY

In 1978, Steve Boyer and Gary Tiller climbed 54 Colorado peaks over 14,000 feet in 21 days 3 hours and 20 minutes, breaking the old record of 33 days. Before attempting this feat, Tiller ran 50 miles a week at a 7-minute-per-mile pace. Boyer ran 235 miles in 25 running days, averaging about 9 miles a day. He ran a total of 70 miles of intervals and 25 miles on steep mountain trails at elevations between 11,000 and 14,000 feet. He ran the other 140 miles at a 6-minute-per-mile pace at an elevation of 5,000 feet.

So Prospect Park doesn't have any 11,000-foot peaks. So you're not going to climb 54 peaks in 21 days either. I just want to tell you that running is not a bad way to get in shape. The basic idea of this exercise is to stabilize pulse and respiratory rates and to prevent excessive fatigue, headaches, and nausea at higher altitudes. (More on this in Chapter 14.) Although Boyer concluded that running is no guarantee against high-altitude sickness, he believes it is excellent training and a good way to maximize climbing time on vacations in the mountains. By the way, Boyer and Tiller wore lightweight, flexible-soled boots, not running shoes, and changed their boots and socks daily. Result: Not one blister.

There is another conditioning tool called yoga. I will confess that I am not a devotee, and when someone first suggested that I try it, I had a mild choking spell. Then, Eileen shared a long canoe trip with me. She was an ardent yoga fan and soon had me doing stretches and breathing and the whole bit. In camp at night, when I couldn't find Eileen, I just looked up or down the river and there she'd be sitting cross-kneed on a sandbar, getting rid of the day's kinks. I have to admit it is a simple way to eliminate the knots that occur in the neck and shoulders when carrying a heavy pack, or in the hamstrings and calves after walking all day. It is also a way to eliminate the cramping that comes from sitting in a canoe all day. So try it—you might like it.

It is not always feasible, but if you can, try to include a short weekend trip or two in your training program. If the going gets too rough, you can turn back when you've had enough, and no one but you will know. Fitness centers also have much to offer prospective packers. In addition to the general exercise routines, some of the machines zero in on key backpacking muscles. One machine is used for thigh extensions and leg curls, both of which strengthen front and back leg muscles for the uphill grind. Sit-ups on the slant board (or anywhere for that matter) strengthen back and stomach muscles. The leg press works on those calves. The bench press works out the pectoral and frontal deltoids (I think that means chest and biceps) on the upward lift and the triceps (the back arm muscles) coming down. Arm pulleys do the same, more or less, and are used by skiers to develop poling strength. The bicycling machine, if you can get it past twenty miles per hour, can do something for stamina. You know of course that you can buy a good book on exercises and do all this in your living room. The flesh is weak and misery loves company, so many hop off to the fitness center. Cross-country skiing at least once a week beats the winter blahs and starts you on the right boot come spring. I start hiking the first day a piece of bare ground shows through. There is a short period of much pain when I switch from cross-country skiing to hiking since skiing requires fewer muscles—my muscles, that is. I know the racers will disagree. But my first springtime assault of a local conditioning peak, which rises from sea level to three thousand feet in four miles, is always marked by faltering steps and pained brow. It takes several weeks to work out the thigh and calf pains.

There are those in the past-fifty bracket who would love to see the backcountry but think hiking is not for the elderly. Age can be a handicap only if you think it is. One of my lesser motives in starting to backpack ten years ago was the onset of a mild form of arthritis. Backpacking has certainly alleviated that condition for me. Just don't be discouraged if you travel with a group and don't see the leader until the end of the day. I usually say goodbye to my kids in the morning and hello again in late afternoon. Find someone to walk or ski with you at *your* speed and watch out for each other. When I "lead" a hike, I always appoint someone else, who I know is a fast walker and familiar with the route, to go ahead; I "sweep trail." This is a wonderful excuse to take my time, stopping often to rest and observe what's around me. I ignore the young machos who still have something to prove. They'll slow down some day when they realize how much they've missed.

Mom and Dad skiers can take their young ones along in this device known as the pulka, pulk, or Fjellpulken. It's wise to test it on trails near home before trying a long trip. (*Photo by Tobben Spurkland.*)

24

CONDITIONING THE BODY

Parents of young children are sometimes hesitant about undertaking the rigors of backpacking. An increasing number, though, bundle up their young ones, snuggle them into a handy back or front carrier, and take off. I know one family who started with their four-year-old, first on short trails, then longer trips; he was soon carrying his own pack for four or five miles without a whimper. I can't boast the same success. There were too many trips when a four- or five-year-old came home on Dad's shoulders sound asleep. By age eight, though, our children were veteran packers and could carry a pack for eight or nine miles. Skiers have a handy device these days for toting very young tots—the pulka. This is a plastic sled with two long, rigid handles that fasten around Pop's or Mom's waist. This is one way to beat the high cost of babysitting. But skiing or backpacking with kids does require patience and flexibility. Think out all the options before you take them to ten thousand feet for two weeks.

No matter what your age, condition that body before you take it off to a mountain. Your program should include: 1) a yearly physical; 2) daily running, bicycling, or some other physical exercise; and 3) a short trip or two to check out your stamina as well as your gear. Even with your conditioning program, don't get overly enthusiastic—plan a trip that won't exceed your endurance. (Seven or eight miles a day is about right for me in terrain that includes some bushwacking and some altitude gain.) And be sure to allow some leeway in your time schedule in case the weather, illness, or unusually difficult terrain delays you.

CHAPTER FOUR

FINDING YOUR WAY

We camped often when the children were small. My husband drove the car. I packed the food, the clothes, the tent, the first-aid kit, the baby's formula, and the spare tire. He observed scenery, plotted the route, and read maps. I broke up fights, sang nursery rhymes, read *Green Eggs and Ham*, and bravely set up a home away from home. Some years later, returning to the same side route, he fondly recalled our first trip. I responded with a blank stare. "Boy, you don't have any sense of direction," said my beloved. That did it.

I now have accumulated a vast storehouse of ways to find your way in the wilderness. My files bear neat labels: route finding, reading maps, estimating distance, using a compass. How not to get lost. What to do if you do get lost. How to signal for help. How to get home without letting your husband know you got lost.

Before heading for the summit, it is always necessary to find the trailhead. It's quite humiliating to wave goodby to your family, then run into them again ten minutes later because you can't find your way out of the campground. But false starts aren't always your fault. In Alaska and other states with growing pains, landmarks are changed or removed for new development. Trails become overgrown with brush, others are rerouted because of new roads or subdivisions, others are blocked off by private home owners. It is the wise backpacker who checks out distinguishing trail markers with someone who has been there recently or with park or forest service officials.

■ Trail Markers

Marking a route through brush with trail tape is frowned on by the purists, but it can mean the difference between returning or staying perman-

26

ently. It beats blazing trees, which was the sign of a real woodsman not too far back. If you are returning by the same route and hope to find the trail again, leave short lengths of fluorescent surveyor's tape tied to brush or tree limbs at significant turns or places you think might be hard to find again. Then you can remove them on the way out. It should be obvious that these suggestions apply to unmarked trails through brush and forest enroute to the summit and not to the Pacific Crest Trail.

Stone cairns are natural trail markers that appeal to even the most rabid environmentalist. They are rocks piled several feet high and are often used above timberline to mark a route. Finding a route above timberline should be easier than doing so in wooded areas, but I always feel a little more secure if I see a cairn off in the distance. Foggy days on the top require additional strategies, to be discussed in a later chapter.

The author sights a cairn (in foreground). Cairns are often used as trail markers above timberline. (*Photo by Bill Wakeland.*)

A rule sometimes neglected when plodding along through brush and on game trails is to look back often. The route always looks different when approached from the opposite direction. I find it's easier going up, because you have a peak or ridge in sight, than it is coming down when your destination is "over the edge" of the contour.

I have in my maturer days resorted to making landmark reminders on my map. The margins of my topos are riddled with such memory prodders as "game trail ends here—veer west" or "lots of blueberries here." When this foresight is lacking, it is headache time in high valley while three different versions are pooled to determine a sure route home. It is usually Nadine with a natural sense of direction who got us lost in the first place, but we also blame Ethel with her false sense of confidence. Mabel with the map bails us out. So let's talk maps.

■ Maps

Modern maps are drawn from aerial photographs and sometimes verified by field surveys. A backpacker needs topographic maps which are available for most areas of the United States and Canada. Each map is drawn to a specific scale. The three most commonly used are expressed as fractions or units: 1:250,000; 1:62,500 (a shorthand designation for the exact scale of 1:63,360); and 1:24,000.

The scale of one inch to 250,000 inches figures to about one inch to four miles. A map with this scale is nice to have if you're sitting on a mountain top enjoying the distant peaks, but it's not very good for identifying features of the terrain in order to find your route. Maps with a scale of one inch to 62,500 inches (more precisely 1:63,360 or one inch to the mile) are more useful for finding your way in mountain wilderness. Because of their greater magnification, though, these maps cover less area. So you may need several of them to cover an area you're hiking in, and this can become cumbersome. I mentioned before that I solve this problem by cutting off edges, taping sections together, and folding them (mapside out) to map pocket size. The inch to 24,000 inches (or inch to 2,000 feet) maps give even greater detail and even more bulk. I have never used maps of this size because they are simply not available in Alaska. Cartographers are still struggling to complete inch to the mile maps for the many quads in this vast state.

I would like to add here one more suggestion from my "do as I say, not as I did" list. For years the lovely ladies at the local USGS Distribution Office have put up with my bumbling requests for maps and information. Had I earlier bothered to learn the meanings for such terms as *index, quadrangle, 1:250,000,* or *1:63,360,* I could have saved much time and confusion. Remember that index refers to a map of your entire state overlain with rectangles called quadrangles. Each of these quadrangles (quads) is divided into twenty-four sections, which usually are identified with a number and letter, beginning with A-1 in the lower right section of the quad and ending with D-6 in the upper left section. The date of the survey on which the map is based appears below each number. This date becomes significant when you must make route decisions based on the map because certain features may have changed if the survey is old. A river could have shifted course, for example, or a forest shown in green on the map may have burned. A quad map has a scale of 1:250,000, or four miles to the inch. Section maps use a scale of 1:63,360, or one mile to the inch. Referring first to the index to determine your quad, you can then page through the section maps displayed at the Distribution Office to determine which ones you'll need for your trip. It's not quite as easy to order by mail, but the index is free and it shows major bodies of water, rivers, and mountain ranges. If you're uncertain that the map you're ordering covers your proposed route, then describe your route on the order form and let the nice people at USGS determine if you have selected the right map.

When you hear someone say he's using a fifteen-minute map, he doesn't mean he used it for only fifteen minutes of hiking before he had to refold it. He's talking about fifteen minutes of latitude by fifteen minutes of longitude and this is just another name for that 1:63,360 map mentioned above. You learned about longitude and latitude in grade school but you may have forgotton that there are 360 degrees of longitude but only 180 degrees of latitude (90 from the equator to each pole). Each of those degrees is divided into 60 minutes and each minute into 60 seconds. You'll find these numbers in the margin of your topo, for example, 70°30' (75 degrees and 60 minutes). You can closely pinpoint any point on earth using this navigational degree method.

Another more precise system of location uses township and range lines. These grid lines were established years ago when land surveys first began. The east-west lines are called base-lines (or township lines). The lines running north and south are called meridians (or range lines). The square formed by these lines, called townships, are exactly six miles long and six miles wide. Each section of a township, thus, is one square mile, or 640 acres. Within a township, the sections are numbered (starting in the upper right corner) from right to left for six squares, then down one square and left to right for six squares, and so on until the thirty-six squares have been numbered. (As I mentioned earlier, the thirty-six sections of a township should not be confused with the twenty-four sections of a quad).

The grid system formed by range and township lines is shown on some topo maps. At the midpoint of each section (*square*), there is a tiny cross. This symbol forms quarters named by their compass direction, i.e., northwest, northeast, etc. By pinpointing your location within one of these quarters, you could quickly return with help for an injured hiking companion. Using range-township designations found in the margins of the map can also be useful when discussing locations on the telephone. As an example, I often question rangers or others familiar with an area about good stream-crossing points or likely passes through mountains. They usually have a map to which they can refer, and I save a lot of excess verbiage and bumbling around by stating the precise range and township number. Unfortunately for backpackers, not all the country is divided into range and township lines, and sometimes the lines on one map do not match up with adjoining maps. Section numbers appear only on 1:63,360 maps. But despite these problems, range-township designations can be an indispensable tool for the high-country wilderness backpacker.

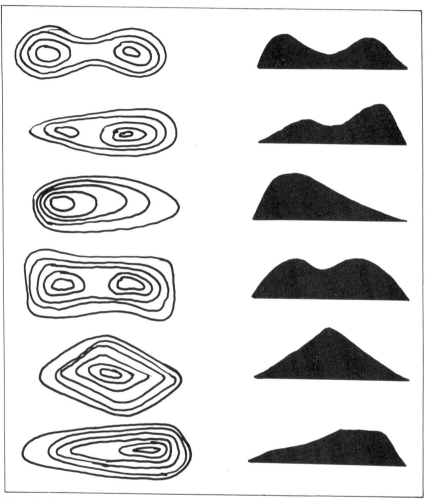

Terrain features shown in silhouette (*right*) are represented by the corresponding contour lines (*left*). (Adapted from *Be Expert with Map & Compass: The Orienteering Handbook* by Bjorn Kjellstrom, published by Scribner's.)

While you were examining your topo, you noticed brown lines swirling their way across the map. These are contour lines which indicate intervals of vertical feet, generally from 20 to 250 feet depending on the map scale. Each fifth contour line is heavier and the corresponding elevation is printed along its length. Widely spaced lines mean a gentle slope; lines that run close together mean a cliff. A valley makes a pattern of Vs pointing upstream. A ridge shows up as downhill Vs or Us. A contour line always meets itself, eventually forming a closed curve. These little brown lines are never fully appreciated until you can translate them into actual terrain. It can be discouraging at the end of a long day when you're expecting to easily reach a lovely meadow and you suddenly encounter a nearly vertical ravine necessitating a long walk around instead of a short one straight ahead. All because you failed to notice those closely spaced contour lines on your map. I've suffered the same lapse, and on a mid-winter backpacking ski tour at that. So watch those contour lines.

There are descriptions to go with the contour lines (other than profanities, that is). A col is the saddle-shaped dip between two hills or in the crest of a ridge. A hill is an elevation shown by two or more closed contour lines. A knoll is a small hill shown by a single closed contour line. A pass is the passable depression between two large hills or mountains. A ravine is a narrow, steep-sided valley, shown by close parallel contours. Ridge is the name given to the spine of a hill and is shown by one or more long, closed contours with almost parallel sidelines. For most beginning navigators, these terms are just so many printed words until they can sit down on a hilltop with map in hand and match up those brown lines with the terrain in sight.

Estimating distance on a map is fundamental to realistic trip planning. In the past, my basic tool was a piece of string that I traced over the planned route, then measured on the map's mileage scale. I have now graduated to using a map wheel, a darling gadget which has a needle and dial with three rings, each scaled to a different map size (1:24,000, 1:62,500, or 1:250,000). By tracing the nose wheel along a proposed route, I can estimate map miles. This works great for the salt flats, but not for the mountains.

One way to estimate altitude gain is to calculate on your map the vertical feet from start to destination and divide this number by 5,280, the number of feet in a mile. For instance, if your altitude gain is about 2,500 feet, divide that number by 5,280. Add this "vertical" mileage, about 0.47 miles, to the "string" mileage of, say, 5.0 miles. This gives you the more realistic distance of 5.4 miles. Backpackers may feel justified in further computing the energy necessary to lift one fifty-pound pack 2,500 feet, one step at a time. If a trail meanders up and down through gully and ridge, I sometimes add a rough ten percent to the total mileage.

After calculating the distance to your destination, you'll want to know how long it takes to get there. If you've timed yourself on similar hikes, you know whether you can walk one, two, or three miles an hour. The art of orienteering, though, is a more exact science: You must calculate the length of your average pace and the time elapsed to complete it. This can be translated into the time it takes to cover a mile.

THE HIGH-COUNTRY BACKPACKER

Jim Benedict, in the August/September 1980 issue of *Backpacker*, described a new method for estimating time and distance in mountain terrain. Using data collected in Yosemite National Park, Benedict devised a chart that shows elevation gain or loss in feet per mile of trail and the time in minutes per mile of trail both uphill and downhill. Mark your map in one mile lengths and using the contour lines on the map, calculate the elevation gain or loss for each mile of trail. Add these up and refer to Benedict's chart, which is reproduced on the next page. He claims this method will give you a realistic time for the distance you want to cover.

Another, less accurate way to estimate time is to add a flat ten percent to the mileage and divide this by your normal backpacking travel time per hour for the degree of steepness indicated by the total altitude gain. Most trail guides estimate that backpackers travel from 1½ to 2 miles per hour. But that doesn't take altitude gain into consideration. Nor other personal idiosyncrasies. So set up your own formula. If you're traveling en-groupe, use the statistics for the slowest person on the trail. A good leader will not overextend his hikers. A good party member will understand if the leader tells him to speed up because there is only one good campsite with water in the next ten miles, and he's got to make it or go thirsty.

Map symbols are another facet of the orienteering game. Each has a distinctive color: Man-made features or cultural features are shown in black; water features in blue; vegetation in green; and elevation in brown.

Various colors and symbols are used on topo maps to represent both natural and man-made features. High brush like this near Lower Russian Lake in the Kenai Peninsula would be shown in green. (*Photo by Emile McIntosh.*)

32

Elevation Gain Or Loss In Feet Per Mile Of Trail	Time In Minutes Per Mile Of Trail	
	Uphill	Downhill
0	29	29
40	30	30
80	31	30
120	32	30
160	33	31
200	34	31
240	36	31
280	37	32
320	38	32
360	40	33
400	41	33
440	43	33
480	44	34
520	46	34
560	47	35
600	49	35
640	51	35
680	53	36
720	55	36
760	57	37
800	59	37
840	61	37
880	63	38
920	65	38
960	67	39
1000	70	39

To calculate travel time going uphill or downhill, mark your trail in one-mile segments on the map and determine the elevation gain or loss per mile from the contour lines. Then refer to the above chart to find the corresponding travel time. (Reprinted from "Shouldn't We Be There Now?" by Jim Benedict, *Backpacker,* August / September 1980.)

Unimproved roads, for example, are indicated by a double dash black line, trails with a single dash line. Utility lines (such as pipelines and underground power lines) are indicated with a longer dash single line. Lakes or ponds are drawn as close to actual shape as possible and tinted blue.

Brooks and narrow rivers are indicated by a single blue line and larger rivers by a blue band. (A mighty important difference when you have to wade across them.) Marshes and swamps show tiny tufts of grass rising from a blue background. (Watch for these booby traps.) Sand dunes or sandbars are pictured with, what else, tiny grains of brown sand. (Sandbars are great mosquito-free campsites in the Arctic.) Vegetation is shown in green, and this bit of color can make or break a trip. It can mean pleasant hiking through a lovely carpeted spruce forest, or ankle-breaking bushwacking through alder, willow, or brush. (Be forewarned when your map shows green bordering a stream above timberline.) These are only a few of the dozens of map symbols. If your map shows some puzzlers, write to the USGS for their free booklet *Topographic Maps.*

In the left-hand corner at the bottom of your map, you will find a triangle with one side labeled "magnetic north" and the other "true north," with a degree number indicating the angle of declination. We'll talk about that later, but first, let's talk about a compass.

■ Compass

When our boys were Scouts, I bought them an army surplus air compass and thought all compass needles bounced and never came to rest. Until I started moving into no-trail country, I paid little attention to compass design. After I'd been lost a few times, I got serious about map reading and bought a modern orienteering compass, one which is a compass, protractor, and ruler combined. My Silva Type 7 has a magnetic needle enclosed in liquid that almost eliminates needle swing. The compass housing consists of a revolving dial (azimuth ring) and a transparent plate that has an arrow inside the housing which points to north. This is the orienting arrow. The rotating dial is marked with 360 degree lines. North is at 0 degrees, east at 90 degrees, south at 180 degrees, and west at 270 degrees. The base plate also has a direction-of-travel arrow.

There are two basic uses of a compass: to take a field bearing, and to take a map bearing. Taking a field bearing is easy. Say you want to head for a distant peak. Point the direction-of-travel arrow at the peak. Without moving the compass, rotate the azimuth ring until the orienting arrow lines up with the red needle. Read the degree number at the direction-of-travel arrow (or index point). This is your bearing. Whenever you want to check to see if you're maintaining your bearing, align the red needle with the orienting arrow and walk in the direction of the travel arrow. Remember that the time to set a bearing is when you have a visual reference, not when you're down in the forest. I'm ashamed to admit that I've had to send my sons shinnying up tall spruce trees to get a bead on a lake when I forgot to do it at the top of the hill.

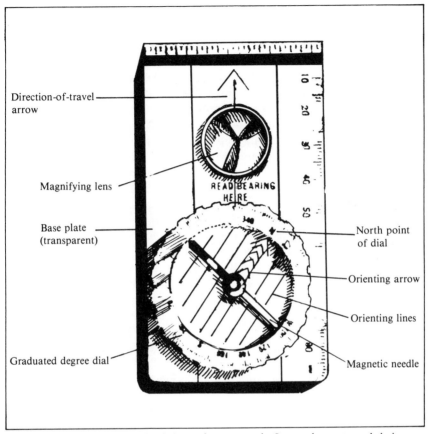

Direction-of-travel arrow

Magnifying lens

Base plate (transparent)

Graduated degree dial

READ BEARING HERE

North point of dial

Orienting arrow

Orienting lines

Magnetic needle

A compass is useless if you don't know how to use it. Learn the parts and their uses *before* you get lost. A typical orienteering compass is diagrammed.

A compass is a direction guide only. It can't tell you where you are, where your compass is, or where a road is if you have no visual point of reference or map. Most of my fellow packers carry a map and compass, but a lot of them fake it when it comes to reading the map. The reason I know they are fake map readers is because it takes one to know one. I had my final Watergate one hot June when it took me ten hours to hike five miles; I couldn't lie to my husband anymore because this time he'd flown into the lake and was waiting for me. So I learned to use a compass and a map to get unlost.

If you're using a compass with a map you must allow for declination, because map directions are true directions and compass directions are magnetic directions. If you paid attention in grade school you will know that magnetic north and real, or map, north vary depending on your location on the globe. In the eastern part of the United States and Canada, the declination will always be west and can be as much as twenty degrees west of true north. In the western part of the United States there can be twenty or more degrees of declination east of true north. Alaska readings are several degrees more. In the continental United States you get a compass reading of true north along the Zero Declination Line, which extends from the tip of Florida through Chicago to the northern tip of Michigan.

The first step in using your map and compass together is to orient the map. If you know where you are on the map, you visually line up features. If you don't know where you are, orient the map using your compass. Spread out your map and lay the compass on it. Be sure it's not near something like your metal cook kit or a flashlight. Align the straight plastic edge with the true north key on the map (on topo maps this should be in the lower left corner.) If the declination key is missing from your map, place the compass edge parallel with the edge of the map, since most maps are drawn with true north at the top. Rotate map and compass together until the needle points to your local degree of declination. Now see if you can match up visible landmarks with the map—say a lake, or set of three peaks, or a river. Take a bearing and head out. This is called orienting the hiker.

If this discussion has gotten you lost, there are masters in the field of orienteering to whom you can refer. These include Bjorn Kjellstrom *(Be Expert With Map and Compass)*, Dwight R. Schuh *(Modern Survival)*, and Anthony J. Acerrano *(The Outdoorsman's Emergency Manual)*.

■ Getting Unlost

You've decided that you're no longer confused or disoriented but plain LOST. What now? You already know what the first words of advice will be: Don't Panic. So with quivering lip and palpitating heart, you set yourself down on or under a rock and take some deep breaths. Here's where you decide whether you're going to sit it out and wait for rescue (you have reached a point of exhaustion and fog has rolled in unexpectedly) or whether you will try to figure out where you went wrong and how to find the route again.

If staying is your choice, set up your tent, drink a hot beverage, crawl into your sleeping bag, and take a nap. These housekeeping chores are great therapy and get you ready to face your problem. Get out that map again and try to locate the spot where you went wrong. Perhaps you ate lunch several hours ago on a prominent ridge that you can pinpoint on the map. Try to trace your route since then. If you're still nervous and undecided, sit tight. If you've simply become separated from fellow hikers, they'll be looking for you. If you're on a solo outing, you should have told someone where you were going and when you'd be back. If fog or whiteout is the problem, all the more reason to cozy up in your sleeping bag and read that paperback you brought along. However, be conservative with your food supplies, just in case.

Next day the fog will probably have dissipated, and you can see some prominent landmarks. Find them on your map. When you find a good one, sight it with your compass and take a degree reading. Draw a line on the map that passes at the same angle through the landmark. Look for a second landmark and do the same. Where the two lines cross is roughly your posi-

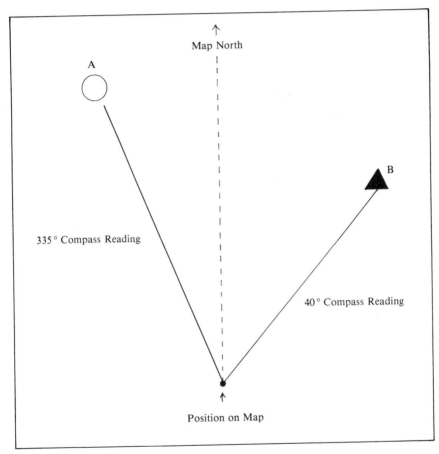

To find your position on the map by triangulation, first spot a landmark and locate it on the map. Then, sight it with your compass and take a degree reading. Next, draw a line on your map that passes at the same angle through the landmark (e.g., 335 degrees for landmark A). Now, look for a second landmark and do the same. Where the two lines cross is roughly your postion.

tion. This is called triangulation. Then, if you find you're roughly three miles off course, set your compas bearing and follow it. Just in case, leave some indication of where you're headed—a note in a plastic bag, an arrow made of stones, or twigs pointing to your line of travel, anything that will tell searchers where you've gone.

If you decide to wait for rescue, there are ways to signal for help. If fog persists, obviously mirrors and other visual signals are worthless. Here's where my trusty whistle comes to the rescue. Since repetitions of three seem to be standard emergency procedure, try blowing three times on the whistle. Or you can use the universal Morse Code distress signal: three dots, three dashes, three dots. On a whistle, that translates to three short notes, three long, and three short. You may find this gets old fast and decide to settle down for clearing weather.

| Pick us up | Do not land here | All okay, do not wait | Yes |

| No | Need mechanical help or parts | Our receiver is operating | Use drop message |

| Need medical assistance | Can proceed shortly, wait if possible | Land here |

When trying to signal an airplane, use these official ground-air body signals.

38

Once visibility has returned, you can resort to other devices such as a signal mirror, flashlight, flares, pistol shots—anything that stands out from the ordinary sights or sounds of the area. A signal mirror is not an ordinary cosmetic mirror. Both sides are mirror-covered and a hole is drilled through the center. Suppose you hear a plane in the distance. Hold the mirror several inches from your face and sight the plane through the hole. If the

N	△	K	F	⋁	II	L
No	Probably safe to land here	Indicate direction to proceed	Need food and water	Need gun and ammuni- tion	Need medical supplies	Need fuel

Y	505	LL	↑	I	X	□
Yes	Inter- national distress symbol	All well	Am proceeding in this direction	Seriously injured, need doctor	Unable to proceed	Need compass and map

Ground signals should be made from some material (white rocks, cut branches, clothing, etc.) that contrasts with the surrounding ground cover.

sun and target are in your view, a spot of light will reflect on your face, and you'll be able to see it in the mirror facing you. Turn the mirror slowly until the dot on your face lines up with the hole in the mirror. You will know this has happened when the dot disappears from view, at which point your signal will be visible to your target. If the sun is behind you, however this method won't work. In this case, gently sweep the mirror back and forth across the horizon. There is the chance the pilot might see your signal and come back to investigate.

If a plane flies overhead and sees you, how do you tell the pilot your problem? The International Ground-Air Body Signal Code is the magic answer. Don't wave your hands wildly as the pilot may think you're simply greeting him, dip his wing and fly off. Instead, stand with your arms direct- ly over your head as high as you can reach, which signals that you need to be taken aboard. Other standard body signals are shown in the accompanying diagram.

There also are some official ground signals, one of which I had occa- sion to use on a remote trip into the Wrangell Mountains. Just three miles out from our drop-off point, one group member sprained an ankle and I returned to the airstrip with her after sending the others on ahead with a new leader. While scouting the area, I found some white plastic in what must have been an old hunter's dump. With this material I formed a huge white X beside the airstrip. Had our pilot flown over, he would have read it as "unable to proceed—please pick up." (Unfortunately, his travels did not take him over our camp until five days later when, at the time of scheduled pickup at the end of the trail, he learned of our predicament from the other group.) I could have gathered white rocks from the creek bed or cut willow branches to make a ground signal had the plastic not been available.

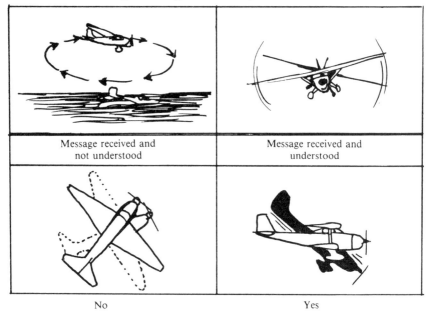

Message received and not understood	Message received and understood
No	Yes

A pilot may maneuver his plane to signal a response to ground or body signals.

■ Final Words on Finding Your Way

In addition to your maps and compass, bring along a whistle, signal mirror, and list of ground-air body signals and ground signals in case the map and compass fail you (or vice versa). Before you leave, write down where you plan to park, where you plan to hike, when you will return, and what emergency equipment you have with you. If you change your mind about route before you leave the trailhead, notify *someone* about your change in plans. I also leave at home with my family a list of the names and telephone numbers of all members of my group. If my family accompanies me, I leave this list with a neighbor or an official of our mountaineering club. Never was the importance of this practice brought out so clearly as when an avalanche tragically caught four members of a five-man ski touring group. The leader was killed and the sole survivor, new to the group, did not know the names of the others. It took me two days to track down the names of the deceased skiers and their home addresses.

All this sounds a bit sombre, so I'll close this section on finding your way with "Murphy's Laws of Orienteering," compiled by Elden Hughes of Whittier, California, for *Footnotes,* a newsletter published by *Backpacker* magazine.

Topo Map Availability
When two or more contiguous maps are needed, you will discover that the adjacent map is (in descending order of frequency):
- A. Not yet mapped.
- B. Mapped, but not yet printed.
- C. Out of print.
- D. On a different scale.
- E. On a different contour interval.

Taking Bearings
All prominent features visible from a given location will be found to be on the adjoining map. Exception: Sometimes they are two maps over.

Contour Interval
The chosen contour interval will be found to be optimum for the terrain on some other portion of the map. The terrain mapped with an 80-foot contour interval will be found to be studded with 79-foot tall cliffs and hills.

Map Alignment
When relying on range lines for north/south map alignment, you will discover that:
- A. There are no such lines on the part of the map on which you are located.
- B. The surveyor was drunk and the lines only occasionally go north/south.

Worn Spots on Map
If the map has worn spots from excessive folding or becoming wet, the worn spots will cover (in descending order of frequency):
- A. Where you are.
- B. Where you are going.
- C. The nearest prominent feature.
- D. The declination arrow.
- E. All of the above (get new map).

Trails

Trails always follow the borders of maps so as to frequently cross between adjacent maps. When trails approach the corners of maps, they immediately curve so as to be on all four intersecting maps.

Locating Yourself When Lost

When attempting to locate yourself, you discover:

    A.   You didn't bring the map.

    B.   You didn't bring the compass.

    C.   Both of the above.

    D.   You brought the wrong map.

CHAPTER FIVE

RULES OF THE TRAIL

Hike leaders are hard to come by. I've never seen a club yet that dared to publish the qualifications for being one. But I can't stand to see a gap without a breech, so here goes the neck to the noose:

A hike leader must be of sound mind and full of self-esteem; a veteran of fifty or more hikes in all types of terrain; a survivor of an emergency or two or three; proficient in first aid; conversant with weather forecasting; able to repair a pack frame or a shoe lace; able to cross a stream and bluff a bear; a listener and a talker with moderate viewpoints; alert to hiker deterioration and a psychological trickster able to coax the trailender over the last ridge.

When I admitted in the last chapter that I appointed a fast hiker to go ahead and leave the trail sweeping to me, I didn't mean to infer that I was deficient in any of the above qualifications. Admitting that someone walks faster than I comes under self-esteem (it also comes with the age). Borrowing from the marketplace, "A good leader must know how to follow." I never did know how you could do this without meeting yourself coming back until I had to go back and find some stragglers who went right instead of left and down instead of up.

■ Getting Along in the Group

There are some unwritten rules of the trail when traveling with a group and the sooner you buckle under, the longer you'll live. A good leader is decisive and firm, but not so intimidating that he broaches no input whatsoever. Although group decisions are great, someone must have the final say on major decisions: rest stops, route, campsite. This last topic can generate enough static to light up a mountain top. Enter leader with tact, good humor, and strong will. Another sticky scene occurs when an individual decides he knows more than the leader and strikes off on his own. I get a trifle testy when some person in my party makes a side trip without telling me where he's going and when he's coming back. This is the guy who, when he gets lost, expects instant mobilization of a rescue group. I don't need to tell you what he does for the enjoyment level of his fellow hikers. Only slightly less exasperating is the ill-equipped walker. If it isn't a new boot that never got broken in, it's a sleeping bag that keeps falling off the frame; or perhaps a forgotten raincoat, which holds up the entire party while everyone tries to improvise with a garbage bag. You can understand why I do equipment checks for longer trips.

Not far down the static scale is morning starting time. There is no war so bloody as the biological rythmn fracas between the day and night people. Naturally, those who stayed up half the night telling bear stories around the campfire will want to sleep in. Those who were in the sleeping bag right after dinner will be clanging cook pots at 6 A.M. I long ago learned to set a starting time the night before, calculated on the distance to be covered, terrain, and temperature. If the thermometer has been hovering around ninety, I plan an early start, with a mid-day stop of several hours, then maybe a few more hours and an early camp. On the other hand, if we've hiked late the night before in order to reach a good campsite, then sleeping in is the order for the day. There are other variables to consider such as threatening weather, steep climbing, time-consuming stream crossings. But by putting out the word the night before, I can soften the shock of an early morning whistle. Still, I learn a lot of new words when I make the rounds of tent city around 6 A.M.

I've found that in larger groups of fifteen or more, some members often prefer to camp apart from the others. Since hikers don't travel hundreds of miles to hear the guy in the next tent snore, I encourage this arrangement. All I want to know is where everyone is. There are exceptions. On one trip in the Brooks Range my party had been sharing the route with two grizzlies all day. I think they were trying to beat us to the blueberries on the Sheenjek. That night I insisted that all eight tents be pitched in close proximity on a river sandbar. I believe there was total unanimity that evening when the grizz ambled on to the sandbar, took one look at eight tents, fifteen people and fifteen cameras, and beat it. I'll admit I had some anxious minutes before he loped off across the mountainside.

Route finding in trailless country is another source of stimulating conversation. Often, hikes take me to areas I have never travled before, but these trips are preceded by months of research. I talk to people who have been there and pester rangers, park superintendents, and wilderness managers for information. Trail guides are available for most mountain ranges throughout the continental United States, but word of mouth is the

44

Facing the challenges and dangers of a backpacking trip brings out the best, and worst, in people. A good hike leader must have multiple talents for dealing with group members. (*Photo by Bill Wakeland.*)

state of the art in much of Alaska's and Canada's uncharted wilderness. I study maps and mark routes. I try to plot the entire trip into daily segments, hopefully arranging a camp near water.

Once on the trail, all your plans may change in a hurry if you run into an unmapped growth of alder or a stream that's running bankful because of rain the night before. This means making up lost time the next day. Backpacking is intended to be an escape from timetables, but if you're dependent on pilot pickup or airline reservations, a certain amount of programming is imperative. During the day, I compare notes with other map readers in the group and decide on route changes. I take a nose count often and blow a whistle periodically in high brush. When the going is rough, I stop to let the tailgaters catch up. There's nothing like the threat of bears to maintain a closely knit group.

A leader learns early that not only must he be a navigator, a physician, and a disciplinarian, he must also be a psychiatrist. The physical functioning of the body is influenced by mental attitudes and vice versa. This usually becomes quite apparent about three hours out as personal quirks begin to surface. I recall one grueling day in the Arrigetch when we had bushwacked for hours through alder that caught at our packs, tripped us up, and was physically exhausting. But we couldn't stop until we reached water and a reasonably flat spot to pitch a tent. A variety of personality traits in the group members became apparent: Some were stoically silent; one filled the air with profanity; one giggled; one wept; another was livid with rage and blamed the leader for not warning that there would be this difficult terrain. The gut reaction to this kind of treatment is to toss out a few negative rebuttals, but a good leader will button his lip, try to bring humor back to camp, and promise that morning will bring relief. And then hope to gosh he's right. Quickly, he gets everyone busy setting up tents, builds a fire if it's permitted, creates some hot drinks or even a cocktail, and asks everyone what they're having for dinner. Friendships have been cemented—and shattered—on hiking trips.

■ Traveling Alone

To solo or not to solo, this is the question. Dozens of backpacking authors have expressed their opinion, and I was surprised to read that many were in favor of the solo experience. I must disagree. I believe it is foolhardy and the solo packer is asking for trouble. I can truthfully say I have never hit a trail alone with the intention of overnighting, although I will admit to an occasional day hike of short duration alone.

But let me tell about my most recent solo venture. While hiding out during the writing of this book, I decided to celebrate the completion of a chapter by hiking several miles up an established trail. I left a note in my camp trailer noting where I was and when I planned to return; I also told some forest service personnel who happened by. About three miles up and on the return trip, my right to the trail was challenged twice by two moose.

The possibility of meeting a protective cow moose with calf is reason enough for not hiking alone. (*Photo by Leonard Lee Rue III.*)

46

The first one decided to vamoose, so I scurried down the trail past him. A few minutes later, my heart started pounding when another moose, this one big and bull, decided I should let him have the trail. (When I first arrived in Alaska, moose were an oddity but nothing to worry about. Now, twenty years later, I give them good distance and expect the worst. Female moose with calf—for that matter, the females of any species with babe—are not to be tampered with. I was charged one time, and not so lucky friends have spent time in the hospital with cuts, bruises, and broken ribs. However, this time it was May, and most cows were in hiding awaiting the birth of calves.)

To get back to my story, this particular bull was a young, but stubborn, one. We stood for over fifteen minutes, eyeball to eyeball (well, maybe twenty-five feet apart) while each waited for the other to move. I threw a stick thinking to stir him. No luck. I snapped my camera. He merely flicked his ears. Finally, I ventured a few feet forward. He moved a few feet into the brush. I tried a few more feet, all the time planning my retreat behind a large spruce along the trail. Finally, I went for it. The last I saw of him and he of me, we were each crashing through the woods—in opposite directions.

This long tale is merely to tell you that I think hiking alone is not without danger. I was lucky this time—my homecoming was merely delayed by half an hour. But I had not met a single hiker on the trail and, since it was preseason and mid-week, chances of anyone coming by were slim. Had I been lying injured on the trail, I probably would have stayed there through a freezing spring night and not have been missed for several days.

■ Sharing the Trail With Others

In Alaska, horse pack trains and hikers don't often share the same trails. We are much more likely to encounter dog teams. Trail courtesy for either is not too different. Since dogs are easily distracted by flashbulbs, other dogs, or someone on the trail, it is established procedure to relinquish the trail to them. This is especially important if the team is racing and one snafu can mean the difference between winning and losing. These encounters usually take place when one is on skis and getting off the trail is not so easy, but it is always appreciated by the driver and he'll usually acknowledge with a silent wave of the hand.

Dennis Gebhardt in his *A Backpacking Guide to the Weminuche Wilderness* has some words of wisdom for those encountering horses in the wilderness:

> If you have not been around horses there are some characteristics that you should keep in mind. Horses are easily alarmed by things they don't understand or recognize, such as a person with a backpack. Swatting mosquitoes or other sudden movements can startle horses into kicking. When walking in dense

cover you should call out a hearty hello to approaching horse-men. The sound of your voice lets the horse know you are a human being. Often you will meet riders who have little or no control over their animals. The horse can follow the animal ahead for miles with the rider holding the reins slack or not at all. Then when a dangerous situation arises, such as a grouse exploding into flight or the presence of cliffs, the rider is caught unaware. I always give horses the trail when in steep and rocky terrain and move off on the downhill side. If the horse begins to turn and buck the rider will have a better chance of bringing him back to the trail. Move off just far enough to avoid being kicked but not into concealment. Stand quietly but not absolutely still and, as said earlier, speak to the riders in a conversational tone.

It is not unusual to encounter dog teams on ski trails in Alaska. (*Photo by Emile McIntosh.*)

In many states, trails are shared with motor bikes, all-terrain vehicles, snow machines, and four-wheel drives. In some places, this has caused such a hassle that designated areas have been set aside for each. Know the rules. One of my favorite trails is open to hunters in the fall, snow machines when sufficient snow cover occurs, skiers in the warmer spring months, and hikers in the summer. When one feisty skier reported an "out of season" snow machiner to the Forest Service, the rule breaker was cited and fined. On the other hand, I often follow snow-machine trails when skiing in backcountry that lacks trails because the machines pack the snow well and the drivers usually know where they are going. If I hear a snow machine in the distance, I step off the trail until it has passed.

I do admit to feelings of sadness when I discover deep ruts in unrepairable tundra where a four-wheel drive or ATV has become mired and the driver has plowed his way through. Or to some annoyance when I awaken in a tent three thousand feet above Anchorage and hear the insistent buzz of a motorbike straining over a mountaintop, very much off limits. I do not belong to the group who wants to preserve wilderness for a selected few—it belongs to all of us. But it is nice when we can divide it up equitably, each to his own.

■ Waste Disposal

The bible of trail etiquette includes rules about disposal of litter. No more can we throw a can in the brush, bury trash, or hide a plastic bag under a tree. Even fire rings are considered a blight. You've heard it before and I'll say it again: If you can carry it in, you can pack it out. Foil burns in a hot fire, but pick out the residue and put it in your garbage bag. Burn cans to get rid of the food odor, but after they are cooled, crush them and carry out. If fires are verboten, you know what you have to do. We'll talk about latrines and toilet paper in a later chapter.

If you're still a skeptic, consider the following estimates (published in the January 1979 issue of *Footnotes*) of how long it takes various types of litter to decompose under trailside conditions:

Item	Decomposition Time
Aluminum cans and tabs	80–100 years
Vibram soles	50–80 years
Leather	Up to 50 years
Nylon fabrics	30–40 years
Plastic film	20–30 years
Plastic bags	10–20 years
Plastic-coated paper	5 years
Wool socks	1–5 years
Orange peel	2 weeks to 5 months

In Alaska, we would probably amend the decomposition time for the above items to one word—never. Or at least, almost never. Arctic conditions are not conducive to rapid decay.

In the end, rules of the trail for both leader and follower are no different than the rules of life. Do unto others, etc., take good care of God's good earth, and use a large dose of common sense.

EQUIPMENT
AND
SUPPLIES

Back at Mile One, Backpacking, I found the game pretty lonely. That's because I was the World's First Backpacker and figured the only way to master this physical fitness thing was to try it and cover up your mistakes. Probably because I didn't look very hard, I didn't find many books on the subject. Colin Fletcher had not yet hatched his classic, *The Complete Walker,* and most of my husband's outdoor magazines told him how to tie a better fly or stalk a bigger elk. I did pick up *Mountaineering: Freedom of the Hills* and carried it to the hairdressers in a brown paper bag. It was my constant companion just before I went off to mountaineering classes where I, nevertheless, was forced to admit that I didn't know a brake bar from a jumar or a bowline from a ring bend. I was one backpacking amateur, I was. A daypack at that.

My good friend and fellow hiker Kay delights in recalling an afternoon atop Bodenburgh Butte, a bump in the middle of a valley, which rises to a dizzy height of eight hundred feet. We had somehow come upon a book detailing thirty hikes in the Anchorage area and one of the hike descriptions advised the hiker to "don crampons" before proceeding. I read this to Kay as we sat upon the heights, but stopped abruptly at that phrase to ask, "What in the world are crampons?" Even Kay knew what they were. That next Christmas I found a gift under my tree from Kay—a set of crampons. In later years, when we reached the expletive deleted stage of a hiking day, all she had to say was "crampons" and the tension melted. All of this is by way of admitting that I really started from scratch.

CHAPTER SIX

MODERN GEAR— NECESSITY OR OVERKILL

The early explorers, pioneers, and prospectors in the western United States and in Alaska struggled with wood frame and canvas over the mountain passes. Let one of them loose in a modern equipment store and you could start another gold rush that would make Macy's after-Christmas sale look like a Christmas tree closeout on December 26.

We now carry bed, board, and shelter, all fashioned from a few ounces of aluminum and nylon. While they were bent over with bags of flour and bacon roped to back, we walk upright over the same trail with a week's supply of food freeze-dried, instantized, and miniaturized to comfortable weights.

The array of gear that greets today's backpacker on entering an equipment store can lead to the "I'll have a little of everything" syndrome or, worse, the "I don't think I'll go backpacking after all" illness. The seemingly endless selection from which a backpacker must choose has led some old-timers to come full circle—right back to the simplicity of cooking from scratch and sleeping under the stars. The rate at which manufacturers find new ways to render last year's equipment obsolete is suspect, and many wonder if the industry is suffering from a case of equipment overkill.

Ignoring some of the picayne "improvements" and focusing on the more spectacular achievements, I confess to being one of the buyers. I am thoroughly impressed with W. L. Gore's Gore-Tex, Celanese's PolarGuard and DuPont's Hollofill II. Though I admit to hamburger fantasy after a week of freeze-dried food, I have no complaints about its weight when I've carried it twenty-five miles or about its taste when I'm hungry. I agree completely with my eighty-year-old uncle who, after borrowing my tent and sleeping pad, marveled at how comfortable he felt during a rainstorm,

Prospectors in the early 1900s put up with leaky canvas tents, bulky bedrolls, and cooking over an open fire. (*Courtesy Anchorage Historical and Fine Arts Museum.*)

snugged down in his sleeping bag on a Therm-A-Rest mattress, in a rainproof, bugproof, windproof tent.

To avoid gear jitters, pick up a copy of *Backpacking Equipment Buyer's Guide* by William Kemsley and the editors of *Backpacker* magazine. (It's available for $8.95 plus $1.05 postage from Wilderness Bookstore, Bedford Hills, New York 10507.) This book was published in 1978, but it's a good basic guide that lists equipment by brand name.

Backpacker, published every two months, also regularly evaluates new equipment. For subscription information write Backpacker, P. O. Box 2946, Boulder, Colorado 80321. Another source of up-to-date information on equipment is Recreational Equipment, Inc. This is a cooperative with a membership fee of five dollars. Its two catalogs a year contain good research information and offer equipment at reasonable prices. Write to REI Co-op, P. O. Box C-88125, Seattle, Washington 98188.

MODERN GEAR—NECESSITY OR OVERKILL

You can further add to your knowledge by talking to experienced backpackers. Visit outfitting stores and chat with the salespeople when they are not busy. Read the ads in outdoor magazines. Borrow someone's gear for a weekend. Check out the army/navy surplus stores, Goodwill, Salvation Army, or charitable thrift shops. (I once found a pair of brand new wool twill pants in a thrift store—cost $2.00.) Our mountaineering club holds yearly swap and sell events.

There's another sneaky way to ease the financial pain of gearing up. Put the item on your Christmas or birthday list. My lists are displayed on the refrigerator months ahead. I also concentrate on acquiring one item at a

Early explorers, pioneers, and prospectors struggled with cumbersome, heavy packs. (*Courtesy Anchorage Historical and Fine Arts Museum.*)

The array of gear in a modern equipment store contrasts sharply with that available in earlier times. For some, today's choices are bewildering.

time, stashing away until I have enough to pay for a tent or sleeping bag. Avoid the temptation of gimmicks and first acquire basics such as boots, bag, and tent.

Once you've acquired some gear, concentrate on taking care of it properly. There is a strong inclination to set your pack aside, unpacked, when returning from a trip. Don't. Hang your tent and sleeping bag in the sun to dry thoroughly, thus preventing mildew. If that's not possible, hang them over a chair or shower rod for a day or two. Check empty containers and set them aside to be filled or replaced. Wash your cook kit. Clean the stove. Throw out the trash. And most important, dry, brush, and grease your boots. Stuffing them with newspaper while they dry helps to maintain their shape.

Planning for a trip is fun, they say, but there's got to be a system. One ill-prepared hiker can spoil a trip for the entire group. Let me tell another one on myself, the Great Leader. Each year when I lead an extended hiking trip, I require every participant to submit to an equipment check. One year, before a trip into the Arrigetch Peaks of the Brooks Range, I had all seven hikers lay out every piece of their equipment on my family room floor.

When we arrived at Bettles, we were delayed by weather from flying out to our take-off point. That night I crawled into my sleeping bag and discovered that the zipper had melted in the dryer. I raced over to the local cooperative store and was advised that the resident native women sewed caribou skins with dental floss, so I figured it should work on my nylon bag. I found a large-eyed needle in my repair kit, threaded it with dental floss,

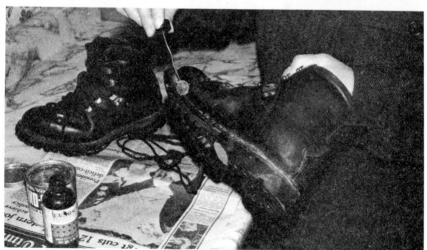

After returning from a backpacking trip, first dry your boots away from direct heat, and then grease them with a wax waterproofing material such as Sno-Seal (*top*). It may be easier to use a liquid such as Leath-R-Seal to waterproof the stitching (*bottom*).

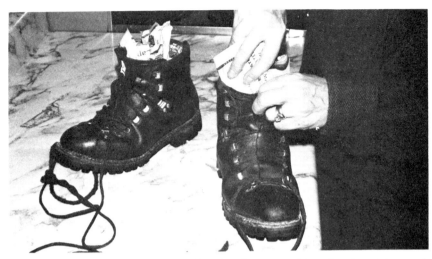

Stuff your boots with newspaper or other absorbent material to absorb moisture and to help them retain their shape.

and sewed up the front of my bag. For the remainder of the trip, I slithered in and out of my bag—carefully. Lesson 1, Check zippers on sleeping bags before departure. Lesson 2, Never put a sleeping bag in a hot dryer.

Make a checklist. It should be posted wherever you keep your outdoor gear and referred to *every* time you pack. There's a tendency to become complacent, especially if items are left in the pack while stored. You won't be very happy when you reach for the sunscreen on a blistering day and discover the tube is empty.

Following is my checklist of equipment and supplies. Edit it as need be to fit your part of the country and your particular needs.

Clothing
- Boots (no waffle stompers, wallabies, or tennis shoes in the high-country)
- Socks (cotton or Quiana undersocks; wool oversocks)
- Underwear
- Shirts (one turtleneck; one short-sleeved open neck)
- Trousers (two pair, one wool and one synthetic; shorts and bathing suit optional)
- Jacket (wool, pile, 60–40, or Thinsulate)
- Rain gear
- Head gear (watch cap, balaclava, rain-sun cap, felt or cotton hat)
- Hand gear (mittens or gloves, or better both)
- Gaiters (in wet brush and snow)

- Tennis shoes, tabbies, or neoprene diver's boots (for stream crossings)
- Parka (down, PolarGuard, Hollofill II, etc.)
- Wool shirt or sweater

Backpack and Pack Cover

Shelter
- Tent, rainfly, tent poles, stakes
- Sleeping bag, stuff bag with inner plastic bag liner, straps with teeth
- Sleeping pad

Food
- Freeze-dried foods
- Beverages (instant packets, in plastic bottles, etc.)
- Fresh foods (oranges, carrots, celery, cheese, peanut butter, sausage, crackers, etc.)
- Snack foods (to supply high-carbohydrate needs)
- Water, purifying tablets (if necessary), and containers (wide-mouth plastic bottle and collapsible container)

Food Preparation
- Stove
- Cook kit
- Matches or butane lighter and firestarter paste
- Utensils (jackknife, opener, spoon, fork)
- Paper towels, pot cleaner
- Cups (one insulated and one plastic measuring)

Safety and Comfort
- Map
- Compass
- Whistle
- Flashlight
- First-aid kit (see Chapter 12)
- Sunglasses
- Sunscreen and chapstick
- Insect repellent
- Repair kit (clevis pins, wire, small screwdriver, manicure scissors, duct tape)
- Other emergency items (rope, carabiner, fishing kit)

Personal Grooming (see also Chapter 12)
* Toothbrush and toothpaste
* Biodegradable liquid soap
* Comb
* High-lanolin lotion (tube)
* Wash n' Dries
* Toilet paper and Kleenex
* Sewing kit
* Mirror

Winter Items
* Skis and poles
* Wax, scrapers
* Skins
* Special cold-weather clothing (see Chapter 21)

CHAPTER SEVEN

FOOTWEAR AND CLOTHING

Rough out, rough in, top grain, split. It's enough to send you hiking in bedroom slippers. Boots were not so all-hallowed important the day I trekked my first trek. It was wet spring time, so I put on my high-heeled plastic snow boots and departed. My leader and mentor eyed them mid-trip and diplomatically suggested there were better ways to go.

Somewhere along the line, I listened to a knowledgeable salesperson and bought my first pair of heavy hiking boots. And my second pair. And my third pair. I was one of the lucky ones who hit it right the first time. Each pair fit and lasted through seven hundred or so miles of rugged use. One of my sons, fresh from a high-school outdoor class and seeking independence, elected to purchase a pair of well-known name-brand boots that split sole-wise on his first trip out. From time to time, I have bought discount-store boots for fast growing children and had them disintegrate before the kid grew out of them. Any parent knows that's fast. In later years, my college-bound kids were presented with good, name-brand hiking boots, and all are well and holding, thank you. The boots, I mean. I don't know about the kids.

■ Boots and More Boots

In the innocence of my early hiking days, I concluded that if a boot fit, you wore it. Today, browsing through literature on the subject, I learn that I should have considered a few additional points, such as leather and how you slice it—top grain (outside), split (any of the other layers), smooth out (the way the cow wore it), rough out (the way the cow didn't wear it). Not to mention the way a boot is built—from a single piece or several; double-stitched or triple-stitched; reinforced, padded, collared; hinged heel, soft

61

toe, hard toe, box toe; gusseted tongue, split tongue; grommeted or hooked lacing or both; leather or nylon laces; insole, midsole, outsole, shank, vibram sole, welts and weight. Depending on where I was going, I should have considered a choice among all-leather boots, half leather-half canvas, half rubber-half leather, all rubber, double vapor barrier plastic, or lined, unlined, and now even hard plastic (à la downhill boots). No wonder one old-timer left his six-pound boots in the closet and took to wearing kletter shoes at two pounds each.

In local hiking circles, I am sometimes referred to as "the lady who won't let you hike in tennis shoes or waffle stompers." Often enough this advice is so intimidating that potential trekkers have gone home to re-shoe. But then there is the renowned biologist who became so weary of wet feet during his summertime research hikes through the Arctic tussocks (bumps of land with water around them) that he threw out his "waterproof" boots and now wears only sneakers—one pair hanging from his pack and drying in the sun, the other getting wet on his feet.

Lightweight hiking boots provide enough support on dry, well-groomed trails, but for wilderness and rocky high-country, a heavier lug sole boot is recommended. Nowadays, many mountaineers who plan to be in snow are choosing a double plastic, rather than leather, mountain boot.

FOOTWEAR AND CLOTHING

Like seekers of the Promised Land, hikers are ever seeking dry feet and waterproof boots. But let's face it, leather breathes (it did on the cow) and no amount of Sno-Seal, Mink Oil, wax, or silicone will permanently seal it. (Early Winters claims their water seal really does waterproof.) I dry and seal my boots after every wearing, and they keep my feet dry until I step into that first wet hole or two or three. So, you're asking, why not wear rubber boots? I tried them on my last kayak trip. The rubber knee highs were great for stepping into and out of the craft in water, but after a day in the hot sun, my feet were wet from perspiration. On cloudy days, they were cold. The final chapter was written when we got hung up on a hidden sandbar and I jumped out to free the kayak. Water poured over the top of my boots and I felt like the Green Giant laboriously lifting each foot shoreward. My fellow kayakers wore tennis shoes, fishing waders, tabbies, and bare feet. So much for water footwear. What about backpacking boots?

With all its shortcomings, I am a strong proponent of the heavy, leather hiking boot. By heavy, I don't mean mountaineering boots with a full shank, but the sturdy hiking boot with a half or three-quarter shank. I maintain that its six pounds are outweighed by the advantages of good ankle support, rock protection, and traction in mud and scree. Try boulder hopping sometime in tennies, (but not too often if you value your neck). Try coming down a scree slope in running shoes, (but only if you're a marathon runner who slides most of the way anyhow). Along with firm leather, I favor such niceties as padded ankles, full gusset closure or gusseted flaps over padded tongue (so I can step in that first ankle-high puddle and stay dry), heavy braided nylon laces looped through D-ring hooks and grommet fasteners, and above all, good fit.

I wear a European boot. Ladies might remember that the European boot-size system doesn't differentiate between sexes, but shoes in American women's sizes are made on narrower lasts than are men's. A woman with medium-wide feet usually has little problem in either a man's or woman's shoe. It's the gals and guys with very narrow or very wide feet who cry and cry. Here's where your friendly shoe salesman is indispensable. Don't leave the store with a pair of boots about which you have some doubts. A conscientious salesperson knows and uses all the tests for correct fit. If all else fails, there are always custom-made boots. (Colin Fletcher recommends Steve Komito, Estes Park, Colorado 80517, for both custom-made boots and repair of your old favorites.)

You'll know before you buy whether you have unusual foot configurations such as extremely high arch or instep, unusually narrow foot, unusually wide foot, bunions, what have you. Be prepared to try on many brands and styles until you are completely satisfied. You will remember, of course, to take to the store with you the inner cotton or poly sock and outer heavy sock that you normally wear. And just in case no one has told you, the reason for two socks is that they rub against each other rather than against you. Don't ask me why the inner sock doesn't rub you—probably it's too busy rubbing the outer sock. I just know it works.

Another indispensable aid to feet is moleskin, that soft, strongly adhesive covering for hot spots or actual blisters. Many hikers apply it before starting out, knowing their potential trouble spots. I've even used it over hip bones and shoulder bones when the pack rubbed. Moleskin comes in sheets and can be cut to size. You'll find it in your drugstore among the foot products.

Apply moleskin at the first sign of a blister. Moleskin also can be used over hip bones and shoulders, where packs may rub. (*Photo by Bill Wakeland.*)

Why mention blisters when good-fitting boots are supposed to prevent them? Because there *are* blister times with any boot: 1) first trip of the year, feet still winter-soft; 2) second trip of the year, feet still soft; 3) after you've hiked all day in the rain through swamp; 4) when you are too lazy and stupid enough to wade through a stream in your boots and you think a pair of dry socks will heal all; 5) when you've been hiking in hundred-degree weather in all wool socks and are too macho to stop and change to lighter socks.

One last word of advice. Beware of those who tell you to break in a boot by soaking it in the bathtub, then wearing it until it dries. This happens fast enough on the trail. Don't speed up the disintegration of a good boot.

Gore-Tex has entered the boot market also. The 1980–81 catalog from Eastern Mountain Sports features a light hiking boot constructed from waterproof, breathable, rugged, foam-padded packcloth with Gore-Tex laminate—weight two pounds four ounces.

So much for hiking boots for spring, summer, and fall. What about winter footwear? Cross-country skiers have no choice, except perhaps between racing shoes and warmer, lined touring boots. If feet still get cold in the latter, try a canvas-foam overboot, which helps some. Buy boots large enough to accommodate two pairs of wool socks. Keep these boots well-greased. Body heat and winter sun quickly melt the snow which then penetrates the porous leather of ungreased boots.

Leather, even in double layers, does not prevent cold feet. It also absorbs melted snow, better known as water. For this reason, many winter hikers and snowshoers choose a combination rubber-leather or neoprene-leather shoe (Sorel brand and L. L. Bean's Maine Hunting shoe are two). The rubber or neoprene sole is stitched to a leather upper, and warmth is added with felt liners and wool socks. Best to take along an extra pair of liners so that one set can be drying while the other is being worn. If you also wear gaiters, you may even keep snow from creeping over the tops. Gaiters are made of Gore-Tex or nylon, with snaps or velcro fasteners at front or back. I prefer the sixteen-inchers because they keep the lower pants leg dry almost to the knee.

For really sub-zero mountaineering, I use the white rubber military vapor barrier boot, often erroneously referred to as the bunny boot. This was the name used for the World War II suede leather boot that was dyed white for camouflage. The present-day vapor barrier boot was born during the Korean War. Its warmth derives from the containment of dry air in felt

Options for winter footwear: *left,* lined ski boots worn with gaiters; *center,* Sorel boots with breathable leather uppers and waterproof rubber lowers; *right,* vapor barrier boots. Felt soles or liners may be inserted for additional warmth.

layers sealed between outer and inner rubber layers. The boot's bloated look (hence the name Mickey Mouse boot) comes from its dual layers and the valve on its side, which allows air pressure within the boot to escape if the wearer is in an aircraft that suddenly depressurizes. However, the valve should be kept closed to prevent moisture from getting in and ruining the insulating value of the dry felt. There is one very important thing to remember when wearing vapor barrier boots: Your feet will perspire heavily in them because they are air tight. Therefore, it is vital that these boots be removed at night, the feet thoroughly dried, and dry socks put on. McKinley climbers have learned this the hard way: The skin on their feet breaks down from the trapped moisture, or their feet freeze as evaporating moisture draws out body heat when laces are loosened at night.

The cost of vapor barrier boots, which are very popular in Alaska, is around $150. Compare this to the rigid plastic boots that provide good foot control for climbers, but cost more than $200 a pair. I bought a pair of vapor barrier boots fifteen years ago from an Army surplus store and paid $15 for them. They are still my favorite boot on the winter trail, even though I look like Minnie Mouse when wearing them. They do, however, require considerable adjustment of the binding when used as a ski boot or with snowshoes.

Lest you wonder if hikers wear only boots, let us proceed to other parts of the anatomy.

◼ Clothing—Inner Layer

The skin is as good a place as any to begin a discussion of clothing. In northern and high-country regions, we tend to think a lot about hypothermia, and likewise long johns. My Minnesota childhood version has been improved upon. No longer the dropseat, one-piece, itchy wool version whose legs stretched and had to be folded over under cotton stockings, to the ever-lasting mortification of my third-grade image. Now we have thermal (Duofold), fishnet, and plastic models, as well as the old standbys, waffleweave cotton and all wool.

Duofold manufactures a two-piece underwear with two-layer construction. The outer layer is a blend of wool for warmth, nylon for strength, and cotton; the soft inner layer is all cotton. Even those allergic to wool can have the warmth of wool with the comfort of cotton. These garments are machine washable but washing must be handled with care. All the rules for wool apply: cold water, gentle detergent, line drying. If you have "helpers" in the family who throw in an occasional load of wash and set the dial on hot, hide your underwear until you're ready to give it proper care. Otherwise you'll end up with half a pair. Wool always has and always will shrink in water over ninety-eight degrees—that's the temperature at which the sheep maintained it. Duofold thermal underwear costs $12 to $15 for each piece, but it is an essential piece of gear. In fall, winter, and spring, I wear one pair and carry another set to sleep in.

Some of my walking companions swear by the open mesh or fishnet underwear, made from cotton, cotton-poly, or even wool and usually worn with a tight-fitting overshirt. They tell me it effectively insulates and keeps body moisture from soaking subsequent layers of clothing. In severe cold, some wear waffleweave cotton or wool underwear over it. SXC Manufacturing Company has come out with polypropylene fishnet.

Another new entry on the market is plain-knit polypropylene plastic underwear by Lifa and Odlo. A friend who has tried it says it is nonabsorbent and feels dry under most conditions. Patagonia (Chouinard) has a much heavier polypropylene—like an old school sweatshirt. Damart of New Hampshire sells underwear made from a fabric called Thermolactyl, a new synthetic of Vinyon and acrylic. Their catalog claimed this was exceptionally warm, elastic, and breathable, so I tried it. I have to admit they weren't lying. As with most synthetic products, washing instructions are simple but precise: Hand wash or machine wash on a gentle cycle using cool water; drip dry; do not place in dryer; always avoid heat of any kind such as a dryer, iron, radiator, etc.; do not dry clean; to remove spots, use a commercial spray or stain remover.

For those of Nieman-Marcus mentality, there is Angoraba—a "luxurious Angora rabbit hair"—at a luxurious price of $24 per piece.

Down underwear is another possibility for the chronic sleeping-bag shiverers. Worn over DuoFold, polypropylene, or Thermolactyl, it makes for a comfortable night. It stuffs into a small space, too.

Both men and women should wear all-cotton briefs or jockey shorts. Nylon gets sweat-wet, feels awful, and never seems to dry. Fit should be loose, to prevent binding and chafing. Women might also be interested in the Jogbra, made from a stretchy combination of cotton and Lycra. It has no hooks or wires and is supposed to eliminate chafing. (It's shown in the 1980 Early Winters catalog.) Another undergarment used by some of my female friends is a disposable liner; it cuts down on both washing and the number of underpants necessary for a trip.

■ Clothing—Top Second Layer

I carry two tops on longer trips. One is a long-sleeved, dark-colored turtleneck; the second, a light-colored, short-sleeved open-neck top. (Dark colors absorb heat, light colors vice versa). Each is a combination of polyester and cotton that dries quickly, whether sweat laden or stream washed. These two styles get me through chilly mornings at altitude or hot tromps across the lowlands. Some turtleneck tops have a zipper in the neck, which is great for ventilation as the day gets warmer. I wear the zipper in the front.

Men can go the same route or opt for cotton-poly button shirts. One hiking male I know always wears a long-sleeved button shirt for all temperatures because he's allergic to sun. Since it is a poly-cotton blend, it dries quickly after a stream washing. (Environmentalists relax—you can wash the shirt in your cook pot and throw the suds away from the stream.)

■ Clothing—Lower Second Layer

Unless I am absolutely certain I will be hiking in high temperatures, with little or no altitude gain, I always carry two pairs of trousers, one wool and one synthetic. Pants can be of woven wool with a soft finish or with a hard finish such as twill. If wool is combined with a small amount of nylon or polyester, it is more resistant to abrasion and tears. Beginning hikers soon learn that wool, because of its tight fibers, is warm even when wet (although its insulating value is reduced by almost half when wet).

Polyester pants, either of a hard-finish knit or with some other abrasion-resistent finish, have always been my choice for hiking. Although the elastic-waist stretch knits move with the body, they boast no pockets. This deficiency I remedy by carrying a small fanny or waist pack to hold items such as money or tickets on the plane, and sunlotion, insect repellent, sunglasses, notebook, and pencil on the trail. Most men and some women prefer cargo trousers, some with six pockets, with belts to hold knives, etc.

Although hiking pants are available in a nearly infinite number of fabrics and styles, I insist that hikers accompanying me into the wilderness carry at least one pair made from a synthetic blend—I'll even settle for "50-50." But I emphatically draw the line at 100 percent cotton denim jeans because they are hypothermic death traps. Once wet, they stay wet for the remainder of the trip. One author also describes them as "the most sophisticated instrument of torture known to man." Contrary to popular opinion, they are not the only trousers made these days. Browsing through the catalogs and shops, I came up with this list of fabrics: cotton canvas, flannel-lined, moleskin, duck, Gore-Tex, poplin (65 percent poly, 35 percent cotton), whipcord, stretch (poly, cotton, and Spandex), corduroy, sailcloth, cotton chino, twill, and Zepel-treated poly-cotton. When I get moans and groans from the jeans crowd, I hand them the catalogs or send them shopping. I also ask them to test the drying time of a pair of cotton denim jeans when the humidity is high or it's drizzling. Then they understand why I am also known as the "no jeans lady." The work clothes department of stores such as Sears, Montgomery Ward, and J. C. Penney has a good selection of trousers in synthetic fabrics.

Some will be surprised to know that I often include a pair of shorts in my pack. For some places in the continental United States (and in other continents), it's the only way to go. But there are disadvantages to shorts.

My daughter, for example, once insisted on wearing cotton poplin shorts on a Sierra trip, which she knew would take us into snow at ten thousand feet. Her brother and I opted for synthetic long pants and even at ninety-five degrees we felt comfortable. We soon noticed that her legs were mosquito-bitten and scratched from brush, even though we were on a well-trod Forest Service trail.

Some authors advise hikers to shun shorts entirely and wear only long pants. These do reduce the amount of insect repellent and Band-Aids used. But again, the choice between long and short pants is a matter of terrain, weather, and personal preference. Wearing shorts provides a modest way to cross streams if it's chilly and you want to keep your long pants dry. It seems, however, that men prefer the women to cross in their bikinis, if the photographic frenzy precipitated on one Wrangell Mountain trip is any indication. On the same trip, though, I was chided by a lady of middle years that I should have warned her to at least wear opaque bloomers. Shorts also substitute for bathing suits if you forgot to include same.

■ Clothing—Third Layer

For years, I've included a standard heavyweight wool shirt (85 percent wool, 15 percent nylon). There also are medium-weight shirts of the same fabric and all wool, hand-tailored shirt-jacs from New Zealand. The Nordic ragg wool sweaters and Icelandic handknit pullovers are gorgeous and practical. I prefer a buttoned front that can be opened for ventilation without removing a pack.

In the past year, I've worn a pile jacket. Its hard outer finish is abrasion resistant. The soft pile inner surface is warm and breathable. It dries fast. Even body heat does the job. It is also machine washable, but has a tendency to pill somewhat. It is not, however, warm in wind or very cold temperatures, so must be layered with a windbreaker (I use my Gore-Tex rain jacket) or other outer garment. To some, it might seem bulky when worn with a down or synthetic parka. These folks should stick to the wool-shirt inner layer.

Outer clothing is designed to protect a backpacker from wind, rain, snow, and bugs. When nylon first appeared, it seemed ideal because it was water repellent and wind resistant when coated. Hikers soon discovered that it was also a private sauna. Then came a compromise: 60–40 cloth woven with nylon in one direction and cotton in the other. Still popular is the classic parka made of tightly woven, breathable polyester-cotton blends. Then came Thinsulate and Gore-Tex. The stories behind these two marvels of the chemical age are interesting enough to tell once more.

Thinsulate, made by 3M Company, is a combination of polyester fibers (thicker filaments are used in PolarGuard and Hollofill II) and extremely

69

Hikers near Klein Creek Ridge in the Wrangells are decked out in rain gear: *left,* jacket of water-repellant 60–40 cloth; *right,* coated neoprene rainsuit. (*Photo by Emile McIntosh.*)

fine polyolefin fibers. 3M claims that it is the ultra thin fibers that allow "thin to be warm." Microfibers trap more dead air in a given space than do the larger diameter, more widely spaced fibers of conventional fiberfills or down. 3M also says Thinsulate is odorless and nonallergenic and can be machine washed many times. Not much is said about water resistance or breathability, but as an insulator, Thinsulate tests well.

Gore-Tex was born in 1969, the result of a chemical taffy pull in the laboratories of W. L. Gore & Associates. Scientists there discovered that they could pull Teflon (polytetrafluoroethylene) rapidly in opposite directions and produce a material filled with tiny holes. First produced commercially in 1975, Gore-Tex is eighty-two percent air, with nine billion holes per square inch. The diameter of these pores is so small that aggregates of liquid water molecules can't pass through and instead bead on the surface. However, molecules of gaseous water, also known as sweat, stay in groups small enough to pass through the pores. Voila, a breathable fabric that keeps out water but lets perspiration escape. When rolled into thin sheets, Gore-Tex is quite fragile, so it's laminated to other fabrics, some sixteen different ones at last count.

Gore-Tex garments serve equally well as windbreakers or rain gear. The product has been around long enough to be field tested by many backpackers. I have worn my Gore-Tex jacket and pants during two seasons of backpacking and skiing and rate it highly, but some of my colleagues

70

disclaim it entirely. They dislike having to seal seams and having to keep the garment scrupulously clean to prevent wicking at dirt spots. W. L. Gore & Associates have now answered the seam-sealing problem by melting a thermoplastic tape over the seams on the inside of the garment at the factory. As for cleaning, I wash my rain jacket and pants in the machine (gentle-wash) with Ivory Flakes (note that's soap, not detergent) and sponge off grease spots with alcohol or spray with K2R spot remover.

I've sealed my Gore-Tex rain gear only twice, but it has kept me dry, even in a Kodiak cloudburst. I climbed a mountain in a rainstorm wearing my Gore-Tex, sweating all the way, and I was dry at the end of the day. My daughter survived a Boston winter wearing a pile vest with her Gore-Tex parka. Another friend wore his Gore-Tex rain pants continuously during a 1,000-mile sled dog race. Although the pants were soiled with trail grime and the gruel he prepared for his dogs, he wore them during the rainy mountain hike mentioned above and had no complaints. Gore-Tex passes vapor well as long as that vapor remains above dew point. However, if the vapor cools enough to condense within the layers before it reaches the Gore-Tex, it will remain there until re-vaporized. Translation: Gore-Tex doesn't work so well in very cold weather.

My friends who dislike Gore-Tex opt instead for rain gear made from polyurethane-nylon laminates, such as Bukflex by Peter Storm. The outside layer of nonwoven polyester coated with polyurethane repels rain; the inside layer of absorbent nylon tricot prevents clamminess. But Bukflex is expensive. And though it's been around for quite a few years and is billed as "condensation free," its breathability is limited. Hike fast and you'll sweat in it.

Neoprene combined with cotton is still available and low priced. Many shops sell a two-ply nylon taffeta with thick polyurethane coating. Vinyl-coated cotton also is available, but expensive. Vinyl plastic, in the $1.98 bracket, may last fifteen minutes in brush, but it's better than nothing.

Greasewool is another name for wool that has not had the natural sheep oil (also known as lanolin) removed in the scouring process. Sweaters made from it are popular in cool, rainy climates. Peter Storm also offers an "oiled wool" in which the lanolin is reintroduced during spinning. In Super Oiled Wool, a synthetic water repellent is added in place of lanolin. Light rain beads up and runs off these sweaters. They're great in fog and drizzle, but not very practical in a downpour.

If you're involved in a budget-holding action, you could consider treating your jacket with a water repellent. 3M still sells its Scotchguard, but treatment should be repeated after each washing. K-Pel, a paraffin coating that is applied in the washing machine, works best on nylon fabrics. None of these repellents, however, will get you through a downpour completely dry.

Some long-time backpackers prefer ponchos. They have the advantages of low price and lots of air circulation. (*Photo by Bill Wakeland.*)

I suppose ponchos will be with us as long as limited budgets. They are the vinyl-plastic specials that have the advantages of low price and venting—lots of it. Wind billowing under a poncho in a rainstorm can make an ex-user in a hurry. Cagoules, defined by Colin Fletcher as "knee length sleeved capes with hood," have a drawstring hem that prevents wind billowing. You can also sit down, draw up your knees, and snuggle out a storm in one. Cagoules also come in urethane-coated laminates or Gore-Tex, but there goes the price.

An anorak is a hooded pullover with or without a short zipper. Although it may be more rainproof and windproof without a zippered or buttoned front, it vents less easily. One of my hiking companions grumbles every time she has to stop, remove her pack, and pull the hood over her head. I opt for easy venting.

If you can't find something to keep you dry among all those suggestions, you aren't trying.

■ Clothing—Outerwear

As an alpine backpacker you will, at some time or other, reach a summit and pitch a tent. This is the moment of truth with respect to outer garments and their warmth. Up to this point, I've been fuzzy as to just how much warmth is needed on mountain tops elsewhere than in Alaska. My experience on the Sierra trip mentioned earlier shows why. The temperature in San Diego was a balmy 75 degrees Fahrenheit; at Lone Pine and Independence it registered 95 degrees on that mid-June day (5,000 plus feet); at 10,000 feet the next day the temperature was 30 degrees in the early morning hours and rose to the sixties during the day. While knocking the icicles off the branches to facilitate reaching stream water, I found it necessary to wear four layers of assorted fabrics, plus a watch cap to keep my ears warm, plus gloves to hold that frigid water bottle. I yearned for my double goose-down parka, my insulated gloves and my balaclava—all back in Alaska.

I now recommend that alpine packers thoroughly research temperature and altitude conditions at their intended destination. If you're the type who climbs a mountain, pitches a tent, cooks a meal, and jumps into his sleeping bag, you'll probably ignore the following advice. But if, after taking care of basic chores, you like to indulge in a leisurely cocktail before dinner combined with spiritual inhalation of breathtaking views and a bit of campfire philosophy afterwards, then prepare to clothe your body appropriately.

Standing around camp cools that sweat fast, so I include my double goose-down parka with hood on late fall, winter, and spring hikes. If I was going to be above 4,000 feet in Alaska or 10,000 feet in the lower forty-eight states, I'd also include it in my summer pack. I say "double down" only because my parka is a pre-space age one acquired in the early 1970s. Today's backpacker can go with a Gore-Tex down parka (the outer shell is Gore-Tex laminated to any one of many fabrics and the lining is filled with goose down.) A browse through the stores or catalogs also will turn up mountain parkas with polyester-cotton shells insulated with synthetic fabric, Hollofill II, PolarGuard, or Thinsulate. (There're even some with wool insulation.) Simply stated, the case for synthetics is their quick-drying ability. Down may be warmer, but not when it's wet. Down also is becoming more and more difficult to obtain, and you know what that does to the price. A ray of hope may be "fake" down, which the fiber industry has

73

developed recently. The manufacturer says it will be a perfect substitute for goose feathers in coats, jackets, pillows, and comforters—and much cheaper than the real thing.

For the down diehards, though, the best solution may be combining it with a breathable, waterproof outer shell. Although my fisherman-husband claims his Gore-Tex down jacket becomes saturated, not every fisherman is as persistent in his pursuit of the finny one. He is completely oblivious to a downpour. I think he also forgot to seal his seams. Perhaps for those who stand knee deep in streams or sit in boats for hours, the polyurethane-nylon laminate (waterproof, nonbreathable) is the better answer. Whatever your choice, be sure that it's with you when you reach those alpine heights.

Add to the above, no matter what the month, synthetic or wool gloves and wool mittens large enough to go over them. When cooking or doing other chores that require finger dexterity, you can pull off the outer mitt. Nothing glaciates those pinkies faster than aluminum pots at forty degrees. With practice, you can even learn to fill a mountain stove without spilling gas on your gloves. In extremely cold weather I rely on L. L. Bean's Double Mitts, which have a ragg-knit outer mitten of all wool and a stitched-in-place inner mitten of wool, acrylic, and nylon blend. The inner mitten is terry lined for comfort and to absorb moisture.

These hikers are suitably dressed for different seasons and activities. *Left,* author is dressed for backcountry ski touring; *center,* hiker is ready for an early spring or late fall outing; *right,* backpacker is bundled up for cold-weather camping.

■ Head Gear

I have saved the most important item of gear for last. Omitting it may contribute to your early demise. The brain receives a fifth of the body's blood supply and even more of its oxygen, and the scalp contains an immense number of blood vessels that lie directly over the bone with little fat insulation. This combination causes tremendous loss of body heat, an estimated thirty to fifty percent of the total. Those hikers who intend to return from the heights will not scoff when told to put on a hat to remedy cold feet.

The varieties of head gear are infinite. The watch cap seems to be a favorite. It can be of 85 percent wool and 15 percent nylon, all wool, or even goose down. I suppose the name *watch cap* comes from the warm head gear used by naval types on the high seas or army types in similar inclement situations. "One size fits all" might be a trifle misleading, or else I've got a big head, so try it on before you buy it. Ski hats ride up more easily than the circular knit caps.

You can also get head and neck protection in the traditional Scottish balaclava helmet, also available in wool or wool-synthetic combinations. This can be worn folded up as a regular cap or pulled down over your head to cover face, ears, and neck. Some have visors. Only the eyes are uncovered when wearing the traditional balaclava. You may at times bear close resemblance to Frosty the Snowman when breathing through the mask on an uphill climb at minus temperatures, but you do stay warm, if only by the heat of your own breath. Silk balaclavas cost $15. They are warm but not hot, they don't scratch, and they roll up into a small ball.

If it's raining and hoods cramp your style, you may prefer the sou'wester rain hat with wide brim and chin tie. It slants downward at the back to prevent rain running down your neck and also interference with your pack. One I've seen is made of nylon oxford cloth coated with butyl. A sou'wester hat also can be used as protection from the sun. It has limitations at higher temperatures, but this gives me an excuse to discuss head protection from the sun's rays.

Two cases of heat exhaustion have convinced me that some protection is necessary, and I've experimented with many types—simply narrow-brimmed cotton hats, hats of wool suede with wider brim, cotton bandanas, terry-cloth hats with floppy brims, straw creations with ventilation holes, and plastic rain caps. Since one of the requirements of effective head gear is its "easy on, easy off" capability, the brimmed hats of stiffer fabrics come up wanting when stuffed in pocket or pack. On the crushability index, I rate watch caps or balaclavas high for cold-weather use. During the summer, bandanas, brimmed cotton hats, and visor caps score well on the crushability index, but they all seem to get sticky at high noon. Perhaps Early Winters has solved the problem with the "Panama Crusher." It's a new lightweight hat that folds for storage in a pocket or pack. It's made by hand of real Ecuadorian grasses and weighs less than two ounces. It comes in one standard size but can be easily shrunk or stretched to fit.

The best protection against the sun involves wearing your favorite head covering and sunglasses, stopping often in the shade, and drinking lots of water. Wearing a water-soaked bandana provides evaporation cooling, but plays havoc with hairdos. If I'm still worried about appearance after slogging for hours up a sixty-degree slope, I wet the bandana, fold it into a two-inch strip, and tie it around my forehead and under my hair. This works great for the guys also, who may or may not be worried about hairdos. All of this presupposes an abundance of streams or a very large canteen.

Again, to insure an extended career in backpacking, include appropriate headwear.

CHAPTER EIGHT

BACKPACKS

In order to be a backpacker, you need a backpack. Question: What kind? Next question: How serious do you intend to get about this body-bruising, soul-enriching pastime which can find you in a mosquito-infested swamp in the morning and on a mind-boggling mountain top at day's end. Let's say you've outgrown the day hike with rucksack category and want to strike out for five or six days in high-country. Then, with an anxious glance at your checkbook balance, you hie yourself off to the equipment store.

There are two basic types of packs for the distance overnighter. The external frame with attached bag has been with us for a few years; more recently, the merchants have featured a softpack with internal frame. The softpack is a modern hybrid that was developed from the rucksack to fill the need of climbers, ski mountaineers, and bushwackers for a back-hugging gear carrier. You will understand this need if you have ever found yourself on hands and knees pulling yourself over a ledge, all the while trying to balance a weight on your back; or if you have ever crawled on your hands and knees under an alder limb and been so hung up you needed a tow truck. You will further understand this need if you have skied cross country to upper regions and on the down run felt your pack shift on a turn, throwing you face first in six feet of snow.

An internal-frame pack is usually constructed with only one or two inner compartments and few outside pockets. This lack of compartments and the tendency of the pack to throw too much weight on the hips are reasons I opt for an external-frame pack for longer summer and winter trips. Softpacks are really too warm for summer use, but I use a softpack for day ski tours.

So what do you look for in a framepack? Varieties abound, from aluminum S-ladder or the newer molded-plastic frames to the hipwrap with

The author, wearing an external-frame pack, views the Chitistone Glacier in the Wrangell Mountains. She attaches sleeping bag with teeth-straps, and tucks rain jacket under back tie strings when threatening weather requires quick access.

arms that hug the hips. Some frames are welded, some are bolted, some have extensions or adjustable crossbars. The hipwrap is great when you take it off because it stands by itself. But try to pack it into the trunk of a small car or into a Cessna 206, and you may have a few cross words about its design. Some say the hipwrap chafes the hips, others love the secure fit. This decision I leave to you. I'll settle for a padded hip-belt with quick-release buckle, padded shoulder straps, and nylon mesh backband. These modern innovations have helped to bring backpacking out of the Prospector Dan era. Not to mention what it's done for Arthritis Ann.

Attached to the pack frame is, what else, the pack bag. If it comes unassembled, you'll learn quickly that it's tricky attaching it to the frame. You can use bag snaps. (They come off easily in a fall or when dropping your bag too quickly from shoulder to ground. Carry extras. The snaps always, I repeat, always disappear in deep brush.) The most trailworthy attachment of bag to frame is made with clevis pins, which fit through grommet holes in the pack, then through the frame, and are held in place by wire rings. These break also, but not easily. Be wise and carry extra pins and wires.

Most pack bags are now made of nylon. Don't believe the claims that they are repellent. Carry a waterproof rain cover that can be placed over the pack on the trail or at night. This cover is open at the lower back to accommodate back straps, but ties together at the base of the frame. Eternal pessimist that I am, I also place all clothing and food in plastic bags inside the pack and carry an ordinary, garden-variety garbage bag to cover the pack at night.

For me, the most important attribute in a bag is the number of compartments. While many of my friends have converted to zip-open or one-compartment packs, I cling to my many-compartment bag. Why? I don't like dumping the entire contents of my pack on the ground in a pelting rainstorm to locate a Band-Aid. This may be good for laughs, but it sure muddies the gear.

I have used the same packing system for so many years that I know what's in each pocket. The lower back storage compartment is used for clothing. It is lined with a cut-off garbage bag because I am neurotic about dry clothes. Into this compartment I can stuff hiking pants, two shirts, underwear (long and otherwise), socks, down booties, mittens, and cap. In the upper inside section I store freeze-dried food and on top of that the tent,

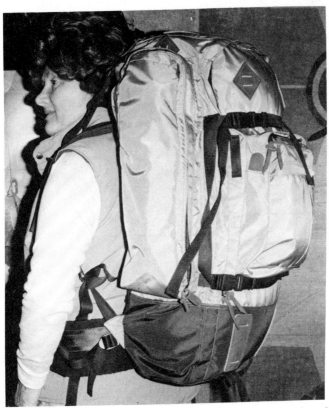

Some internal-frame packs, like the one shown, have several external pockets. Also known as softpacks, they tend to throw weight onto the wearer's hips, which can be tiring on long trips.

rainfly, poles, and stakes. On top of the tent goes my plastic food bag, which also contains knife, fork, spoon, and cups; beside this goes the cook kit containing stove. On top of this and within the extension drawstring top of the bag, I place my folded raincoat and jacket. I either wear or tie around my waist a pile jacket or wool shirt. In one upper side pocket goes a wide-mouth plastic water bottle. In the other upper side pocket are a fuel bottle and stream-crossing tabbies. In one lower side pocket, I carry all first-aid items; in the other lower side pocket, all personal grooming items. The outside back pocket contains compass, pencil, flashlight, carabiners, pocket novel, whistle, etc. The map is stowed in its obvious location—the map flap.

Attached to the frame below the upper pack is my sleeping bag stuffed *inside* a plastic garbage bag *inside* a stuff bag. I emphasize this because some beginners have shown up with the garbage bag over the stuff bag and seen it shredded on the first raspberry bush. You will sleep in a wet sleeping

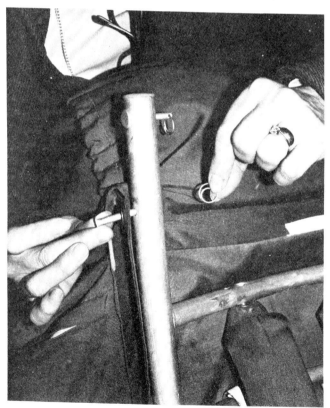

The most secure method of attaching bag to frame is with clevis pins and wire rings. It's easy to lose these gadgets, so be sure to bring extras.

bag only once before becoming extremely cautious about waterproofing same. Also attached to the frame in the same location is my ground pad. Both items are lashed with two teeth-straps threaded behind the crossbar of the frame. I am rather fanatic about teeth-straps. Too often have I waited and waited and waited for bungee cord users who stopped to tighten and restrap or backtracked to find a lost sleeping bag. I also have unkind words for straps without teeth that require a master's degree to release. The advantage of stowing bag and pad in the lower position is that the heavier items (tent, cook kit, etc.) are then placed higher on the body.

Total pack weight often provides miles of trail conversation. Colin Fletcher handles this weighty matter with some simple rules: If you need something, take it. Pare away relentlessly at the weight of every item. If you look after the ounces, pounds will look after themselves. I have always advised hikers to carry about one third of their body weight, then religiously avoided my own advice. Thirty pounds is great, forty, fifty, sixty—well, that's your decision. Weigh yourself on your bathroom scale, then step on it with loaded pack. This is guaranteed to help you remove accumulated trivia. But don't get so carried away that you rip labels off of food packets. You might find yourself eating pudding for breakfast and pancakes for dinner. One thing I have learned is that it is nearly impossible to carry a two-

Lining the clothing compartment of your pack with a plastic bag insures dry clothing despite heavy rain or a fall in a stream. Place food items used daily in a plastic or fabric drawstring bag in the top compartment where they can be reached easily. Always use a checklist when packing.

week supply of food on your back. Some solve this with caching or mailing food to stops along the way. In Alaska, there are darn few wilderness post offices, so I arrange for airdrops. When the cost is shared by five to ten hikers, it's not so bad.

By now, you have probably realized the importance of choosing a frame size (small, medium, large) that is right for you. The length of your torso is a more important consideration than your height. Have the salesperson load the pack with gear before you buy it. This will give you a better idea of its loaded fit.

Finally, you will have to decide which pack you can afford. Blushingly, I admit to buying my first pack in a discount store. It was made you-know-where and looked just like the more expensive brand I'd seen in the equipment store. It lasted two summers. The first season, the pockets ripped and the zipper jammed; the next summer, the frame broke when I dropped it too quickly one exhausting afternoon. My present pack and frame, in the hundred-dollar category, has taken me through five seasons and one thousand miles of wilderness hiking with yet a repair required. Berry and repellent stained, yes, but broken no.

If all of the foregoing is too elementary, I urge you to consult *Backpacking Equipment Buyer's Guide,* mentioned earlier. The editors carry you through picking a pack, loading a pack, caring for it, and carrying it aboard a plane; then they tell you about design and construction. Four frame styles are pictured, and 128 packs are evaluated. The packs are rated in three categories: those for extended expeditions, for general hiking, and for weekend jaunts.

CHAPTER NINE

TENTS

In the summer of '60, a family of six (mine) and a pilot with aircraft plus family of seven took on the great outdoors of fly-in Alaska. Landing on a lake in the soggy Susitna River flats, we pitched tents—after a fashion. Ours was an army-surplus, six-man cotton duck job, purportedly waterproof, with center pole and no floor. Its weight required two men to lift, and it rolled into a "compact" package abut six feet long and three feet wide. The pole wouldn't fit in the airplane. It took four trips to fly all of us and gear to the lake. The spongy tundra, leaky roof, and floorless tent provided a challenge what with an infant in cardboard crib and little people who kept popping out of sleeping bags.

In the summer of '70, one mother (me), one daughter, and one friend took to the mountains in search of Dall sheep. We pitched our two-man, one-wall, "waterproof," discount-store economy tent on the ridge top and proceeded to wait out two days of continuous downpour. We discovered what the tent wasn't, and that was waterproof. Not only did the outside leak, but the inside condensation gave me my first real lesson in that peculiarity of tent living. The body really does respire a pint, maybe a quart, of liquid per night.

In the summer of '80, one backpacker (me) sat in her double-wall A-frame on the sandy beaches of an Arctic river and allowed that the time had come to investigate this upstart in tenting circles known as the free-standing tent. The count up and down the beach went thusly: one A-frame with wind tunnel and cooking vestibule identical to mine; one vintage A-frame; four freestanding dome tents; and one Gore-Tex, one-man tunnel tent. As a sort of last-ditch stand during this thirteen-night trip, I always tried to be the first to pitch my tent. I claimed it was because of bugs or threatening weather or whatever. But I really wanted to time the domers

Over the years, the author has grown attached to her Eureka Mountain II A-frame tent, set up here in the Brooks Range. (*Photo by Chuck Heath.*)

from my secret vantage point inside my tent. I disguised my smugness when they struggled to insert the fiberglass poles in a high wind, or when their tent tumbled down the beach the minute they turned their back. I wasn't quite so smug when they invited two guests into their tent for a game of cards and no heads bumped the ceiling. I was secretly impressed when they spread out two sleeping bags and two backpacks, and still found space inside to cook.

I have had such a love affair with my A-frame with its zip-out cooking vestibule and tunnel entrance that I have over-looked being slapped in the face with a sagging wall. I also have a secret, told here for the first time. When encamped upon slopes with unlimited view or on beaches besieged with gnats, mosquitoes, and fellow campers, I sometimes solve the problem of modest elimination by simply unzipping the cookhole. Needless to say, this minimizes its further use as a cookhole but sure saves long walks on buggy or rainy nights.

Ah well, the A-frame has served me well; still one must look forward. That seems to be in the direction of the self-supporting domes or geodesics. Manufacturers have eased the transition for us diehards by producing a tunnel-design, freestanding tent—the familiar A-frame with a rigid pole wrapped around its middle. This will woo the A-framer gently away from his flapping, sagging tent and into the well-ordered spaciousness of the new tenting world. Tunnel tents also make good wind tents, but alas, the sides have to be guyed out.

Fiberglass poles also seem to break more easily than aluminum. Some companies have solved this by offering anodized aluminum poles with shockcord. One disadvantage of the new poles is their longer length when folded. Since that extra five or six inches won't fit horizontally into the top of your pack, you'll have to lay the poles either across the top of your gear under the flap or push them through the corner openings of the upper compartment into the lower compartment. Some people strap them to leather accessory patches along the side of the pack.

As if attuned to the laments of tall hikers who want stretch-out length along with head room, Recreational Equipment, Inc. features the Ellipse tent in its 1980–81 catalog. This freestanding tent has a rectangular floor, 64 inches by 98 inches. The catalog describes it as a lightweight (6 pounds 7 ounces) three-season tent, which provides "great spaciousness and unparalleled ventilation." Note that it says three-season: The roof is a snow-catcher. The Ellipse not only has plenty of head and shoulder room but also is longer than the standard A-frame. It has two large, arch-shaped doors in the longer sides. In addition to this innovation, the roof has two large triangular panels of no-see-um netting to provide a view of the night sky. As expected, this marvel has a far-out price also: $250 for tent, rainfly, stakes, poles, and stuff sack. I must admit I was impressed by the design of the Ellipse. On its first outing, it performed superbly during a hurricane.

The author's new REI Ellipse tent got a five-star rating during its initial outing in Kauai, Hawaii. The tent and occupants survived a hurricane, 100-mile-per-hour winds, and torrential rains. *(Courtesy Recreational Equipment, Inc.)*

Eureka has also been listening to the laments of backpackers who want a little more leg room. The new four-season Eureka Sentinel, featured in 1981-82 catalogs, is self-supporting, measures 72 inches by 96 inches (two-person model), and has a door on each end. The aluminum frame breaks down into rods no longer than 20 inches, so the frame can fit inside most backpacks rather than having to be lashed to the outside. This is an important feature, especially if you travel by air to your starting point.

Above-timberline campers (or even unsheltered coastline tenters) need a tent that will hold up in a gale. Low-profile tents spill wind better than high ones. This would seem to rule out the larger dome tents. But in wind tests conducted by REI, dome tents fared as well as the A-frames and arched-sidewall types.

Tent sizes often are described as two-person, four-person, six-person, which mean little. Better to ask what size person. Two toddlers take little sleeping space, but sure use up lots of it when they're awake. On the other hand, not many toddlers reach ten thousand feet, but in this day of energetic parents, you can't be sure. By far the greater worry is how long will you remain in the tent? If you're a one-nighter no matter the weather, then low head room won't be a critical factor, unless you're a social butterfly whose tent is the center of evening card and grog parties on buggy or rainy

This scene at Lost Lake, near Seward, Alaska, shows a North Face VE 24 dome tent in foreground and two Eureka timberline tents to the far right. (*Photo by Bill Wakeland.*)

nights. It's hard to drink grog and play cards while lying on your stomach. Sit-up space is great, but stand-up space (a feature of some tents) may not be worth the extra pounds on your back. Weights of freestanding tents range from the 10 pounds 8 ounces for the geodesic wonders to 6 pounds 1 ounce for the A-frame models. The economy model one-wall weighs in at 3 pounds 2 ounces, but most standard A-frames weigh around 6 pounds. If you're sharing a tent, weight can be divided: poles and fly in one pack, tent and stakes in the second.

You won't need to think too much about fabric these days. Most backpacking tents are made of coated and uncoated nylon. The coated waterproof nylon is used for flys and floors (the bathtub design keeps out ground water). The uncoated nylon walls of the tent body are designed to allow vapor from your body and breath to ventilate out, eliminating inside condensation. The airspace between the inner wall and the outer fly permits moisture to escape through the wall, while the waterproof fly keeps out rain and snow. Most tents are rot-and mildew-proof, but don't push it. Always air your tent before storing. Netting seems to come in two colors, white and khaki. The latter provides one-way privacy, but keeps out light as well. Check the zippers for ease of operation.

Gore-Tex is everywhere and that includes tents. In tent fabrics, it is sandwiched between ripstop and rayon which adds weight. But a Gore-Tex tent needs no rainfly. (A fly weighs around 1½ pounds.) A Gore-Tex tent works best with the vents closed so that body heat can warm the air and create a slightly higher vapor pressure inside the tent. This pressure pushes water vapor through the Gore-Tex and out of the tent. With the vents open, there is no pressure buildup and moisture condenses on the cool outer surface just as it does on uncoated nylon. And in cold weather, body heat may not be able to keep air in the tent warm enough to prevent frost from accumulating on tent canopies. Although uncoated nylon canopies and frostliners also frost up, Gore-Tex seems to accumulate more frost under similar conditions. A second problem arises if you cook inside a Gore-Tex tent. Steam is not a problem because it pushes through the pores of the canopy. However, because of the necessity to keep the tent sealed tight to increase the inside pressure, carbon monoxide poisoning is a real danger. If you cook inside a Gore-Tex tent, open the doors. Finally, Gore-Tex is expensive.

Tent frames come in either anodized aluminum or fiberglass. Metal poles may bend (mine never have, even during a sixty-mile-per-hour wind), fiberglass will split or fray with misuse. One aluminum and one fiberglass tent pole bit the dust in REI's wind tests.

The stakes sold with your tent may have to be supplemented, depending on where you tent. Aluminum skewers are okay for most purposes. I found that my U-shaped staple design held better in sand and tundra than the single-nail shape. However, they are a dog to push into rocky ground.

Gore-Tex Light Dimensions tent (left foreground) is outnumbered by A-frame tents in this camp at 3,700 feet along the Chitistone Goat Trail in the Wrangell Mountains. (*Photo by Bill Wakeland.*)

Here the single stake is better. In very loose ground, such as sand, high-impact plastic stakes with I-beam sections provide more holding power, but you'll need a rock to pound them in. Another solution in sand, as in snow, is to deadman, or bury, the stake in a deep hole. So fierce was the wind in one sandy campsite that I wrapped the guy line around a three-foot piece of driftwood and buried the whole mess. But one is more likely to encounter tundra or rock above timberline. Tundra is a joy; rock is a pain. If the location defies staking, it is sometimes necessary to tie the guy lines to boulders or large rocks collected from the surrounding area. Another way is to tie the line to the stake, lay it flat, and pile a few rocks on top. For snow, it is best to use twelve-inch aluminum pegs or anchors buried in the snow. One winter camper of my acquaintance pours a little water in the hole, but there's hell to pay in the morning when de-staking.

Other tent goodies include tunnels, cookholes, inside pockets, and vestibules.

Lest I be criticized for mentioning only one equipment house, Eastern Mountain Sports, Inc. (Vose Farm Rd., Peterborough, New Hampshire 03458) also puts out an informative catalog featuring many freestanding tents. For even more detailed information, consult the *Backpacking Equipment Buyer's Guide,* which evaluates sixty-eight tents from thirty-two manufacturers.

TENTS

Before we fold our tents and quietly slip into the next chapter, I'd like to pass on some hints for pitching a tent. Wherever possible use designated campsites. That means checking local regulations before heading into the wilderness. Where you can't use a designated campsite, make your camp at least one hundred feet from a trail or from the shores of lakes and streams.

If you can't find a level spot, remember that you'll want to sleep with your head uphill. Avoid crests or depressions which place the two ends of the tent on different slopes that will make the tent hang badly. Common sense dictates avoiding gullies or depressions that carry or receive runoff, but I've failed to do so on occasion. In choosing a campsite, remember that it's warmer halfway up the hill than at the bottom (where cold dense air settles during the night) or at the top (where you'll be exposed to wind). An eastern slope exposed to morning sun will warm up and dry out faster at dawn; it's also likely to be sheltered from prevailing westerly winds (southwesterly winds in southcentral Alaska).

Pitch your tent into the wind (the door end in the case of geodesics). A rectangular tent should be staked at the windward end first; then carefully role it out flat and firmly stake the other two corners before attempting to raise it up against a gale. Freestanding tents require a whole new set of wind-pitching rules. It helps to have two people, one to hold the tent and

A level site like this is ideal for pitching a tent. Remember to test the ground underneath and to remove rocks or other debris that could damage the tent floor, and make for rough sleeping. (*Photo by Bill Wakeland.*)

89

one to insert the poles. Some loners place their pack on the inside floor of the tent to hold it down while inserting poles. This is still tricky after two or three poles are inserted and you're trying to lock the ends in place. It is prudent to stake a freestanding tent in windy conditions, as a female friend of mine learned one windy night in the mountains above Anchorage. A fellow camper noted her tent lifting and nearly soaring during the evening, but refrained from knocking on the lady's door to comment. Finally, my friend stuck her head out and allowed that she hadn't dared to come out of the tent because it might take off. Guy wires and stakes stabilized the situation. Another story is told about the beach tenter who returned to find his tent site minus tent. It had rolled down the beach and into the river.

There is one dramatic attribute of the freestanding tent. If you don't like where you pitched it, you can pick it up and move it. Owners like to show off this feature. A-framers solve this problem by stretching out the tent, lying down on it, and squirming their posteriors to check the terrain beneath, before pitching a tent.

You can tell by all of the above that tent-pitching time is a merry occasion in group camps. It also furnishes an endless source of conversation.

CHAPTER TEN

SLEEPING BAGS
AND PADS

Knowledge of sleeping bags grows in direct relationship to the number of miles one is carried on the back. I can't believe I was still fooling around with bulky, flannel-lined kapok bags in the 1960s. The situation improved somewhat when I discovered that the Air Force surplus store sold down-filled mummy bags, but they were covered with a cotton shell and weighed a ton.

About five hundred miles up the backpacking trail, I purchased my first lightweight down bag with a gorgeous blue nylon shell, rated to zero degrees and weighing all of four pounds. I slept blissfully through many more nights on the trail until two things happened: The tent leaked, and a zipper broke. The zipper was repaired, but I think that bag was still soggy weeks later. Anyone who has followed the directions for handwashing a down bag in the bathtub knows that it has the lead weight of a dead body. Manufacturers prefer that you line-dry the stinker but will reluctantly agree to mechanical drying in air—no heat. Some will even agree to dry cleaning, Stoddard solvent, that is; no perchlorethylene, please.

Just about the time I experienced my soggy night, the catalogs and stores were touting the new synthetic insulations—Hollofill, PolarGuard, Kodofill, Thinsulate, and Fortrel, to name a few. I bought my first PolarGuard bag along with an extra large stuff bag. That first monster weighed over six pounds and I huffed and puffed my way through every stuffing. My second PolarGuard bag (necessitated by the melted zipper mentioned earlier) is much more stuffable.

Since then, thousands of words have been written about down versus synthetic insulation, and for a while it looked like synthetics had won, not because of fancy rhetoric, but because of cost. Two factors may change this: The world petroleum crisis may cause the price of polyester to skyrocket; and new trade agreements with China, which supplies the lion's share of the world's down, could provide more down at lower prices.

So who's a body to back—the goose or the oil well? God forbid that we return to the shortages of World War II and its take-what-you-can-get black-market nylon. But black-market geese? Who knows?

Down will probably always be a popular insulator. It is the fluff growing next to the skin of a goose or duck. It traps air, allows body moisture out, and is resilient enough to withstand many compressions and expansions. But down does accumulate moisture in time—say, after a week of tenting in rainy weather—and there goes the loft and insulatory value. The Federal Trade Commission says down is supposed to be comprised of eighty percent goose down; the rest can be chicken, turkey, or pigeon feathers, or even floor sweepings.

PolarGuard and fiberfill sleeping bags are bulkier and more difficult to stuff than are other types. Try using a large stuff sack lined with a plastic bag. This makes stuffing easier and insures that the bag will stay dry.

Polyester fibers are petrochemicals that are extruded into thin fibers. When polyester fibers are crimped and layered into batts, they create loft. The greater the loft, the more dead air; the more dead air, the more warmth. Polyester is able to retain its crimp after repeated compressing, and unlike down, it maintains its loft when wet. It's many times cheaper per pound than down, and absorbs less than one percent moisture. It is non-allergenic, odorless, and mildew resistant.

Both PolarGuard and down bags should be hand washed, preferably in a bathtub. Warm water and a mild soap such as Loft are recommended. Gently press the sudsy water through the fabric, but avoid lifting it because this tears the stitching. Drain the water and rinse, then press the bag against the side of the tub to remove as much water as possible. It will not damage the bag to spin it dry in a washing machine. Hang the bag to dry for several days, preferably outdoors. Then you may finish the drying process by placing it in a machine dryer set on low or no-heat. Toss in a clean tennis shoe to help break up clumps of down.

A fiberfill bag may be machine washed at low temperature and dried in a dryer on the low or no-heat setting. NEVER USE HOT DRYERS. Heat over 140 degrees Fahrenheit destroys the loft of synthetic fills by removing the crimp in the fibers.

After you've puzzled over the down versus synthetic controversy, it's time to consider construction of a sleeping bag. Terminology for this phase relates to shape (mummy, rectangular, barrel, tapered); temperature rating (forty below to twice that above); baffles (this baffling subject includes 101 kinds of sewing—slant tube, slant wall, overlapping, sewn through, double quilt, straight box, slant box, V-tube, cross block, ad infinitum—when all you really want to know is if there are any cold spots); zippers (ladder coil, continuous coil, tooth); and other characteristics, long into the night.

My condensed version follows: A tapered bag hugs the body and leaves less air to be body-warmed but it's not easy to change your socks inside it. A drawstring hood helps to keep out cold, as does a baffle on the inside of the zipper. I prefer a zipper to go only halfway down because this cuts the odds on broken, jammed zippers by fifty percent. Two-way zippers allow for summertime ventilation of hot feet. Coil zippers don't glide as well as tooth zippers, but they are less likely to jam; some manufacturers claim tooth zippers are more durable. I've melted two nylon coil zippers and am still holding on a metal tooth job.

High-country temperatures on the coolish side dictate a three-season bag rated to about twenty degrees Fahrenheit. If the temperature drops, you can put on more clothes to add warmth. If a heat wave moves in, sleep on top of the bag. (Prudent alpiners are inside a bug-free tent.) Camptrails at one time solved the summer-winter problem with the Thermal Couple. The light-weight Simple Sack was right for summer sleeping, and the Sandarac was ideal for autumn and spring nights. Together they became a warm winter bag. Both, made of PolarGuard, cost less than many down sleeping bags. So the ad read.

Liners, vapor barriers and layering are another story. I'll tell it in Chapter 21 on winter camping.

Sleeping bags should be aired after use. Scrub willows at this camp near Skolai Pass in the Wrangells make good airing spots; so do tent tops.

Beneath every sleeping bag is a good ground pad. Plastic-and fabric-covered urethane pads were still around in the 1981 catalogs, as were Ensolite, Blue Foam, and coated nylon air mattresses. The newcomer on the ground pad scene is the Therm-A-Rest mattress. It combines open-cell foam insulation and air, but the neatest trick of the year is its self-inflating capability. Open the valve and air is sucked in; lock the valve; then open it, roll it up, and the mattress deflates. When a Therm-A-Rest is new or you're in a hurry, you can speed things up with a few puffs of your good hot air. Caution: Not too much hot air, please; moist breath leaves moisture inside which can freeze in winter. Fellow users tell me it can spring a leak, but not easily, and can be patched. Mine has survived two rough trips, a total of twenty-three nights of camping on sand, eight-inch river rock, birch forest, alpine tundra, sharp-edged mountain rocks, and soggy swamp. Rating: Five star.

If you still believe that pine boughs make superior insulation under a sleeping bag, forget about it. This greenery is in short supply these days (well, not really in Alaska, but we want some left for looking). I'll fudge a bit and say that it should be used only in extreme emergency—say, if your plane goes down or if extreme weather forces a bivouac (that's without tent, folks).

Back to that sleeping pad. Its purpose is to keep ground cold and moisture from penetrating your sleeping bag and you. Closed-cell foam (Ensolite) contains tiny, closed air pockets inside a poly-vinyl-chloride (PVC) material. Neither air nor water can penetrate. It's thin (1/4, 3/8, or

94

1/2 inch) and not as comfortable as the thicker urethane foam used in open-cell construction. To beat this problem, the EMS Super Pad combines 1/4-inch closed-cell and 1-1/4-inch open-cell foam. Blue Foam is the market name for a ground pad constructed from another of the miracle chemicals. It's cheap and provides good insulation, but bouncy comfort no. Because open-cell foam wicks water, it is usually encased in a waterproof, coated nylon cover; to prevent wicking of body moisture, some manufacturers make one side of a breathable fabric and the other of a waterproof material. You'll usually find moisture under your pad in the morning anyway. If you've ever slept on an unheated waterbed, you'll know that feeling. As for air mattresses, they are too bulky, too heavy, too much bother to inflate and deflate and their insulation value is almost zilch. High-country backpackers should leave them at home.

Size is another choice you'll have to make in the marketplace. The three-fourth length insulates from your shoulders to your hips and rolls into a smaller package than a full-length pad. I make up the shortage with a raincoat, stuff bag, or whatever under my lower legs and feet and a wool shirt or down jacket under my head. Some folks I know carry a pillow; others make one out of stuff bag and clothing. There have been nights when I longed for a longer pad (say, when the thermometer was at fifteen degrees Fahrenheit and I was pitched on wet snow), but for three-season use the three-fourth length usually suffices. Word of warning: At extremely low temperatures plastics break like crackers, with the possible exception of Valorfoam which is rated to minus fifty degrees.

Therma-A-Rest, Ensolite, urethane, urethane foam, Blue Foam— that's not as bad as fifty-five sleeping bags or sixty-eight tents from which to make a choice.

CHAPTER ELEVEN

STOVES AND FOOD

The modern kitchen in the wild has been reduced to a marvelous minimum of fuss and muss. The basic implements are a backpacking stove, a pot, a tool to eat with, and a cup to drink from. If that's too basic, read on.

I've added and subtracted over the years until my upland kitchen now includes a Sigg Tourist Cook Kit (the cover doubles as a frying pan or plate, the extra pot as a water container); a Svea 123UR stove, which fits inside the cook kit; an aluminum, cylinder-shaped fuel bottle with screw cap and additional cap with pour spout; waterproof matches; soft plastic measuring cup (with pour spout); insulated plastic cup; utensil kit (knife, fork, spoon); jackknife; can opener (which doesn't get used much on long trips); sponge, small amount of detergent, and scouring pad; a calculated number of sheets of paper towel; wide-mouth Nalgene water bottle; and a six-inch (one gallon) collapsible plastic water jug. Food containers include a square polyethylene box with snap-on lid for wheat thin crackers or pilot bread; an eight-ounce Nalgene wide-mouth bottle for instant coffee; plastic squeeze tubes for peanut butter, margarine, or shortening; and miniature salt and pepper shakers. A day's supply of food and eating-cooking utensils are carried in a drawstring heavy plastic or nylon bag. This can be pulled out of your pack with an astonishing swiftness that will impress fellow campers who must fumble through two or three sections of their packs to find their things. It also hangs well from a high tree limb, out of reach of even a Yosemite bear.

■ Stoves

The heart of the kitchen is, of course, the stove. *Backpacking Equipment Buyer's Guide* says there were thirty-five to forty models on the market in 1976. The authors admit, however, that the list boils down to seven good ones for winter and ten for three-season use. When *Backpacker* evaluated stoves in its April/May 1979 issue, several new models were available, including the Coleman Peak 1 Model 400 (with fold-out tripod legs), the MSR Model G (with new burner and flexible cable), the Optimus Princess Model 323 (with a hand pump instead of priming), and the Phoebus 725 (with a welded, rather than screw-on, burner attachment).

In 1980, Wonder Corp. came out with a compact butane stove/cookpot, the Globetrotter. It operates for about one hour on a six-ounce GT 100 cartridge. Average boiling time for a pint of water is seven minutes. The set includes two pots, a handle, the burner, support arms, and windscreen, which all pack together in the pots. Total weight is one pound.

An added feature to the very popular Coleman Peak 1 stove is the brand new Sigg P-1 Cook Kit, which appeared in 1981-82 catalogs. This kit is designed to fit the Coleman Peak 1 but otherwise is the same as the old standby.

One important way to classify stoves is by the type of fuel used: white gas (Coleman fuel, Blazo), propane, butane, kerosene, denatured alcohol, or solid fuel (Sterno, Heat Tabs). Availability of fuel is a real consideration

The Coleman Peak 1 stove, fueled by white gas, has been used by backpackers for some time, but the Sigg P-1 Cook Kit is new, designed to fit the larger dimensions of the Peak 1. (*Courtesy Recreational Equipment, Inc.*)

97

when backpacking. Most scheduled airlines will not permit passengers to board with campstoves filled with gas or with filled fuel bottles. Some airlines even insist that stoves and bottles be purged with carbon tetrachloride. Charter companies generally will carry gas as a necessary risk. This means that long-distance trekkers should call ahead to their destination to determine what fuels are available. I have found that even the smallest bush village in Alaska generally has white gas for sale, but on at least one occasion, it came from a large fuel tank and was contaminated with water. Since white gas is not as commonly used in trailhead villages in the rest of the United States, it is imperative that you find a fuel source *before* starting your trip when getting to the trailhead requires air travel. Kerosene is more readily available than white gas. The butane-filled Gaz cartridge is sold almost everywhere in Europe, but is not so easily purchased in the United States. Although airlines will not accept fuel cartridges on passenger flights, most will carry fuel on freight flights, so it may be possible to have fuel cartridges air freighted separately to your flight destination.

Weight is a factor to consider when selecting a backpacking stove, but don't let a few ounces more or less strongly influence your decision. Some very lightweight stoves don't work well, nor do some of the heavier ones. *Backpacking Equipment Buyer's Guide* rated thirty-six stoves whose weights ranged from sixty-nine ounces to six ounces. You may complain (or exalt) along the trail, but I-Day (Ignition Day) tells the final story.

Besides weight, and type of fuel, you should consider a stove's ease of packing, durability, safety (such as tank placement, fuel volatility, starting, refueling, fuel connections), stability (does it tip easily), reliability, boiling speed, cold-weather performance, AND PRICE. Very few stoves listed in the *Buyer's Guide* came through this battery of tests unscathed, but seven made it to the five-star category for three-season use. Of these seven, five were fueled with white gas, one with butane, and one was a multi-fuel unit. Add to this the more recent evaluations in *Backpacker* (April/May 1979) and the score stands at eight white gas, two butane and one multi-fuel. Yet one author claims butane stoves far outsell all others.

I won't get into the white gas versus butane-propane hassle. Proponents of each defend their choices vehemently. Some stoves lack stability but put out a blow-torch flame. Some do a fantastic job in summer, but fail in winter. Some poop out at altitude; others take forever to do the job at sea level. The ultimate questions are at what altitude and temperature do you plan to use your stove and what price are you willing to pay for this basic creature comfort.

If I had it to do all over again, I think I'd opt for the MSR Model GK multi-fuel stove, for which I'd need $74.50 or $69.75, depending on who sells it to me. Add to this $6.00 for a fuel bottle. This price might send me

FUEL COMPARISON

WHITE GAS
Caution: Do not use automotive fuel

Advantages	Disadvantages
Spilled fuel evaporates readily	Priming required
Stove fuel used for priming	Spilled fuel very flammable
Fuel readily available in U.S.	Self-pressurizing stoves must
High heat output	be insulated from snow
	or cold

KEROSENE

Spilled fuel won't ignite readily	Priming required
Stove can sit directly on snow	Spilled fuel does not
Fuel sold throughout the world	evaporate readily
High heat output	

BUTANE

No priming required	High cost
No fuel to spill	Cartridge disposal a problem
Immediate maximum heat output	Fuel must be kept above
	freezing for effective
	operation
	Gaz cartridges cannot be
	changed until empty
	Lower heat output

(Courtesy Recreational Equipment, Inc.)

right back to my old reliable Svea 123UR, which goes for "only" $26.95 or $29.95, again depending on who sells it to me. And then I would also have to purchase a Sigg Tourist Cook Kit and put up with the Svea's several drawbacks: difficulty of priming (I threw out the pump and now use paste), vulnerability to wind (I add an aluminum foil screen around the *outside* of the cook kit's own windscreen), and malfunctioning because of improper use such as overheating or letting the stove run dry, thus scorching the wick. To overcome starting problems in snow or cold weather, I place a square of Ensolite beneath the kit and warm the stove inside my jacket for as long as I can stand it.

The advantages of the MSR multi-fuel stove are its weight (one pound four ounces for stove, fuel bottle, and screen) and its ease of starting, aided

The MSR Model GK will burn a variety of fuels. For this reason, it should be carried as survival gear in every private plane, snow machine, or car traveling in backcountry or during severe weather. *(Courtesy Recreational Equipment, Inc.)*

by a flint lighter and self-contained priming pump that works at high altitude and in the cold. Moreover, the stove burns almost anything: Blazo, Stoddard Solvent, #1 stove oil, #1 diesel fuel, JP-4. The manufacturer says it will also burn leaded gasoline fuel for two hours before gumming up, and that it can be ungummed in the field. That's a lot of performance, even for the price. Just one reminder: Bring along ear plugs if you're seeking quiet with your solitude. The machine sounds like a freight train coming over the peak.

I got so carried away about the MSR stove that I pinned its description on the refrigerator door. And what do you know, six months later I received the MSR as a birthday gift. Now, after a season of use, I give the MSR stove a four-star rating. It always started promptly and boiled water rapidly, albeit noisily. The MSR's single deficiency, as I see it, is its lack of simmer capability. Here the Coleman Peak 1 excels, but its boiling time is longer than that of the MSR and it weighs more. If you're a freeze-dried/hot water proponent, then the MSR Model GK stars; if you're a gourmet, stir-fry cook, Coleman Peak 1 wins.

I write all of the above knowing that my butane-propane using friends may attack me on the next trip. They will claim fast starting, powerful flame, simmer capability, and moderate price for their favorite. They may forget to mention its greater weight, poorer stability, longer cooking time at

100

sea level, and tendency to leak fuel. Not to mention the difficulty in obtaining fuel or knowing how much is left in a cartridge.

STOVE COMPARISON

Stove	Fuel	Stove Weight without fuel (in ounces)	Capacity in Pints	Burning Time at Max. Flame (in minutes)	Average Boiling Time (5) (in minutes)	Boiling Time (6) at 14,000 ft. (in minutes)	Stability	Ease of Operation	Cold Weather Use	Compactness
Optimus 8R	White Gas	23	.30	45	8	8-11	G	G	F(1)	G
Svea 123	White Gas	16	.35	60	7	8-11	P	F	F(1)	E(2)
MSR G/GK	(7)	15	2.00	240	3.5		E	G	E	F
Purist I	White Gas	25	.35	45	4.5		G	E	E	G(2)
Coleman	White Gas	32	.60	60	3.5		G	E	E	F
Gaz S200-S	Butane	11	10(4)	180	11	12-15	P	E	F(3)	F
Optimus 00	Kerosene	24	1.00	150	5	8-9	G	F	G	G(2)
Optimus 96	Kerosene	17	.50	120	8		G	F	G	G(2)

E = Excellent, G = Good, F = Fair, P = Poor
(1) Stove must be insulated from snow and cold.
(2) Stove will fit inside cooking pots.
(3) Fuel must be kept above freezing.
(4) Weight of cartridge in ounces.
(5) Time needed to bring 1 qt. water at 70 °F to boil 212 °F in uncovered pot.
(6) Time needed to bring 1 qt. water at 35 °F to boil at 187 °F in covered pot.
(7) Burns a variety of fuels.

(Courtesy Recreational Equipment, Inc.)

■ Using Your Stove

Even more interesting than the ratings in *Backpacking Equipment Buyer's Guide* were the astounding bits of information the editors dredged up during their research. They recount some sad stories about people who suffered accidents because of misuse of stoves, then offer pointers on how to use a stove safely. They tell you to try your stove at home in order to iron out problems and to always be sure of adequate ventilation. Staff researchers measured levels of carbon monoxide inside a partially closed tent using eight stoves (liquid propane gas, propane, butane, methanol, and white gas) and concluded that high-output stoves produce high levels of carbon monoxide in a partially vented, breathable nylon tent as a result of incomplete combustion caused by flame quenching. Final concentrations of carbon monoxide ranged from 70 to 130 parts per million. Exposure to such levels of carbon monoxide probably is not dangerous at low altitudes, but above 10,000 feet it poses a potentially dangerous hazard. Normal oxygen saturation in human blood at sea level is about 97 percent; at 10,000 feet it lowers to 90 percent; at 20,000 feet, to 70 percent. Combine this with further reduction of oxygen while using a stove in a closed tent, and the danger becomes extreme. Collapse from carbon monoxide poisoning is generally preceded by dizziness, headache, nausea, and vomiting.

To prevent carbon monoxide poisoning while cooking in my tent, I tie back the tunnel entrance even in rain, and flip back and tie the vestibule door. Netting on each entrance remains in use. After the stove is started and the cooking commenced, I move to the rear of the tent near the tunnel entrance to do other tasks. If I feel the slightest twinge of a headache, I place my head outside the tent and breathe deeply. I avoid long use of the stove by preparing quick-fix meals. The gourmet operations are left for sunny, clear evenings outside the tent.

Always make sure to place your stove in a safe place. That means on a level spot where it can't be knocked over and away from combustible grass, dry leaves, tent walls, mosquito netting, and sleeping bags. A few other hints for safe use of a backpacking stove follow.

Don't overfill. Three-fourths full is better than full. I had always thought this was to leave space for compression, but the *Buyer's Guide* authors add that when a tank is too full it can build up too much pressure while the stove is burning. The safety valve is supposed to prevent the stove from exploding, but when it blows, watch out. This happened to me, and the stream of fire was not so safe. I was in the tent, but cooking outside the door. My neighbor in the next tent pushed the inferno away from my tent with his walking stick. We eventually doused the bonfire with water, but a heavy piece of fabric would have worked better. At times like this, you realize there is very little in the way of flame-quenching fabric in an alpine camp, unless you want to use your good wool shirt.

Avoid overpriming, which may cause a flare-up, and always close your fuel bottle before striking that first match. I once saw a flame jump six feet to an open fuel bottle. Ribbon starting-paste is far safer than priming with liquid fuel, even if the latter is applied with eyedropper precision.

Don't use over-sized pots. They are too tippy. (I have hip scars to prove it.) If you use the Sigg Cook Kit, be sure it is on stable ground and that each of the sections is fitted together correctly.

Avoid overheating the fuel tank. A gas tank must be warm to generate pressure, but if it's hot, turn it off. Propane and butane cartridges should feel cold to the touch.

Do not refuel a hot stove. If the fuel runs out in the middle of cooking a meal, wait for the stove to cool before refueling. Not only is there a risk of a hot stove catching fire, but in the case of attached fuel bottles, they too can go up in flame.

Those are the most often neglected safety points. Memorize them.

Altitude and wind affect a stove's starting capability and boiling time. At 5,200 feet, water boils at 201 degrees Fahrenheit; at 9,500 feet at 192 degrees; and at 14,000 feet at 186 degrees. This may sound like increased efficiency, but veterans will know that a three-minute egg at sea level becomes a six-minute egg at 9,500 feet. There is also the strange sensation of pouring a cup of "boiling" water into your instant coffee cup only to find it's lukewarm when you drink it.

At higher elevations less oxygen is available for combustion. So, at a given stove setting the flame will burn "hotter" at sea level than at 10,000 feet.

A third factor applies to butane stoves. At sea level, butane will not vaporize below 32 degrees Fahrenheit. But at greater heights, where air pressure is less, butane vaporizes at lower temperatures, e.g., at 12 degrees Fahrenheit at 10,000 feet. Butane users may have an easier time of it the higher they go.

Svea stove in foreground is protected by a folding aluminum windscreen. (*Photo by John Nevin.*)

103

Wind adversely affects stove performance in several ways. When a pot of water is not covered, wind blows away the insulating layer of warm air and steam from above the surface of the water. This cools the water and increases boiling time from ten to twenty-four percent. Wind cools the surface (sides) of the pot and therefore its contents. Wind pushes the flame to the side away from the bottom of the pot and drives heat out of the flame. Wind cools the stove parts and fuel tank, which is crucial with white-gas models because their fuel tanks must be warm to maintain pressure.

How do you solve these wind problems? One way is to use a windscreen. The MSR aluminum foil screen can be bought separately and cut, bent, folded, and scrunched to fit other stoves, but you must be careful not to enclose the fuel tank so tightly that it overheats.

Now, would you ever have believed that so many words could be written on this simple little replacement for a campfire? But wait—there's more for your gourmet pleasure. Optimus sells a teflon-coated fry pan with a fold-in handle that fits most stoves and provides scorch-free pancakes, fish, and omelettes. (Eggs can also be cooked in the Sigg lid-frying pan in double-boiler style. Just set the pan over the cook pot of boiling water. Pancakes and fish might take until the next day using this method.) The teflon pan requires the usual plastic spatula. Optimus also sells a truly luxury accessory, the Optimus mini-oven. It bakes coffee cake, hot brownies, and biscuits. It looks like a bundt pan, but has a cover and plate for use beneath the pan and over the flame. Can you imagine what a prospector of '98 would have to say about that?

■ Food

If you think backpacking equipment generates heated conversation, throw in the subject of food and stand back. I thought I had heard all during the years of dealing with picky toddlers and teenage food faddists, but that was before I began leading group backpacking trips. The battle lines are divided thusly: the too-much versus the too-little protagonists; the weight conscious versus the skinnies; the nutritionists versus the handful-of-gorp eaters; the freeze-dried fanatics versus the gourmands. And on past bedtime.

Obviously, there is the middle-of-the-grocery aisle, and one over-riding question: Can the food be carried without breaking your back? High-country hikers use much energy getting to the top and, at times, take a few days to get there. This narrows the plot, but does not ordain emulation of St. John in the desert.

As with their equipment, veterans tend to relax the preparation schedule. This can cause some hungry last days on the trail. On a trip this past summer, I carried what I thought was food for fourteen days; for-

One way to ration food for a long trip is to pack each day's entrees in a Ziploc bag labeled with day and date. Place these in lower part of top section of the backpack, and transfer one day's rations to the drawstring lunch bag each morning.

tunately, the trip lasted only twelve days or I would have been forced upon the generosity of my companions. This frugality was prompted by sixty-pound packs on previous trips and a tendency to take too much food. There is something about spending a week far from supermarket or refrigerator that triggers fanatic insecurity in novice and veteran alike. Intense care is taken to insure that not one "necessary" item of food is left behind, and preoccupation with food preparation becomes absurd at times. Then, on the other end of the scale, there are trailwise veterans who take twelve days of food for fourteen days of camping.

Most of the thirty million hikers in this affluent society can afford to lose weight. For the three-season hiker, protein and fat are not absolutely vital requirements for a one- to two-week trip. Calories for energy can be provided by carbohydrates, and ordinary sugar does it quickly. Pure glucose or sucrose does it even faster. However, adding fat or protein to your diet will cover long-term needs. Fat provides about 250 calories per ounce, digests slowly, and gives you a longer "full-feeling." Cheese (fat and protein) has about 100 calories per ounce, and peanut butter (fat and protein) about 100 per tablespoon. Fat is absorbed better when combined with carbohydrates (for example, rice with butter, bread with cheese, chocolate with nuts). Protein is necessary for cell construction and repair, but not for physical activity unless you're injured, sweating profusely, or particularly susceptible to cold. Lacking calories, the body slows down to a stumble,

THE HIGH-COUNTRY BACKPACKER

judgment falters, and the system loses resistance to cold. For safety's sake, hikers are told to keep eating and drinking: snacks frequently, water often (preferably sweetened with a sugar drink and whether you "feel" thirsty or not), and three meals a day. How then does one care for the walking body, calorie-wise and weight-wise?

Dieters on crash diets know that a body can survive on 1,000 calories a day (less if you're really crashing). On the other end of the scale is the Nordic skier who can expect an energy loss of between 8,000 and 18,000 calories a day.* Add a gale at minus 70 degrees and the energy loss can increase to 1,800 calories per hour. Choose any number in between to calculate your personal calorie needs.

My food consumption on one hiking day this past summer included instant cereal with powdered milk and honey, instant coffee with a packet of Pream, and an orange for breakfast; gorp snacks (M&Ms, mixed nuts, and raisins); cheddar cheese, sausage, wheat thins, and Gatorade for lunch; candy bar snack; freeze-dried lasagna (for two persons), two carrot sticks, pistachio pudding, and Gatorade for dinner. That totals about 3,000 calories, I think. If it had been a hot, bushwacking, bug-fighting, steep-climbing day, I would have had to force myself to consume that quantity.

Those, like me, whose muscles retain carbon dioxide and whose stomachs acidify to a point of nausea during strenuous activity will understand my eating problem on the trail. These physical failings are the excuse I use to indulge in a leisurely cocktail hour before dinner. The most interesting news in this category was an announcement that the Japanese had been able to freeze-dry alcohol. But bureaucracy intervened and most Americans must do without this innovation. I called a local bureaucrat to find out why the item could not be sold in Alaska and learned that "we have enough problem with alcoholism now. Think how easily freeze-dried alcohol could be bootlegged into the villages." But think, also, how easily it could be carried in old ladies' backpacks.

More seriously, the delay before eating does give the body time to rid muscles of carbon dioxide and the stomach time to settle down. Those who are so exhausted they can think only of crawling into a sleeping bag might discipline themselves to a two-hour nap, then prepare a full meal. I know at least one person who perished in her bag overnight because of hypothermia, intensified by lack of calorie intake. She was too tired to cook a meal.

Backpacking foods can be selected from the same seven or so categories used in home kitchens, with due regard to weight, spoilage rate, and preparation time. These categories are roughly fresh, processed, dried, dehydrated, canned, freeze-dried, and natural.

---

* From "How to Stoke Your Inner Fire," by Magda Krance, *Mariah,* December 1978/ January 1979.

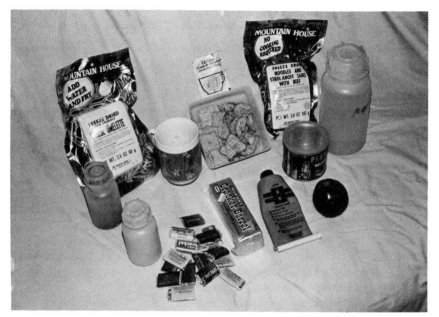

A day's typical food supply.

Fresh foods that have held up well for me on the trail are oranges, apples, cucumbers, green peppers, cherry tomatoes, and avocados, all of which must be protected from crushing and used early in the trip. Carrots and celery sticks last longer and aren't so fragile.

I include under processed foods foil-wrapped natural cheddar cheese, summer sausage, pumpernickle bread, homemade cranberry and apricot bread, stickbread, crackers, jam, and honey. Examples of dried foods are beef jerky, raisins, prunes, peas, and beans.

Dehydrated foods are made by several different methods of rapid hot-air drying. Many of the "instants" are in this category, including milk, mashed potatoes, coffee, vegetable and fruit juices, cereals, jello, puddings, and soups (such as Top Ramen and Cup-o-Soup).

Canned foods light enough for the backpacker might include individual-sized puddings, fruit cocktail or other fruit, canned meats such as Spam, meat and vegetable combinations such as Beans and Franks, Chicken and Noodles, spaghetti, and on down the supermarket shelf.

And then we have freeze-dried foods, much praised and much maligned. Mountain House and Richmoor between them offer such exotics as Cheese Omelette, Spaghetti with Meat Sauce, Chicken Chop Suey, Beef Stroganoff, Beef Almondine, Turkey Tetrazzini, Chicken with Rice, Cheese Romanoff with Ham, Vegetable Beef Stew, Turkey Supreme, Tuna Salad, Blueberry Cobbler, Pineapple Cheesecake, and Chocolate Ice Cream, in addition to more mundane mushrooms, apples, peaches and strawberries. Need I recite further?

Natural foods are best sought out in a reputable health food store, preferably one that doesn't indulge in rip-off prices. One company, Granite Stairway Mountaineering (120 Woodland Ave., Reno, Nevada 89523), offers natural-food backpack items, such as their Middle Eastern Style Dinner, Curried Bean Pilaf, Meadow Mushroom Soup, Country Corn Chowder, Hearty Lentil Soup, Loch Ness Stew, and Mexican Style Dinner.

Alternating and combining foods from these categories helps to alleviate bored palate. I have been known to leave a warm sleeping bag for a piece of coffee cake freshly baked in an Optimus oven. Likewise, I never turn down a piece of cranberry bread baked at home by my friend Emile. This same friend prepares homemade entrees and places them in seal-o-meal bags, which can be trusted to hold hot water for rehydrating or even be submerged in hot water for heating.

Once I caused a near riot beneath the Arrigetch Peaks when I tried to divide a cheesecake with graham cracker crust and fresh-picked blueberries. Fresh blueberries in pancakes or cereal can draw out the worst sackhound. A can of corned beef tastes positively fresh following a week of freeze-dried entrees. Fresh fish, caught along the trail, seasoned with proper spices, and fried over a campfire, can perk up even the most disconsolate eater. Fresh mushrooms, other than poisonous ones, make eggs taste like eggs again. What some folks can do with a fresh green pepper is just short of miraculous. And finally, there was the man on another Brooks Range trip who on the sixth day out had a six-pack of beer air-dropped. The rest of us settled for Russian tea (Tang, instant tea, lemonade mix, sugar, cinnamon, and ground clover).

CHAPTER TWELVE

SAFETY, COMFORT, AND PERSONAL GROOMING

When teaching equipment classes, I lump a mixed bag of essentials under the title of safety, comfort, and personal grooming. Presupposing that all backpackers have had a sobering experience or two and *always* carry an extra wool shirt or sweater and rain gear, and presupposing that high-country hikers know enough to toss in some extra candy bars or even a small survival kit (I carried one for ten years and finally opened it out of curiosity), I'll proceed to some other essentials.

■ Map and Compass

Even on trips into the Chugach Mountains twenty-five minutes from Anchorage, I include an inch to the mile USGS topographic map. Admittedly, four maps taped together are rather bulky, but when folded flat into a Ziploc bag, they slide easily in and out of the backpack pocket. Then, if curiosity beckons me into a new drainage, or if I merely want to check out the altitude of a distant peak, the information is at hand. In less remote terrain, trail followers carry one of the many good guides available for almost every moderate bump in the continental United States (see Chapter 1 and Appendix II for sources). On cross-country wilderness trips, maps are absolutely essential.

The need for a compass has already been explained in Chapter 4. Learn to use it and take it whether or not you *think* you need it. You need it.

■ Whistle

My fondness for this piece of equipment approaches fanaticism, to the point where I have been quoted on the subject in the local press and on television outdoor shows. I have had ten bear encounters (grizzly, brown, and black), and on each occasion, whistles alerted them to my presence and reduced our relationship to a Brief Encounter. All of these bears were wilderness types, not people bears. I have it from former Alaskans that bear encounters in Yosemite and Yellowstone parks utterly destroyed their faith in the whistle. More on bears in Chapter 17.

Whistles are invaluable when one is lost in the deep woods. Rescuers have reported hearing whistles in gale winds. Anyone who has yelled to someone a few hundred yards upwind with absolutely no response knows the futile feeling. When a group is spread out, a leader can check out the position of the tailender with whistle signals. That may sound ridiculous to those who use only well-trod trails, but I find this safety procedure essential when bushwacking the alder and willow so often encountered enroute to a summit in Alaska. And finally, to the everlasting chagrin of my sackbound trailmates, I use a whistle to rouse camp in the morning. Every good leader should have one.

■ Flashlight and Head Lanterns

Twenty-four hours of daylight should eliminate the need for these items during the Arctic summer, but I carry a pencil flashlight even then to help find things in my tent during dusky midnight hours and to read by. In fall, winter, or spring, I include a metal flashlight with two C-size heavy-duty alkaline batteries, though others tout the lithium battery.

Mountain Safety Research in their March 1976 catalog gave high ratings to D-size lithium cells. They say these don't fade and, because you need only one D-size battery, weigh less. They further claim that lithium cells are excellent at low temperatures because they contain not water but a liquid that doesn't freeze until the temperature reaches minus sixty-five degrees Fahrenheit. Even though lithium batteries cost more than other types, the researchers claim they are cheaper when all factors are considered. Others, however, claim that the jury is still out on lithium batteries because of their unreliability and leakage. Whichever type you choose, start out with fresh batteries (admittedly not so easy to determine since you don't know how long they've been on the store shelf). When it's cold, batteries usually can be resuscitated by warming them to about seventy degrees Fahrenheit, in an armpit or other suitable place, but not in the campfire.

Skiers and hikers in northern latitudes can extend the daylight hours in winter by wearing headlamps. I neglected this bit of advice one February day when our group underestimated the distance to a turnaround point and got caught by darkness. My flashlight got us back to a return trail, but it was impossible to hold it and two ski poles at the same time. Lucky for us, the moon came out and gave enough light to see the faint outlines of the trail. It did not, however, light up the valleys and ravines of the trail. I had a few cheap thrills that night when skiing into those "black holes," flying blind to the crest of the up-slope and miraculously staying upright. I also learned that my spills on similar slopes in daylight probably were caused by tensing up in anticipation; when I couldn't see the bumps and grade, I sailed over them without a falter. That digression is not written to encourage you to ski in the dark. There could have been some dangerous trailblocks leading to my early demise. If you ski tour, carry a head lantern.

This headlamp has four D-size cells in a plastic case which is clipped to the belt or inside jacket pocket to keep it warm. Cord can be threaded down the back and under the arm so it won't get in the way.

■ Sunglasses

I refuse to divulge the number of sunglasses I have lost or broken on the trial. Too often, while learning over a stream to get water, they have skidded off my nose and disappeared; or I have set them on the grass at a rest stop and never seen them again; or I have removed them to better photograph a scene and left them lying on a rock. To accommodate this advanced state of senility, several suppliers provide mountain glasses that not only stop ninety-eight percent of the infrared and ultraviolet rays and have adjustable wire bows and leather side shields, but also feature an elastic head strap. This strap is long enough to rest gently on the back of the neck or jacket when you're wearing the glasses and to hold the glasses at chest level when you're not using them. The flexible, covered wire bows are comfortable and warm in winter and prevent glasses from sliding forward on the nose. The leather side shields keep out side light during long tours in brilliant snow. If the leather shields are too warm for summer use, remove and store them (carefully). I'm sorry I didn't discover these all-purpose glasses long ago. I could have saved much discomfort as well as strain on my pocketbook.

Climbing glasses with leather side shields keep out side light.

■ Sunscreen

Along with saving your eyes you might want to save your skin. In Alaska, some form of skin protection from the sun and wind is needed all year. For that matter, alpine hikers everywhere are wise to protect themselves year round. Even if you find a lovely, large boulder to shade you, the reflected burning goes on. Likewise, skiers above timberline are subjected not only to the natural breezes, but to the ones they whip up themselves on the downrun.

Glacier people and skiers who expect to spend the better part of the day on sunny (and cloudy) slopes use PABA (para-aminobenzoic acid), the clown-like white paste you see plastered all over the noses and faces of expedition climbers. In proper concentration, it blocks out all ultraviolet rays. Chapstick gives lip protection if applied often enough to counteract lip-licking. Spend some time in the sunscreen section of your drugstore or supermarket. Read the labels to determine the skin-protection factor of the different products. I like tubes because they require less space and it's easier to know when they're on empty. Apply sunscreen often when you're perspiring and on windy days. And sleep happier at night.

■ Insect repellent

If you have been laboring under the premise that mosquitoes, flies, and gnats had eyes only for you, read on. In 1942, the United States Army discovered that malaria and yellow fever mosquitoes were as mean as enemy bullets. The Bureau of Entomology by 1947 had tested over 7,000 different repellent compounds; by 1951, that number was up to 11,000. By 1960, the most promising repellent was a material called N,N-diethyl-meta-toluamide. It was nicknamed DEET and repelled mosquitoes, ticks, chiggers, and fleas by confusing the insect's nervous system and numbing its sense of timing, thus preventing its zoning in on your carbon dioxide beam. DEET was safe on skin and cotton clothing, and at full strength, it was effective from twenty-four hours to a week, depending on conditions. The bottom line is which commercial repellent available today contains the most DEET. To save you from squinting at the fine print on sundry bottles, I report the following DEET concentrations in the best-known brands: Muskol, 95 percent; Mosquitone, 50 percent; Off, 50 percent; Cutters, 30 percent; Woodsman's, 25 percent; Skram, 15 percent. Although 6–12 contains no DEET, it is 75 percent E-Hex (ethyl-hexanediol).

The makers of Muskol advise that you spread seven or eight drops evenly over exposed skin. Note, they do not advise application on clothing and caution that it may damage synthetic fabrics, some plastics, etc. So, be careful with glass frames, watch crystals, Ziploc bags, and knife handles. I have used Muskol for two seasons. Because I failed to read the small print

113

and because I used the plastic bottle with the flip top which leaked, my side pocket now has a large oily spot. The Muskol "ate" right through the plastic sandwich bag in which I had placed it. (Muskol now comes in a container with a screw-top lid that is leakproof.) This kind of potency causes one to wonder about Muskol's safety, but I've used it during two seasons and had no allergic reaction or other skin irritation.

Despite claims to the contrary, many repellents are ineffective against some flies. Which flies, you ask. By conferring with Dr. Mark Osgood, a stream ecologist and zoologist at the University of Alaska, I learned a bit about the nature of these winged enemies. Some pertinent information, gleaned from Dr. Osgood, about the members of Order Diptera follows:

No-see-ums (Family Ceratopogonidae). This is the almost invisible member of the fly family that bites, sometimes causing swelling and sometimes leaving long-lasting itchy red marks.

Black fly (Family Simuliidae). The not so invisible black fly also bites humans. Sometimes white sox are included in this category, but not all black flies have the "white sox" distinguishing feature.

Deer fly or Horsefly (Family Tabanidae). This large fly bites, then laps up the blood of its victim. We could not determine if the moose, or elk, fly described by some backpackers belongs in this category.

Midges (Family Chironomidae). This insect is non-biting, but it can induce loss of sanity by swarming in droves around the head, the body, or just everywhere. It is found near aquatic habitat (lakes, Arctic tundra, etc.).

Gnats (About a half-dozen families). This name is commonly misapplied to many flying insects. Generally speaking, most do not bite.

Housefly (Family Muscidae). The housefly does not bite and, despite its name, can be encountered in the out of doors.

The black fly, deer fly, horsefly, and, possibly, the moose and elk flies are often confused by victims. The Muskol label states that "unsolicited tests including other major insect repellents have shown that Muskol is far superior in repelling mosquitoes, chiggers, ticks and black flies." The company cautions, however, that the product does not work very well with flies, but does repel deer and moose flies for approximately three hours. My experience has been that Muskol works reasonably well against all types of flies but is totally ineffectual in repelling gnats.

My companions on a recent trip claimed relief from mosquitoes and gnats by taking two tablets (100 milligrams each) of Thiamin (Skeetertabs) every eight hours. While they picked blueberries unaffected by the insect world, I huddled in my Gore-Tex jacket with hood up and hands in pocket, suffering swarms of gnats.

When chemical defenses fail, physical ones may succeed. On more than one occasion, a head net has gotten me out of my tent into the insect world, enabling me to become a more sociable camp person. Fellow campers

The author, armed with head net to keep out insects, enjoys the Arctic evening snug in her down booties, pants, and parka. The ground pad provides a cushion and wards off chill. (*Photo by Chuck Heath.*)

delight in photographing me in "evening dress," complete with down underwear, down booties, heavy jacket or shirt, and head net, usually with a cup of toddy held in hand under the net. I have also heard tell of, but have not used, the head-to-waist garment constructed of no-see-um netting doused in repellent. This garment, though it provides a marvelous bug-free environment, might contribute to my further delinquency by prolonging fireside imbibing.

■ First Aid

The very first item of first aid should be a book on the subject. My daughter, the doctor, sent me *Emergency Family First Aid Guide* (Simon and Schuster), which is printed in unusually large type and yet is compact enough to carry in a pack. In bold, black letters a quarter inch high, the index tells you where to find what to do in all kinds of emergencies; the corresponding text tells you how to do it. I had to use this book when one of our party injured an ankle in the Wrangell Mountains. The precise instructions and pictures helped me first to determine whether it was a fracture or a sprain, then how to treat it. I used the book again midway through the Arctic Wildlife Range when a hiker dislocated her elbow.

I also recommend that anyone who intends to backpack into high-country take a course in first aid. The Red Cross, local schools and colleges, and mountaineering clubs sponsor first-aid courses in many communities.

As for the first-aid kit itself, here are the items I generally include:

- Moleskin. This tape adheres to the skin better than Band-Aids. It should be applied to hot spots *before* blistering occurs. It can be purchased in the foot-care section of your drugstore.
- Band-Aids. Useful for small cuts and scrapes. Butterfly Band-Aids are best for closing cuts.
- Gauze pads (sterile, 4-inch squares). These individually wrapped squares are more sterile than rolls of gauze bandage, and are useful for covering larger wounds or burns.
- Adhesive tape. Holds dressing in place. Also helpful in splinting.
- Elastic bandage (3 inches wide). For sprains, and when pressure is necessary to reduce bleeding. I also carry an elastic knee bandage to relieve mildly pulled ligaments or tendons. Elastic bandages should not be worn while sleeping because they may restrict blood flow.
- Antiseptic. A local pharmacist recommends Betadine swabs or Zephiran. I do not recommend straight iodine or other antiseptics that burn or color the wound red.
- Aspirin. Take one or two for mild pain.
- Pain Killers. Dr. Michael Armstrong advises, "If I were going on a short hike (near air rescue facilities), I would not include this item. Co-

deine impairs judgment and might compound the problem. However, for longer trips into remote areas, it might be a reasonable approach to obtain from your personal physician a prescription such as codeine, *to be used as prescribed.*''

- Antibiotics. Dr. Armstrong suggests taking a broad-spectrum, oral antibiotic, recommended by the hiker's own physician, for infections secondary to cuts, abrasions, and burns and for non-viral respiratory infections. Neosporin is an effective non-prescription antibiotic ointment.
- Antacid. For settling stomachs upset by exertion or altitude. (See Chapter 14 for more on this subject.)
- Antihistamine. For pollen and food allergy or reactions to bee stings. Chlor-Trimeton relieves my itchy eyes and sniffles but makes me sleepy.
- Needle and tweezer. For removing splinters, thorns, etc.
- Scissors. Very necessary for cutting moleskin and adhesive tape. Small manicure scissors or fold-up scissors fit into a small-sized metal Band-Aid box. Some pocketknives have a scissors attachment.
- Snakebite kit. Not necessary in Alaska, where reptiles are noticeably absent. If you're heading for snake country, though, take one along and consult *Medicine for Mountaineering* by Dr. James A. Wilkerson, as well as Chapter 14, before you leave.
- Diamox (Acetazolamide). Several sources report that this prevents acute mountain sickness. Fortunately, I've never had to use it.
- Other personal medication, all clearly labeled.
- Disposable fever thermometer. Tempa Dot is made by Physical Measurements, Inc., 601 W. 41st Street, New York, New York 10036.

■ Miscellaneous Items

I carry fifty feet of six-millimeter nylon rope which has a tensile strength of 1,650 pounds. It's made by a French firm (Mammut) for Chouinard. It can be used for stream crossings, to hang food bags on high tree limbs, as a clothes line, to tie makeshift crutches or stretchers, and to raise or lower accident victims when heavier mountaineering rope is not available. A snapping caribiner is handy for hooking into a stream-crossing rope, for ferrying your pack across a stream or chasm, and for other pulley duty.

Ice axes and crampons are more than emergency items on a winter trip: They are essential gear. An emergency repair kit should contain extra clevis pins and wires for backpack repair, a small screwdriver and pliers, safety pins, and a few inches of light steel wire. I can usually push all of this into a metal Band-Aid container. Other often-used items are cloth tape (duct tape), long-burning candles, several feet of trail tape, and a clothespin or two for wet socks. A thermometer is a must in winter. A small nylon day-pack comes in handy to carry your lunch, water, and a sweater on those side trips out of base camp. Don't forget an emergency hand-signal chart.

If you feel absolutely inadequate without a gun in bear country, and firearms are permitted, then by all means carry one. Bear repellents will be discussed in Chapter 17.

In the nice but not essential category are cameras and binoculars.

And finally, don't forget coins for that emergency phone call.

■ Personal Grooming

Although personal needs and preferences vary from person to person, a basic toilet kit includes the following items:

- Toothbrush and toothpaste (some stores sell small plastic travel kits which contain a fold-up brush and small tube of paste)
- Dental floss
- Small comb or folding brush
- Mirror (in a pinch, can double as a signal mirror)
- Wash n' Dries or quick-drying washcloth
- Kleenex
- Toilet paper (remove from roll and compress to an inch or so)
- Eye drops such as Murine or Visine
- High-lanolin lotion (in tube) for wind- and sun-dried skin
- Biodegradable liquid soap
- Nail file
- Towel (if you don't plan to use paper towels from kitchen supplies)
- Sewing kit containing needles, thread, and safety pins (scissors can be borrowed from first-aid kit)

At times, women will need to carry menstruation supplies. Fastidious men will carry razors. Both may want to include deodorant and foot powder. Include your driver's license or some kind of identification. I forgot this necessary item once when hiking the Chilkoot Trail which runs between Canada and the United States. (They don't meet you at the summit, but they do ask for ID when you ride the train between Whitehorse in Canada and Skagway in Alaska.) My good friend Kay also claims that carrying her driver's license will enable rescuers to identify her body.

Any more than all this and you'd better start weighing your pack.

WHAT TO EXPECT AT HIGHER ELEVATIONS

The days of planning end and the magic moment arrives. You hoist home on back. Correction. You *try* to hoist home on back. Let's do that again. There are two basic ways to get into a pack. You can grab it by the shoulder straps, hoist it onto one knee, slip an arm through a strap, and swing it around to your back. Or you can sit on the ground against the pack, slip into the straps, turn onto your knees, and stand up.

After discarding ten pounds of necessary gear, such as leftover potato salad and a bottle of wine, I usually end up with a pack weighing fifty pounds. The two methods above then require amendment. If I have properly developed my Somebody's Mother routine, I prevail upon Somebody's Son to lift the pack to my back. If the group is short of willing young people, I proceed to the first-method described, out of direct view of fellow strugglers. On occasion, I even resort to the second method, also inconspicuously, while hoping that my trailmates won't see me fall on my face when I turn onto my knees. At rest stops, I am overjoyed when I find a log, boulder, or dirt bank to sit on. I don't need to mention why.

Phase one completed, a backpacker commences walking. His pack weighs about one third of his body weight, his boots fit, and he has conditioned his body according to the gospel of Chapter 3. He moves at a moderate pace, ever upward, and refers to his guide or map when in doubt. Without incident, he reaches timberline. Without warning, or so he claims, there is an abrupt change in the weather. He seeks shelter from lightning and rain. He shivers and wonders about hypothermia. After the rain, continuing upward to higher altitude, he is beset with fatigue and nausea. About that time, the trail crosses a stream, running fast and rising because of the rainstorm. Beyond the stream lies a boulder field and, at the pass, a scree slope. Adding to the tension, someone spots a grizzly meandering not too many yards away. Finally, the day's hiking ends: Packs are dropped and it's time to build a home. But first, there is an urgent need to find some private spot in this endless vista to attend to the call of nature.

Follow me, fellow alpinist, through the next few chapters and know that others before you, of all ages, have bit the bullet and met the challenges of high-country without a whimper, yea, even with enjoyment. Anyone who has potty trained a three-year-old or said no to a teenager is emotionally equipped to handle anything nature has to offer. For that matter, so is anyone whose powers of concentration have been honed by dodging traffic in New York City or driving the Los Angeles Freeway.

CHAPTER THIRTEEN

MOUNTAINS AND THEIR WEATHER

Approaching high-country without some knowledge of weather could be dangerous to your health. Weather is discussed so much on the nightly news and used as a conversational space filler so often that it's easy to be bored by the subject. I recall the endless discussions about weather by rural Minnesotans gathered around the pot-bellied stove in my father's place of business. For those farmers, weather dictated their livelihood and the prosperity of the surrounding community as well. I also remember vividly the day they carried in the frozen body of a farmer who failed to make the trip from farm to town during a blizzard. Perhaps that was the day I gained respect for the life-and-death power of weather.

Even with that youthful background, it took a few spells of adverse climate to imprint upon my prairie-oriented mind that mountains brew some significant weather, too. My first Alaskan overnight was in winter, in the mountains, and with an all-male mountaineering group. Any one of those circumstances should have deterred a first-time backpacker, but I had prepared with the determination of a K–2 expeditioner. I submitted to an equipment check, during which such deficiencies as lack of wool, too much weight, and a synthetic parka were called to my attention. (This was in the pre-PolarGuard-Hollofill II era.) Deterred by the expense of both down and wool, I substituted as best I could. This oversight and my lack of expertise were etched in ice as I suffered through a night alone when the temperature fell to zero degrees Fahrenheit and the wind roared down the peaks at thirty miles per hour. My wind-chill chart tells me that is equivalent to minus fifty-five degrees. This was the night I learned about weather and mountains.

How much should you, a beginning or intermediate alpine backpacker, know about mountain weather? You won't need a doctorate in meteorology, but knowing that south-facing slopes are more apt than others to brew a thunderstorm can be helpful. So is the rule that the temperature drops about 3½–4 degrees Fahrenheit for every 1,000 feet of elevation. If you live at sea level and plan to camp at 10,000 feet, better plan for a 40-degree drop in temperature. Then put that wool shirt and down jacket in your pack, along with your rain gear.

Although predicting weather is chancy, even the most cautious forecaster will admit to a few general rules. Rain showers, which often occur during late afternoon and evening during the summer months, are heaviest in the hills and lightest in the valleys. Wind flow is channeled by valleys and peaks. At higher elevations, there is a summer of three months; spring and fall are almost inconsequential; the rest is winter. Because severe cold is a potential problem to winter mountaineer's, it is useful to know that clear skies and light wind usually portend cold weather. In the northern hemisphere, a rapid rise in temperature, together with a south wind and clouds, usually precedes snow and rain. Western hikers who frequent the Cascades, Coastals, and Sierras will recognize the late afternoon shower phenomenom, but the Appalachian hiker who has experienced five kinds of weather in one day may question the theory.

The National Weather Service, a division of the National Oceanic and Atmospheric Administration (NOAA), maintains an office in one major city of each state. Ask them for a "climate package" for the area you intend to visit. If that doesn't get action, write to the National Climactic Center, Federal Building, Asheville, North Carolina 28801.

Many cities have a twenty-four-hour recorded phone service that provides local weather information. Some also have an avalanche information number. If you own a radio with a special weather band, you will be able to use the VHF-FM radio service offered by the National Weather Service. Forecasts are issued at scheduled times and broadcast tapes are updated and amended as required. The broadcasts, in general, contain forecasts and warnings for the local area and nearby coastal waters, severe weather bulletins, tsunami (earthquake-tidal wave)) warnings, a description of the weather patterns as it affects the state, and weather reports from selected weather stations.

■ Air Masses and Wind

One of the basic components of weather is the air mass, which is defined as an extensive body of air, sometimes a thousand miles wide, whose temperature and moisture are similar at a given altitude throughout the body of air. Generally, during the summer a cold air mass is characterized by cumulus and cumulonimbus clouds and by local thunderstorms, showers, hail, sleet, or snow flurries; during the winter, though, a cold air mass is accompanied by fair skies. On the other hand, a warm air mass is characterized by haze, fog, stratus clouds, and drizzle.

The locale where an air mass acquires its identifying properties of temperature and moisture is called a source region. The most common air-mass source regions are large snow or ice-covered polar regions, tropical oceans, and large desert areas. From this comes the terminology polar, continental, maritime, and tropical air masses.

Residents of the northcentral states know about the Polar-Continental mass—usually cold, dry, and stable—which flows from Hudson Bay and stays east of the Rocky Mountains. Southwesterners are aware of the Tropical-Continental mass, which is hot, dry, and usually unstable in summer. Southern Californians experience the Tropical-Maritime-Pacific mass, which brings warm, moist, and sometimes neutral air. Northwesterners are familiar with the Polar-Maritime-Pacific and the Northern Ocean masses, which bring cool, moist, and unstable weather in winter, but fairly stable air in summer. Texans and southeasterners know about the Tropical-Maritime-Gulf and Atlantic masses, usually warm, moist, and unstable. Northeastern hikers and fishermen have felt the effects of the Polar-Maritime-Atlantic mass, the cool, moist nor'easter of storybook legend.

Alaska, often accused of being the weather factory for the lower forty-eight states, is kept quite busy with four climate zones of its own. Formed by geographical features such as the Brooks Range and the Alaska-Aleutian Range, these zones are known as the Arctic, the Continental, the Transition, and the Maritime. Annual precipitation can vary from the record 269 inches of snow and rain in the southeastern panhandle of Alaska to 6 inches in the Arctic "desert." A total of 974.5 inches of snow fell during the 1952–53 season in Thompson Pass on the highway out of Valdez, a port city whose weather is influenced by the Gulf of Alaska. In that same location, 62 inches of snow fell in twenty-four hours in December 1955. But the North American high was recorded at Paradise Ranger station, Mt. Ranier, Washington, where 1,000 inches of snow fell in one season.

Which brings us to the subject of air-mass modification, a fancy way of saying that when air masses collide or interact with each other, weather results. The meteorological fallout may include winds, clouds, fog, rain, thunderstorms, or snow.

In the interior of Alaska, and perhaps in other places, there is a weather phenomenon that supports the wisdom of scaling a peak early in the day, if you wish to avoid being thunderstruck by more than the view. In a study of thunderstorm activity in central Alaska over a ten-year period, National Weather Service researchers concluded that thunderstorms were least likely to occur in the early morning and were most prevalent in mid-afternoon. Even though precipitation often occurred during the night, it tapered off around 7 A.M., according to the study.

Although I have experienced thunderstorms at 5,000 feet in the Arctic Wildlife Range (Brooks Range) and at 4,000 feet in the Wrangells, thunderstorms are not as common in Alaskan mountains as in the forty-eight continental states. However, I have a notorious reputation among my fellow packers for blowing the whistle at 5:30 A.M. in order to get a group moving before the heat of the day or because of a long day ahead. I may incorporate the NWS results into my early-morning strategy in the future.

Whether you are the sackhound-late-day type or belong to the ambitious, early-morning risers you should know that mornings may dawn brilliantly, but when the weather factors go into operation, late afternoon can bring startling changes. Even in the Arctic with twenty-two hours of daylight in July, the exposed upper slopes of a mountain are heated during midday and become warmer than the surrounding valleys. Convection currents or thermal upslope winds result. As the rays of the sun slant, these upper slopes cool and the wind reverses to a downslope direction in late afternoon and evening. A similar situation occurs in coastal areas where offshore-onshore breezes switch directions during the day. I live near Cook Inlet in Anchorage and the 4 P.M. breeze in summer comes up as regularly as the dinner hour. Since breezes have a way of becoming winds, it behooves a wise backpacker to take note of the hour, quit early, and get his tent set up.

The wise high-country backpacker will also learn about *chinooks,* the warm, dry winds that blow downward on the lee side of a mountain range. Before a chinook comes over the mountain, it is forced upward along the rising slope of the mountain and cooled enough to drain it of moisture before beginning its downslope run on the lee side. That's why windward slopes often have heavier vegetation than leeward slopes. (A seemingly opposite situation occurs in winter when windward slopes are blown clear and the snow comes to rest on the lee or protected side of the mountain.) The rapid rise in temperature associated with warm, chinook winds can dramatically change conditions for a winter or spring ski tourer who suddenly finds that the lovely powder snow encountered on the ascent turns to slush on his homegoing run. This is the time to be alert for avalanches. (More on that subject in Chapter 22.)

Another unpopular wind is the *williwaw.* It has been described as a violent, cold drainage wind that swoops down a mountain peak sounding like a freight train, then abruptly stops. Its sudden gusting probably is caused by higher pressure on the other side of the mountain. When it blasts your tent after you've fallen asleep, you soon discover whether you planted the tent stakes securely.

◼ Clouds

Clouds are another obvious weather sign. In *The Outdoorsman's Emergency Manual,* Anthony Acerrano describes the main cloud types and the kind of weather associated with each.

Cirrus clouds

Cumulus clouds

Nimbus clouds

Stratus clouds

Each of these common cloud types accompanies certain weather patterns. Many hybrid forms also occur.

"Cumulus clouds," Acerrano says, "are the billowing puffs of white that you often see against a backdrop of clear blue sky. Cumulus clouds are good news because they forecast fair weather if they drift about without changing form. But if they begin to build up vertically, forming prominent 'heads' they are turning into storm clouds."

Acerrano describes cirrus clouds as "long wisps of condensed moisture that float high in the sky looking as though they were painted there with thin, feathery brush strokes. Cirrus formations are also known as 'mare's tails' and are generally fair weather clouds, but keep your eye on them." The author, who writes from a Montana viewpoint, says that "if the wind is steady from the northeast, east or south they spell trouble." He admonishes late-season outdoorsmen "to beware of increasing mare's tails because they portend blizzards and snowfalls."

"Stratus clouds are low clouds having little or no layering in a vertical sense, often appearing more as a gloomy gray blanket covering the sky and obscuring the sun. Stratus clouds bring long sessions of drizzly rain or light snow flurries, but coupled with northeast to south winds [and in Alaska, southwest winds], are capable of heavy precipitation."

"Nimbus clouds are low and formless, usually have large patches of dark blue or gray, usually accompany precipitation or are direct forerunners of it."

Mountaineers also should learn to recognize cap or lenticular clouds which form due to strong winds passing over mountain peaks or ridges. These clouds are lens-shaped with smooth tops and can be a warning of increasing winds even when the winds are still light at lower elevations.

■ Fog and Whiteout

In the mountains, when clouds come in contact with the ground, we call it fog. Because of its high moisture content, fog can be a bone-chilling experience. When fog moves in rapidly, it limits visibility and can cause sheer panic.

False bravado, rather than panic, were my undoing during one hiking trip I led in the Chugach Mountains. I confidently moved forward through the fog because I thought I knew the terrain well enough to navigate in any weather. Several hours later I discovered, with profound embarrassment, that I had traveled in a semicircle and ended up several miles from our intended destination.

There is a solution for the backpacker who finds himself suddenly engulfed in pea soup. Stop. Get out your map. Get out your compass. Get your bearing. Set a course. Then proceed. If you're still unsure of yourself, set up camp and wait it out. This latter advice might not apply in the case of supercooled fog which is composed of unfrozen water droplets at temperatures below freezing. These drops freeze on impact with anything, icing up equipment as well as terrain. Provided that no member of the party is hypothermic, it would be far wiser in this situation to descend to a lower elevation and shelter as quickly as possible, else you might become an unwilling ice sculpture.

Another related condition, called *whiteout* or flat light, occurs when light becomes so diffused in a snow-covered area that there is no visual point of reference, just a uniform flat light. Ground features disappear and you may not see a cliff until you ski over it. I experienced whiteout while skiing out of the Talkeetna Mountains one February. There had been no problems with visibility while skiing up the valley, but outward bound we

When fog is heavy, it's best to stay close to your companions, as these hikers are doing near the summit of historic Chilkoot Pass.

could not even distinguish contours beyond the tips of our skis. Luckily, the descent was gradual. If you encounter whiteout in unfamiliar territory, the best approach probably is to wait for better conditions before proceeding. If you must keep moving, then party members should keep in touch by voice. You may not be able to see your companions, but at least you'll be able to hear them.

■ Thunderstorms

When warm, moist air is forced upward, either by gradually sloping land or by abrupt uplifting of winds as they strike mountains, thunderstorms can result. However, the occurrence of thunderstorms is more often caused by parcels of air heated so that they rise rapidly, like a hot air balloon.

During summer months, violent thunderstorms are numerous in mountainous areas of the country. It can take as little as thirty minutes for simple cumulus clouds to mature to the cumulonimbus stage characteristic of a thunderstorm. Vertical motion of the clouds and rapid condensation of moisture cause strong ion fields to develop, and lightning results. Lightning is a rapid electrical discharge of voltage (a) between two clouds, (b) between a cloud and the ground, or (c) between ground and cloud. It was easy for me to understand how voltage could travel between clouds, and between clouds and the ground, but I could not understand how the ground built up its charge for that ground to cloud event. Elliott Barske of our local weather service explains that the earth is negatively charged. Why it stays that way is complex and not completely understood. But simply stated, it is believed that enough negative charge is brought down to earth by lightning to maintain that charge.

Because thunderstorms are not very common in the maritime climate in which I live, my experiences have been limited to the Wrangell Mountains and the interior Alaskan ranges. There I've seen only cloud-to-cloud and cloud-to-ground lightning. But the experience of two friends while hiking in a valley in the Chugach Mountains demonstrates the potential of the third type. Although dark clouds hovered over the peaks near the end of the valley, my friends were not particularly concerned about rain. They began to feel what they thought were cobwebs and brushed them off their faces repeatedly. Then their skin began to "crawl" and one of the girls observed that her partner's hair actually stood straight out from her head. At this point, they realized spiders were not responsible for their discomfort and hastily returned to their car. This is an example of ground current, and these hikers were extremely fortunate that they were not exposed to an electrical discharge between ground and cloud, which is almost always fatal.

Electrical storms are one of the hazards feared most by mountain backpackers because it is not easy to take evasive action. I recall the feelings recounted by a fellow hiker on the Horsfeld to Chisana trail, four thousand feet up in the Wrangell Mountains. She said she had never felt so helpless as at that moment when lightning cracked while she stood, amid pouring rain, ankle deep in water—the highest object on an alpine slope—with a metal pack on her back.

One way to estimate the proximity of a thunderstorm is to count the seconds between lightning and thunder. Since sound travels one mile every five seconds, count the time between the time you see the lightning and when you hear the thunder and divide by five. If that time gets shorter, you know the storm is coming your way. This was a useful bit of information during a three-hundred-mile kayak trip down the Porcupine River in arctic Alaska. After several days of hot sunshine, the clouds moved in from the southwest, and lightning flashed through the sky. We beached our kayaks and found shelter from the cloudburst, but were undecided as to when we could safely continue paddling. Most undecided were those in metal canoes. Finally, after someone remembered to use the second-counting system, we discovered the storm was moving away, not towards us. We continued our trip, but for over an hour lightning flashed, ever farther away.

There are safety rules to follow if you are caught in an electrical storm. If your tent has aluminum poles, get out of it, because aluminum is a good conductor of electricity. If you are on the trail, remove your metal pack frame and unroll your Ensolite or foam pad. Crouch on the pad, feet somewhat apart and hands off the ground. Rubber-soled boots and the Ensolite or foam should provide resistance to ground currents. Get off exposed peaks and ridges and stay away from tall trees, especially that lone spruce sometimes found above timberline. Stand away from the face of a cliff.

If you are caught in an electrical storm, remove your metal framepack and unroll your Ensolite or foam pad. Crouch on the pad with your hands off the ground. The pad, plus your rubber-soled boots, should prevent passage of ground current.

Although a cave or overhanging rock may seem to be a safe refuge, current running along the surface will follow the path of least resistance, which could be you if you're near a wall. As hinted at earlier, stay away from south-facing slopes, which because of solar heat buildup, are ten times more likely than valleys to be the site of thunderstorms. Most of these suggestions seem to run contrary to a natural desire to get out of the rain. This is why it is important to carry good rain gear. You can be downright smug squatting out a thunderstorm in the open if you're warm and dry under waterproof clothing.

■ Flash Floods

After a thunderstorm or heavy rain you have a new worry and that's a flash flood or rapidly rising water. Mountain streams can rise with unbelievable speed. An ankle-high rivulet becomes a thigh-high torrent within hours. If your map shows a stream ahead with broad drainage and many feeder streams, it would be smart to extend the day's hiking in order to cross it before the next morning's runoff. If it has been raining steadily, it would be wise to cut short a weekend of hiking rather than attempt a flood-stage crossing.

Would that I had followed my own advice one summer. Our group had negotiated with a rafting service to take us across a deep, glacial stream in order to climb a mountain on the other side. After climbing for several hours in a drizzle, we set up camp near an alpine lake and waited for the mountain top to reappear. It never showed. The steady patter of rain on our tents must have hypnotized every one of us because we didn't get moving until the following noon. We skidded down the mountain to our scheduled raft pickup point and were shocked to find the river at flood stage. It was moving fast and deep, creating holes that looked as if they would swallow a

Small mountain streams may rise quickly after a rainstorm. Sometimes it's best to wait until the water has receded before trying to cross. (*Photo by Margaret Leonard.*)

raft, and carrying trees and other debris in its way. We noticed cars lined up across the river and saw people gesticulating wildly but could hear nothing above the roar of the stream. A rescue helicopter flew low over us. Finally, we saw our raftsman swirl around a bend upstream and maneuver through some deep holes to our side of the stream. Catching the tossed anchor was a feat and so was stopping the boat downstream at the landing site. It took three prone men to stop the boat and you never saw passengers evacuate a boat faster. I was glad we had put the river crossing in the hands of professionals. We later learned that two hikers had been stranded by rising water on a river bluff a few miles from us, necessitating a helicopter rescue. We also heard about two canoers who drowned on the river that day.

Knowing that mountain streams rise rapidly can help you plan safe crossings. Knowing that water also recedes after runoff, you may decide that your best, perhaps only, alternative is to stop and wait it out. The same rules apply if that rain turns to snow. Finding your way in driving snow is nearly impossible. Better to set up camp and keep warm than risk hypothermia and death. (More on hypothermia and its prevention in the next chapter.)

■ Helpful Gadgets

These words about mountain weather only scratch the surface, but they should be enough to alert you to the meaning of cloud and wind changes. If you have a short memory, jot down in a small note pad some of the key weather signs discussed in this chapter and use your notes when faced with decisions involving weather in high-country.

If all this fails, you can resort to an item in the Early Winters catalog, a Weather Wizard pocket computer, which will make you an instant weatherman. Just line up the slide-chart indicator to match existing cloud and wind conditions and you have an instant weather prediction. Or for only nine ounces of extra weight and thirty dollars you can carry the new weather radio that automatically pulls in the results of NOAA weather stations.

With this chapter-full of information and those gadgets, you will be one less victim who has to be rescued by helicopter because he didn't know mountain weather could change so fast.

CHAPTER FOURTEEN

HEALTH IN THE HIGH-COUNTRY

They call him Goal-Oriented. He must cover this many miles per day, at this rate of speed, by this certain hour. Failure gives him fits of depression.

There is also Tailend Tillie. She's that dot back there on the horizon who strolls leisurely, photographs often, takes two-hour lunches, and gives the leader fits.

Then there's us, the Moderates. With great good humor, we pace ourselves, covering six to eight miles a day on a reasonable gradient. We use the rest or lock step on the upgrade, never cut switchbacks, sometimes zig our own zag on trailless slopes. We use a relaxed, loose-kneed step on the downslope. We usually arrive in camp before GO (Goal-Oriented) finishes dessert. Our day's end features the cocktail hour (more hour than cocktail) and, if bugs and rain do not deter, dinner around the fire or campstove.

It takes guts to be a Moderate. Always, there is the nagging fear that you might lose the trail or, worse yet, never catch up with the leaders. Psychological stress can bring on quick physical deterioration. That's where the sense of humor comes in. Anyone who can laugh at himself after tripping over his own boots for the third time, or when he is the only member of the party who sits down on the log to cross a stream, usually makes it to camp, sanity intact.

I wish there were some humorous way to cover the subject of health hazards in high-country, but it's too serious to take lightly. Hundreds of medical papers, books, articles, and pamphlets have been written on mountaineering medicine. If you're like me, you rarely read them—until you get in trouble. I sincerely hope the following pages will alert you to the possibility of medical problems at high altitudes and encourage you to prepare for problems. This knowledge might even save your life some day.

134

■ Skin and Eyes

The skin burns quickly at higher altitudes because there is less atmosphere to screen the sun's ultraviolet rays. Sunscreen should be applied often, especially if you're sweating heavily. The eyes must also be protected from ultraviolet and infrared rays. Heavy perspirers may find sunglasses or goggles a pain to wear because they're uncomfortably hot and skid down the nose bridge on a path of sweat. Better a little inconvenience than sunburned eyeballs and temporary blindness. The flexible bow goggles recommended in Chapter 12 will stay comfortably secure on the nose. Hikers who cross snowfields without glasses are asking for trouble. Skiers who don't wear goggles risk freezing the very surface of the eyeball when running downhill at high speeds, even when it is not very cold. Remember that snow stays late and comes early in high-country. Sometimes it never leaves.

■ Dehydration

A backpacker must be ever alert for dehydration, especially on very hot or very cold days. If there is a breeze, you may not notice you're perspiring heavily because of rapid evaporation. If drops of sweat are running down the face, the rate of water loss could be one quart per hour. As much as a gallon of water a day may be lost from the lungs during heavy breathing brought on by exertion or high altitude. Substantial water loss, if not

Stopping to rest often, drinking plenty of fluids, and wearing some sort of head gear all help to prevent dehydration, heat exhaustion, and heatstroke.

replaced, can cause muscle cramps, nausea, listlessness, and headache. Dark yellow urine is another sign of dehydration.

The remedy for dehydration is not to gulp two quarts of cold water during a stop (which reduces blood circulation in the muscles because blood rushes to warm your stomach), but rather to drink small amounts often. Keep your water bottle filled and accessible. Anticipate a waterless camp and carry extra water in your fold-up plastic water carrier.

A sweating backpacker loses salt, as well as water. Replacing salt loss has stimulated much controversy and considerable research. There was a period a few years back when it was thought inadvisable to take salt tablets. For one thing, taking them after the fact (that is, when nauseated) usually causes vomiting. Some thought (and still do) that normal food intake supplies ample salt. There were other complicated reasons, involving levels of sodium, chloride, and bicarbonate in the blood, advanced for not taking salt tablets. Then came coated or wax-impregnated salt tablets, which eliminated the vomiting problem because they passed through the stomach before dissolving. Others took to drinking Gatorade, but it contains only 0.6 grams of salt per quart. One authority on mountain medicine says that unconditioned hikers may lose up to twenty grams of salt per day. Another advises that muscle cramps can be prevented by providing a daily supplement of ten to twenty grams of salt together with a generous fluid intake (one cup of water with each 0.5-gram tablet). This may be feasible for a sweating giant in a steel mill but is an almost impossible amount to down for others. A local doctor, an experienced mountain climber, advises that a more conservative dosage of five to ten tablets should be adequate. Remember to count the salt intake from meals before you start wolfing down tablets. If you eat much salt, you may become puffy. In the final analysis, your sweat output should be the guiding criteria.

■ Fatigue

Fatigue, a common problem on the trail, can cause injury and impair judgment. One cause is an inadequate supply of sugar, an important energy source. Maintain energy with this simple regimen: A light breakfast of cereal and hot drink; high carbohydrate snacks throughout the day; a light lunch of crackers with peanut butter or cheese and fresh or dried fruit; a dinner at night containing some fat or protein which will digest overnight and give you energy the next day. Freeze-dried foods contain little fat, but a dab of margarine or cheese compensates. As noted in Chapter 11, physical activity does not require protein unless you're injured, sweating profusely, or particularly susceptible to cold, so most hikers can easily withstand a week or two of limited fat and protein intake. But calories are necessary to prevent fatigue and maintain energy; carbohydrates are the answer.

■ Stomach Distress

Closely associated with hiking exertion in some individuals is that burning, burping distress in the upper abdomen and lower chest known as heartburn, or hyperacidity. My medical adviser sees no harm in neutralizing stomach acid with your favorite antacid pill. Some researchers believe that antacids containing aluminum hydroxide and sodium carbonate (Rolaids), which combine with stomach chloride to form common salt, are superior to those containing calcium carbonate (Bisodol, Titrilac, Tums, and many others). I suppose this will generate argument from the calcium carbonate folks. I would not stick my neck out on such a detail except that it seems to be a lively subject among mountaineers.

■ Heat Exhaustion

Heat exhaustion and heatstroke are sometimes confused. Both are serious, but the latter can be deadly. Heat exhaustion is caused by dehydration and salt loss and is characterized by painful cramps in the large muscles of the legs, shoulders, and arms. Other symptoms are fatigue, weakness, irritability, headache, dizziness, and vomiting. The skin is *pale, cool, and clammy with sweat,* but body temperature is usually normal. An exhaustion victim should seek shade, lie on his back, and drink fluids containing salt. Go easy on the salt until nausea passes, then increase the amount of salt until you feel well again. The body can be cooled by sprinkling water on the skin or using wet cloths. Anyone who has suffered heat exhaustion should stay out of the heat and remain quietly at rest for at least a day if possible.

I have experienced heat exhaustion on two occasions, both in Alaska. One incident occurred on an eighty-five-degree day when our party lost its bearings in interior Alaska and wandered for hours through dense spruce. The second time, I was climbing steep and fast on a hot June day near Anchorage. During the first experience, I suffered unbearable leg cramps and vomiting. Salted water would not stay down. Shade, rest, and wet towels improved my condition enough to allow our group to move on to its destination, where I dived into my tent and stayed until morning. A doctor happened to be leading our hike the second time I experienced heat exhaustion. Since we were above timberline where there was no shady spot, he advised that I get into my tent and open both ends to allow the breeze to flow through. He also advised rest, water, and no salt. I avoided vomiting this time. Several hours later, I was able to keep down salt tablets.

■ Heatstroke or Sunstroke

More serious than heat exhaustion is heatstroke, also called sunstroke. It can kill a person and people have died because their companions thought collapse was due to a heart attack or other cause. Early signs of sunstroke are profuse sweating, irritability, and fatigue. Then the mouth temperature rises to 100 degrees Fahrenheit or higher. The person feels weak, dizzy, nauseated, and confused. Then he stops sweating. When his temperature reaches 105 degrees, the victim will collapse. The skin is *hot and dry.* (Notice the difference between these symptoms and those for heat exhaustion.) Although dry skin, which indicates that sweating has stopped, is a positive sign of heatstroke, some victims may still be sweating upon collapse.

Begin treatment for heatstroke at once. The body temperature must be lowered immediately. First place the patient in a shady, cool, airy place in a prone position. Then remove his clothing and pour water over his entire body. Fan him vigorously to promote evaporation. Continue to pour water and fan until body temperature returns to normal. A heatstroke victim should stay out of sunlight and heat for several weeks after recovery. He should see a doctor as soon as possible.

As important as knowing how to treat heat exhaustion or heatstroke is preventing it in the first place. One way to beat hot weather is to start early and stop for several hours during the hottest part of the day. For this reason, some hike during the evening hours. Others rest often, maybe ten minutes during every hour, and set up camp early in the afternoon. It is wise to wear a ventilated head covering. Or soak a bandana, fold it triangularly into a strip, and tie it around your forehead. Douse your arms and legs often and let the water evaporate. Replace salt if you're perspiring heavily.

■ Altitude Sickness

The most common types of altitude sickness are acute mountain sickness (AMS), high altitude pulmonary edema (HAPE), and cerebral edema (CE). Frankly, in years past I had assumed that the only likely victims of altitude sickness were dingbat mountain climbers who land at 10,000 feet on Mt. McKinley and set out to bag the summit immediately, if not sooner. But then came my mid-June trip to the eastern Sierras in 1980 and a personal experience that convinced me to include these topics in this book.

On that trip, we drove from San Diego (sea level and 75 degrees Fahrenheit) to the Independence trailhead (5,000 feet and 95 degrees) and climbed to 6,000 feet that same night. The next day, we hiked, in hot sun, to the 10,000-foot level where I suffered my first case of altitude sickness. I had a number of the standard symptoms: headache, vomiting, and shortness of breath. The last symptom told me that this was not just another case of heat exhaustion. Aspirin and fluids saw me through the night, but the next day, while my daughter and son continued upward to Baxter Pass, I moved down to 9,000 feet. My recovery was immediate. I do not know whether another day of acclimatization at 10,000 feet would have resulted in the same recovery.

Before 1960, very little had been written on the subject of altitude sickness in any of its forms. In that year, Dr. Rodman Wilson, an experienced mountaineer and member of the Mountaineering Club of Alaska, was descending from the summit of Mt. McKinley when four experienced mountaineers from Washington and Oregon were injured in a fall on the same mountain. In the ensuing week, the four injured men, a seriously ill woman climber of Dr. Wilson's party, and an ill man in a ground rescue party were evacuated from the mountain under difficult, dangerous conditions. All were suffering some degree of altitude sickness. The story of the rescues made Alaska headlines, and accounts appeared in *Life* and *The Saturday Evening Post*. Dr. Wilson also published an account of the incident together with his findings concerning acute mountain sickness and pulmonary edema suffered by the victims.

Since then Dr. Wilson and other researchers have continued to study the symptoms, treatment, and prevention of altitude sickness. Among their findings is that acute mountain sickness victims are as diverse as the climbers who tackle the summits. Some climbers tolerate oxygen lack very poorly, while others experience no problems under the same conditions.

The symptoms and treatment of mountain sickness are discussed by Dr. Peter Hackett in his pamphlet, *Mountain Sickness,* which is availble from the American Alpine Club, 113 East 90th St., New York, New York 10028. I strongly recommend this pamphlet to anyone who plans to hike above 6,000 feet.

The symptoms of acute mountain sickness (AMS), which typically are seen in people who have recently arrived at altitudes greater than 10,000 feet, include headache, insomnia, lassitude, loss of coordination (ataxia), edema of the eyes and feet, cough, shortness of breath, fullness or tightness in the chest, irregular breathing (especially at night), loss of appetite, nausea, vomiting, reduced output of urine, weakness, and "heavy" feeling legs. Dr. Hackett states that "the real bell-ringing warning sign is a headache, usually moderate to severe, that persists despite aspirin or acetaminophen and perhaps 30 mg. codeine, and *despite a night's rest.*"

The symptoms of AMS may appear a few hours after arrival at high altitude, worsen for a while, and then slowly improve. Light activity, plenty of fluids, aspirin for the headache, and *no* additional altitude gain are the best treatment. The patient should be watched for more serious developments. Like all forms of altitude sickness, AMS is minimized or prevented by ascending slowly, but susceptibility varies tremendously from person to person.

High altitude pulmonary edema (HAPE) is the most dangerous form of altitude sickness. Its symptoms are shortness of breath, increased pulse rate, dry cough, and a chest rattle, followed by frothy pink sputum, cyanosis, ataxia, stupor, and coma. Dr. Hackett gives three rules for treatment: 1) Descent, 2) Descent, 3) Descent. If for some reason descent is delayed, the administration of oxygen at a high flow rate will help. But, since most backpackers do not carry oxygen, descent is the only truly reliable, and practical, treatment; it should not be postponed because of darkness or dubious weather. Getting down even a few thousand feet usually has a dramatic beneficial effect, unless the illness has gone too far. In that case, further descent to hospital care, oxygen treatment, and medication are necessary to save the life of the victim.

A third form of altitude sickness is cerebral edema (CE), which is fairly uncommon and usually does not occur below 12,000 to 13,000 feet. The cardinal symptom of CE is a severe and increasing headache. Vomiting also is common. The climber may stagger as if drunk and experience hallucinations. Behavior becomes irrational and simple tasks impossible. Lethargy leads to stupor, and the patient may drift into coma and die. Cerebral edema demands immediate descent under almost any conditions.

There is no way to predict who will or will not develop altitude sickness. The best advice is to ascend slowly (say, 1,000 feet per day above 8,000 feet); even this rate may be too fast for some people. There are drugs such as acetazolamide (Diamox) that can prevent mild forms of acute mountain sickness, but no drugs have been found that prevent high altitude pulmonary edema or cerebral edema. For these, the best, and possibly only effective, treatment is immediate descent to a safe altitude.

Reflecting on my own experience with altitude sickness, I've concluded that, in addition to the "it can't happen to me" fallacy, there is another factor that may lead hikers to tempt fate once to often. That's unreasonable time limitations. Too many hikers, including my family on that fateful Sierra trip, try to squeeze trips in between work-a-day schedules and don't leave themselves enough time to acclimatize to the high-country environment.

■ Carbon Monoxide Poisoning

The danger of carbon monoxide poisoning is greatest at high altitudes and when cooking is done inside a tent during adverse weather. The symptoms, which are similar to those for altitude sickness, include breathing difficulties, headache, and drowsiness; the skin, lips, and nails may be bright red; collapse is generally preceded by dizziness, nausea, and vomiting.

The best first aid for carbon monoxide poisoning is prevention—using a stove carefully with lots of ventilation (see Chapter 11 and Chapter 21 for additional discussion). If you feel the symptoms coming on, or observe them in a friend, immediately shut off the stove and get to open air. If a victim stops breathing, mouth-to-mouth artificial respiration should be started. When help is not too far away, oxygen should be obtained and administered.

■ Hypothermia

In the mountains, more weather-related fatalities are caused by hypothermia than by lightning, dehydration, sunstroke, or frostbite. With thirty million backpackers heading for the hills, hypothermia has almost become a household word. Yet, I wonder if its true significance doesn't escape the average alpinist until real experience comes along. Therefore, THINK HYPOTHERMIA. It describes the rapid, progressive mental and physical collapse accompanying the chilling of the inner core of the human body. It is caused by exposure to cold, aggravated by wet, wind, and exhaustion.

CHILL FACTOR CHART											
LOCAL TEMPERATURE (°F)											
WIND SPEED (MPH)	32	23	14	5	-4	-13	-22	-31	-40	-49	-58
EQUIVALENT TEMPERATURE (°F)											
CALM	32	23	14	5	-4	-13	-22	-31	-40	-49	-58
5	29	20	10	1	-9	-18	-28	-37	-47	-56	-65
10	18	7	-4	-15	-26	-37	-48	-59	-70	-81	-92
15	13	-1	-13	-25	-37	-49	-61	-73	-85	-97	-109
20	7	-6	-19	-32	-44	-57	-70	-83	-96	-109	-121
25	3	-10	-24	-37	-50	-64	-77	-90	-104	-117	-130
30	1	-13	-27	-41	-54	-68	-82	-97	-109	-123	-137
35	-1	-15	-29	-43	-57	-71	-85	-99	-113	-127	-142
40	-3	-17	-31	-45	-59	-74	-87	-102	-116	-131	-145
45	-3	-18	-32	-46	-61	-75	-89	-104	-118	-132	-147
50	-4	-18	-33	-47	-62	-76	-91	-105	-120	-134	-148
LITTLE DANGER FOR PROPERLY CLOTHED PERSONS				CONSIDERABLE DANGER		VERY GREAT DANGER					
				DANGER FROM FREEZING OF EXPOSED FLESH							

The combination of cold temperatures and wind, which is common in mountains, increases the risk of both hypothermia and frostbite for alpine backpackers, as shown in this chart. Wet clothes and fatigue also compound the possibility of suffering hypothermia or frostbite.

Prevention is your first line of defense against hypothermia. Stay dry. When clothes get wet, they lose about ninety percent of their insulating value. I discussed the attributes of various kinds of clothing in Chapter 7, but you must also *use* clothing to the best advantage by adjusting it frequently for heat or cold. Don't wait until your underwear is soggy from perspiration. Button or unbutton, zip or unzip, layer or unlayer as conditions change. Wear a hat, take it off; wear mittens, take them off. When you stop, add a wool shirt under your windbreaker. Put on rain gear before you get wet. If you fall in a creek, change clothes. If you get wet feet, change socks. This all sounds gaily glib. It's not so easy to discipline yourself to these procedures if you're compelled to keep up with the crowd or, worse yet, show off.

Moisture evaporating from the skin draws heat from the body. Wind blowing through clothing draws even more heat. It also refrigerates wet clothes causing evaporation of moisture from the surface. Loss of heat accelerates as the wind speed increases and the temperature drops. A windchill chart makes this very clear. The Army's "Thirty Rule" is a succinct reminder: A temperature of 30 degrees Fahrenheit together with 30-mile-per-hour winds will freeze the flesh in 30 *seconds.*

Most hypothermia cases develop in air temperatures between 30 and 50 degrees Fahrenheit. Most outdoorsmen can't believe that such temperatures can be dangerous because they underestimate the danger of being wet at such temperatures. Try soaking yourself in a 50-degree bath tub. Cold, wasn't it? Cold water held against the body by soaked clothes is a hypothermia bathtub.

Learn to recognize the progressive symptoms of hypothermia. At a body temperature of 97 degrees Fahrenheit, uncontrollable shivering begins. At 92 degrees, the following symptoms become evident: vague, slurred speech; memory lapse and incoherence; immobile, fumbling hands; frequent stumbling and lurching. Drowsiness and stiffening of the muscles begin at 80 degrees. When the body temperature goes below 80 degrees, a trance-like stupor, accompanied by slowing of the pulse and respiration rates, sets in, and death soon occurs.

Your second line of defense against hypothermia is to terminate exposure as soon as the *early* symptoms appear. Watch for persistent shivering; do not continue if you are near exhaustion. Production of body heat drops unbelievably fast with exhaustion and you can slip into hypothermia in minutes. Have the guts to give up a planned destination and to set up camp where you are. Build a fire.

Your final line of defense is treatment. The victim may deny he's in trouble. Believe the symptoms, not the patient. Here's what you should do:

1. Get him out of the wind and rain.
2. Strip off all wet clothes.
3. If the patient is only mildly affected, give him warm drinks and get

him into dry clothes and a sleeping bag. Well-wrapped, warm rocks or canteens placed against his body will hasten recovery.

4. If the patient is semi-conscious or worse, try to waken him and give him warm drinks. Remove his clothes and put him in a sleeping bag with another person (also stripped). At a body temperature of 95 degrees or less a person can not produce enough heat to replace heat loss. If you have a double bag, put the patient between two heat donors. Skin to skin contact is the most effective means for transfering heat to the victim.

5. Place the victim near a warm campfire.

■ Frostbite

Another major hazard of mountain hiking is frostbite. Severe cold alone is seldom responsible for frostbite. Rather, *cold plus dehydration* is usually the cause: When the body lacks sufficient fluids, circulation slows and frostbite on fingers and toes results. So, dehydration is not only a problem in itself, as discussed earlier, but it also increases the potential for frostbite.

I emphasize dehydration because I have found among my hiking companions an almost perverse reluctance to take fluids. Admittedly, melting snow and ice to obtain water is a tedious, sometimes difficult, chore. Furthermore, climbers affected by thin air often do not feel thirsty even when their bodies crave water. But when you consider the possibility of dehydration leading to frostbite, taking the necessary precautions assumes more importance.

For example, in 1976 three climbers on Mt. McKinley (Denali) had their feet frostbitten while they were in their sleeping bags, primarily because they had eaten too little and were dehydrated. Two of those climbers subsequently lost portions of their toes. Most likely, others of the fifty-three reported cases of frostbite on Mt. McKinley that year also were caused in part by dehydration. A friend of mine also has suffered frostbite on Denali. Although she was in excellent physical condition, her toes froze while she was standing around camp during periods between ferrying trips.

Of course, during extremely cold weather it is important to wear proper clothing. McKinley authorities strongly advise that the military vapor barrier boot be worn to prevent frostbite. You will recall that in Chapter 7 I mentioned wearing those bunny boots the night the chill factor plunged to minus fifty degrees Fahrenheit, and I'm hear to tell about it with all toes intact. I emphasize again, though, that preventing dehydration is an important part of avoiding frostbite.

The first sign of developing frostbite is a feeling of painful cold in the affected area. The pain becomes even sharper, then fades as numbness sets in. The area will begin to feel warm, even. The skin will look waxy and yellowish to dead white, but the flesh will still be pliable. At this stage, there's trouble ahead if you don't treat quickly. Warm the affected parts WITHOUT RUBBING. Ears, cheeks, nose, and chin can be warmed with the hands. Fingers can be placed in armpits; feet, against the abdomen of a willing donor. Once a part is warmed, make certain there is no refreezing. Thawing is usually followed by a tingling and burning sensation and a blotchy red appearance.

When the affected part freezes hard *(deep frostbite)*, do not treat the victim in the field. Rather, make plans to get him to a doctor. Once a part is frozen, the damage is done, although further exposure may extend the freezing upward. Do not rub a frozen part before, during, or after rewarming. Never try to warm a frozen part by heat from an open fire or stove. Severe burns could result. The procedure for warming frozen flesh should be done only by a doctor or experienced first-aid technician. It should not be attempted in the field or by the inexperienced.

When filling stoves, be careful not to spill gas on your skin. This can result in almost instant frostbite. Also, wear gloves when handling cook pots in freezing weather. Wear mittens on the trail. Sit on a insulating pad to minimize heat loss by conduction. Some Alaskan winter campers wear mukluks or other insulated foot gear in camp, then put on ski boots just moments before departing. They warm socks over a campstove or fire to further minimize chance of frostbite.

■ Burns

It is often difficult to find a level spot to set up cook kits and stove in sloping mountain terrain. The result may be a tipped kit and boiling water spilled on the cook seated beside it. Or the pot gripper may slip while you are lifting the pot of hot water. Whatever the cause of the mishap, if you are near a stream, immerse the burned area in cold water. Otherwise, pour water from your drinking bottle over the burn. Leave the burn exposed to air as long as possible. If the skin is broken, take precautions to prevent infection. Spread Neosporin antibiotic ointment on the area and cover with clean gauze squares. Change dressings often. The same procedure should be used for burns incurred from an open fire. Use your first-aid book to determine the severity of the burn. If it's second or first degree, get off the mountain fast and get to a doctor.

■ Sprains

Sprains are common in high-country and frequently occur when a backpacker loses his balance coming down a steep incline or when a boulder tips, sending him sprawling. In these cases, wrists and arms are usually involved. Ankle sprains are often the result of rushing across or between braids of a stream in foot gear that does not have the grip of your boots' lug soles. Use extra caution at these times.

If a sprain occurs, first apply cold compresses to reduce the swelling; then after the swelling goes down, warm the area to encourage circulation. You can't walk to the refrigerator for ice cubes on a mountain top, but you can use a cold mountain stream, or you might even find a snowfield from which to make a cold compress. You can use your plastic water bottle filled with hot water in lieu of a hot compress. After several days, the victim should be able to walk with the aid of a crutch, which can be fashioned from a notched branch. Two hiking staffs, one in each hand, also can be used to give the victim the support he needs to hobble to the trailhead.

■ Broken Bones

There is a decided feeling of helplessness when someone injures a bone and you can't tell if it's broken. Here are some signs that indicate a fracture:

The arm or leg is swollen in the area of the fracture.

The area is black and blue. (The discoloration may not show at first.)

Finger pressure on the fracture causes severe pain.

The hurt part can't be moved without pain.

The area looks deformed. If the bones are not displaced, it will not look deformed, but there still may be a fracture.

It is important to know the difference between a compound fracture and a simple fracture, because a compound fracture is an emergency. A fracture is called simple if the skin is unbroken, because there is little danger of infection. If the skin is broken, it's called compound, because the exposed blood vessels, nerves, and muscles are in great danger of becoming infected.

Once you have determined the seriousness of the injury, decide whether the victim will have to be evacuated by helicopter or other means. In the case of a simple arm fracture, the victim may be able to finish the trip under his own steam, although he will, of course, need help with his pack if he decides to walk out. Then refer to your first-aid manual for splinting instructions. A bandana or towel can be fashioned into a sling.

■ Lightning

Because high-country backpackers often are exposed in regions where thunderstorms are common, they may run more risk than hikers in lowland areas of being struck by lightning. A person who has been hit by lightning can be touched right away without any danger. First aid is to begin mouth-to-mouth resuscitation at once. As little as ten seconds can tip the scale between life and death. The average person may die within three minutes of the time breathing stops unless artificial respiration is administered.

I repeat that a wise backpacker will enroll in a first-aid class to learn mouth-to-mouth resuscitation, cardio-pulmonary resuscitation (CPR), and other life-saving procedures. The day you need to use one of these is too late to learn it from a book.

■ Snakebite

The poisonous snakes in the United States are rattlers, copperheads, moccasins, and coral snakes (quite rare and found only in the South). Although most snakes in this country are nonpoisonous, between six and nine thousand harmful snakebites occur annually. And high altitude doesn't eliminate the danger entirely. Several species of rattler have been observed above ten thousand feet in New Mexico, southern Utah, Arizona, and southern California.

How do you know whether a snakebite has come from a poisonous species? Severe swelling or instant sharp pain in the bite area usually means the snake was poisonous. Most poisonous snakes leave two puncture marks in the skin caused by their fangs, but swelling may hide them. Non-poisonous snakes, which don't have fangs, don't leave these telltale marks.

Controversy reigns about the best treatment for snakebites, probably because it is often botched in the field and the patient is overtreated. All agree that it's best to administer an antivenin shot in a hospital because it can cause a severe reaction. But if you are in an isolated region you may have to give the shot yourself.

The general procedure for treating a snakebite victim is to place a tourniquet between the bite and the heart. Loosen the tourniquet every fifteen minutes. Keep the victim as still as possible as movement spreads the poison through the body faster. DO NOT give stimulants such as coffee, whiskey, or any alcoholic drink, which also spread the poison faster. If you must move the patient, use a stretcher. If you are alone, carry the victim over your shoulder if the bite is on the upper part of the body or seat him on your lower back if the bite is on the lower part of the body. The bitten part should hang lower than the rest of the body to slow down the spread of poison.

If medical help is hours away (five or more), use the incision-suction method described in your snakebite kit to remove the poison from the victim's body. The wound should be swabbed with disinfectant; likewise the knife or small razor with which you cut. Make short, light cuts across the puncture marks, following the direction of the limb. DO NOT cut deeply, just enough to draw blood. Suck out blood coming from the cuts. Continue this procedure for at least one hour, resting as needed. Use a suction cup or pump from the kit if you have one, otherwise suck the blood by mouth. The poison only acts through the bloodstream, so sucking by mouth should not harm you. However, the poison could enter a sore in your mouth, and your mouth also has many pathogens that could be transmitted to the wound. As in all serious emergencies, get the victim to medical help as soon as possible.

CHAPTER FIFTEEN

ON MAKING
TERRA FIRMER

Judging terrain in the mountains begins back home. Once you've finished playing with the trail guides, maps, regulations, permits, airline schedules, and equipment catalogs, you read this chapter on what to expect in the way of booby traps under foot at higher elevations. I'm here to tell you that sometimes the trail becomes unexpectedly impassable to the backpacker. Canyons, suddenly flooded rivers, slides that have occurred since the map was drawn, overgrown areas, changes in the course of a river, icy slopes, fresh scree slopes, all may obscure trails and advance a hike's rating from intermediate to technical. How then do you fool Mother Nature? There are a few tricks of the trail.

Let's go back to sea level. Camping above timberline requires getting there. Finding a trailhead for established trails is usually just a matter of asking the right person and reading signs. In wilderness areas, it's not so easy. Here, as explained in Chapter 4, you must orient yourself on the map, set a bearing, and constantly refer to your compass. Sometimes, I look for game trails. Four-legged types have an uncanny way of knowing the easiest way up and over a mountain. But game trails have another noticeable feature: They vanish. I suspect lunch stops have a lot to do with it—the animals, not yours. If you can find a moose trail *out* of a willow patch, you're in luck. Above timberline, sheep make great traverses around canyons. They're scary to follow at times, but better than side-hilling it on your own. Another trick I use to get above timber is to climb a dry or almost dry stream bed. Even if it has some water flowing in it, it's easier than bushwacking—unless the route is interrupted by a waterfall or logjam. Be careful, though, not to slip on wet or moss-covered rocks.

Once through the brush, alder, willow, aspen, scrub hemlock or pine, and what else, you break into alpine groundcover. Sometimes you wish you

ON MAKING TERRA FIRMER

Alpine ground cover becomes sparse at several thousand feet. Along well-trod Resurrection Trail in the Kenai Peninsula, it presents no problems. But where there are no trails, hidden pea-sized rocks and tangled roots wait to trip you. (*Photo by Mel Monsen.*)

were back in the brush. This stuff is deceptive. From a distance it looks flat and inviting, but walking on it is a different story. You discover that the princess's mattress has lots of rock-sized peas under it and that it tangles under foot and turns ankles. Top ranking on the ankle-breaking charts goes to those precarious bumps of grass called by many names in the Arctic, but formally known as tussocks or hummocks. They are foot high and surrounded by swamp. Walk on 'em and you tip; walk between 'em and you sink into the muck. They often are found in Arctic alpine meadows or where runoff hits the flats and can go no further. Striking out across this stuff, indicated by those familiar tufts on a topo map, generally is not the quickest way to your destination, as I learned on one trip in the Arctic Wildlife Range. Those hikers who followed the meandering river beach, rather than our "shortcut" through tussock land, arrived long before us, though the distance was twice as long. We finally arrived, exhausted and unnerved from stumbling on the tussocks and sinking into the muck. At one point, with our Sheenjek River destination a few hundred yards away, I made a run for it and sank to my thighs in the goo. I yelled so loud that a caribou, which had been sitting on some late-summer ice in the middle of the river to avoid the mosquitoes, got up and raced off to rendezvous with the enemy.

God willing, you will progress upward to lichen- or moss-covered slopes. Here a word of caution. Lichen is fragile and very slow growing (one

Soggy tundra flats in the Skolai Valley in the Wrangell Mountains are invitingly devoid of cover, but may not provide solid footing. (*Photo by Bill Wakeland.*)

inch every hundred years). Modern-day ethics mandate that if there is the slightest hint of a trail you stay on it and let the lichen live. In Alaska, we must defer to the caribou herds who gobble their way across the lichen landscape, but their subsistence use we understand.

You'll know you've arrived in real mountain country when the green changes to boulder, talus, and scree. Boulders you more than likely know about. They are the rocks from stepping-stone size to house size. Talus is the name given to rubble in the intermediate range; scree is the pebble-sized rock and sand. In volcanic and young mountains all of these can be dangerous. Rocks teeter and scree slides, and one misstep can set the entire slope moving. Careful backpackers fan out when crossing slopes, and leave a safe distance between hikers when moving upwards. If you do start to slide, ride it out in a standing glissade, shuffling your feet to keep them on the surface.

There was a time when soft scree slopes petrified me and I would walk great distances up and around a gully rather than cross an exposed area. After watching fellow packers shuffle their way across, I finally decided it could be done safely. It does require practice. You must keep the feet moving, especially when the fine scree slides ever downward. If you're really skeptical about your ability and afraid you might panic midway, have a companion belay you with rope. (We'll talk about this technique in Chapter 16.)

One of the dangers of boulder hopping is the tipping stone that throws you off balance and sometimes into a serious fall. I calculate each step, and

Hikers negotiate a scree slope along Chitistone Goat Trail. The trick is to keep the feet moving forward if the scree starts to slide downward. (*Photo by Bill Wakeland.*)

if the field is unstable, the next *two* steps. Then, if I falter on the first step, I know where to put the next foot in a hurry to prevent being thrown. With a pack on your back, you will find it is easy to lose your balance. Don't hurry through a boulder field. The ankle you save may be your own.

Snow slopes can look like freeways after you've picked your way over a boulder field. They can provide a safe, easy route up and over a mountain. They can also be deceptive. The degree of slope and texture of snow are two concerns when gauging the safety of a snow pathway. Not only must you eye them for avalanche danger, but for degree of hardness. Can the slope be safely kickstepped or are crampons necessary? If you get up, can you get down? Or will late afternoon chill freeze the noontime soft snow and precipitate a slip? Do you have an ice axe and can you use it correctly to stop yourself? Should you rope up, just in case? I'll discuss avalances and winter equipment later, but herewith a word or two about method.

When walking straight up a snow slope, use an ice axe for support.

Kicking steps in soft spring or summer snow is not difficult. But it is tiring and hikers should take turns pounding out steps. If you're wearing sturdy hiking boots, one or two toe bumps per step should do it. Tailor the length of stride, upward or sideways, to the leg length of the shortest member of the group. Long-legged types should consider the shorties in the party.

Other rules apply when going down. The technique here is to face out and walk down, leaning slightly back and plunging your heel in at each step. Nervous beginners may want to lean way back and almost sit down, but the

The wise winter mountaineer will attend classes to learn self-arrest techniques for stopping headfirst and feetfirst falls. (*Photo by Margaret Leonard.*)

safest position is to stand straight up with your weight over your feet, and dig in. No respectable author would tell his fellow backpackers that there is a faster way down, but it's so much fun that I forgo respectability. Glissading speeds up the descent, but it is also a good way to break your neck. Before trying it, practice—a lot—on short slopes. Glissading involves sliding down a snow slope in a crouch position *on your feet, not* on the seat of your pants or on a ground pad, piece of plastic, or article of clothing. You should have an ice axe and know how to arrest a slide that gets out of hand (or foot). Most beginners cannot believe the speed with which a slide becomes an uncontrolled fall. Nor do they realize that when the snow runs out, the rocks and boulders at the bottom do not a mattress provide. Have fun, but don't say I didn't warn you.

When I first started mountain climbing, experts in the crowd would point out a gendarme or a bergschrund and I would knowingly nod but secretly respond, "Okay, if you say so." Who cares whether it's a gully or couloir. All I care about is getting over it. Aha. Therein lies the rub. Knowing what it is will sometimes aid and abet the process of passing over it.

The second edition of *Mountaineering: The Freedom of the Hills* contains an excellent sketch of a mountain with the terrain features labeled and, on the facing page, the same mountain as seen on a contour map. I found these illustrations so helpful I've included them so that you can learn to identify the typical features of a mountain area.

The summit is the highest point in an area. It can be a peak two feet square or a broad ridge. A saddle, pass, or col is the low point in a ridge through which most backpackers pass when moving from one drainage to another. If a glacier has melted, a tarn (mountain lake) may remain. Where a glacier once entered a main glacier from the side, it may have left a hanging valley. Backpackers find these to be great campsites. The upper end of a glacial valley is usually marked by a cirque. Freezing and thawing cause the snow and ice to pull away from the headwall surrounding the cirque, causing a cleft called a bergschrund (from the Swedish). Gauging the possibility of a bergschrund might save you the necessity of backtracking from a cirque.

A glacier is usually fronted by an ice cliff, ice falls, and crevasses. Medial moraine, terminal moraine, and a glacial stream trace the end of the glacial sequence. In Alaska, glaciers are as plentiful as are mountains and knowing this sequence can alert you to the terrain ahead. Standing on a far-off peak, a glacier doesn't look that complicated; walking on it is something else. Crevasses eat hikers with regularity.

Glacial streams may be more than a trickle. Once when we were camping on the terminal moraine of a glacier, two men in the group left to explore the glacier several miles away. They traversed the steep valley wall on the right, and soon we saw them hopscotching across the crevassed surface of the glacier. Their further progress was unmarked by us. It began to grow dark, and as the leader of the group, I became concerned about the men's safety. I walked in the direction of their travel and finally spotted them across the glacial stream a mile or more from camp. The stream was fast and high and I could not hear what they were trying to tell me. Finally I deduced that they were going downstream and would wait until daylight to come across. I knew they carried only daypacks and I worried about hypothermia. Early the next morning, they crossed the stream on a raft constructed from birch trees and their climbing rope. Although they had kept warm with a space blanket and fire, they were ravenous, having run out of snacks the day before. Better assessment of the glacial terrain and the time required to travel in it might have prevented their uneasiness, and mine.

Calculating the time needed to reach the only flat campsite within miles becomes imperative with darkness or a storm approaching. After a few episodes in wilderness terrain, you will learn that traveling through it is much slower than hiking well-used trails. Accurate calculation of distance and time was discussed in Chapter 4, but a few points are repeated here. Unexpected changes in the terrain (flooded rivers, new overgrowth, fresh rock slides, etc.) can blow a schedule. Your computations also may be disrupted because of inadequate information, such as a stream that didn't show on the map or a forty-foot cliff that's not shown on a fifty-foot contour map. I have spent over an hour getting six people across a stream that did not appear on my map.

This may be one way to make a three-day weekend out of two days, but it doesn't set so well with those who wait. They may decide to call out the National Guard. To avoid the embarrassment of frequent association with your local rescue coordination center, learn all you can about the terrain you intend to cover, and estimate the distance and time with all those neat ideas I gave you in Chapter 4.

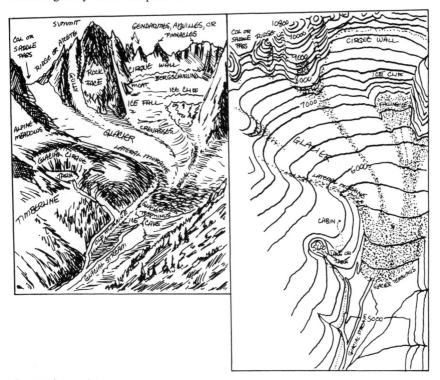

Comparison of how mountain terrain would look visually (*left*) and on a corresponding contour map (*right*). (From *Mountaineering: The Freedom of the Hills*, edited by Peggy Ferber, published by The Mountaineers, Seattle, WA.)

CHAPTER SIXTEEN

CROSSING STREAMS

Bodies of water come in assorted sizes, shapes, and colors. Ways to cross them are just as varied. The preferred plan is via boat or bridge, but backpackers don't always have those options. Enter the art of crossing a stream.

You will notice that I used the word stream rather than river. In Alaska, we generally categorize moving bodies of water as creek, stream, or river. Now that I've said that, I think of a midwesterner with whom I crossed a creek and his comment after the event was *"That's* a creek?" This should tell you that there can be an enormous difference between eastern and western streams. Terrain and gradient make the difference. Western water crashes over boulders, and even in flatland moves with a fair current. Eastern and midwestern water is usually shallower, and underneath is a mixture of gravel and clay. In Alaska, we learn to expect anything from treacherous glacial silt, which will suck you down like quicksand, to tippy, algae-covered rocks, which will upend the most balanced backpacker. But wherever you are, the first necessary skill in crossing water on foot is to be able to read it.

Rivers are beyong the scope of this backpacker. I place in this category such waterways as the Yukon, Susitna, and Matanuska Rivers, to name a few in central and interior Alaska. Most rivers are deep, wide, and fast and are fed from either vast drainages or glaciers or both. I know hunting guides manage to negotiate them on horseback, but I prefer to cross rivers in a rubber raft, starting well upstream from the trailhead across the river. I add here that what I call *streams* may be called *rivers* on a map. It is obvious that the name of a body of water may not have anything to do with its crossability, which is the criterion I've used in these classifications.

Backpacker in Chugach Mountains near Anchorage crosses a stream without getting wet feet. (*Photo by Bill Wakeland.*)

Creeks and streams are usually crossable on foot, provided it's not the morning after a cloudburst or the height of spring runoff. Throw a stick into the stream to gauge its velocity. If it's moving only moderately fast, spend some time finding the easiest and safest place to cross. Look for submerged rocks. If you see a V pointing upstream this should clue you to the presence of an underwater rock. Best to cross downstream of either a submerged or projecting rock, maybe even rest in its eddy. But beware of very large eddies which may trap you in their circular current. When you have a choice, cross at the braided section of a stream. Obviously, when the force of a stream is spread into several channels, the current is slower, so pick a braided section, rather than a single, narrow channel. Then decide if crossing is worth the risk and within the capabilities of every person in your party.

Don't be dismayed if you botch a crossing. Even the experienced make mistakes. On one trip, we had begun hiking from the highway hoping to find a short route to the Peters Hills in interior Alaska. This plan required a romp, or slog, across the soggy Susitna flats. I had skied there the previous winter and decided it was a piece of cake. Piece of frozen cake, that is. It had defrosted somewhat by July. Eight hours later we had covered only four miles and were up against one of the most unusual streams I had ever encountered. It was one of those narrow, deep, quiet tundra creeks that you don't see until you nearly step in it. We took off our boots, rolled up our pants, hoisted our packs, and stepped into the oozy mud. About three feet in, we were up to our waists. Back to square one. Next my partner donned swimming trunks, hoisted his pack to shoulder, and began to wade as I belayed him. Midway, the water reached his neck and he backtracked. Then we tried building a bridge across the twenty-foot chasm. The dead spruce poles cracked with the first step. Next plan: He would walk downstream to see if there were some way to cross this bugger. I waited patiently for over an hour. Finally I heard a shout and my friend returned with the answer to the entire mess. The reason the creek was so high was because there was a beaver dam downstream. The dam also provided a shaky, but crossable bridge.

There are occasions when the creek itself is not the only obstacle; bad weather can cause a usually normal crossing to become an adventure. One Independence Day weekend, our group was returning from Devil's Canyon in interior Alaska to Gold Creek, a station stop on the Alaska Railroad. The weather had been ideal for several days, but as we reached our Gold Creek stream crossing, the clouds opened and rain fell in torrents. Lightning cracked and thunder rolled. It was impossible to get into rain gear before we were drenched. The final insult was a hailstorm, and we scrambled in bare feet across the icy ground. I had considerable misgivings about crossing a body of water while lightning flashed, but one of the women commenced crossing, hailstorm and all. When she reached midstream, a bolt of lightning flashed, thunder cracked, and more hail poured out of the heavens. Her classic remark later was, "I'll never forget this Independence Day. I've never felt so dependent in all my life." This leader will be forever indebted to the man with belay rope who stood in bare feet with hail up to his ankles in order to assist everyone across. Although this combination of weather phenomena was highly unusual, it's an example of what a backpacker might experience almost anywhere in the United States or Canada.

■ Rope Crossings

The belay method, which saved us at Gold Creek, is one of the simplest methods for crossing a stream with the aid of a rope. I use this technique often when the current is fast. I do not carry heavy mountain-climbing rope, but rather six-mil braided nylon, which is strong (1,650-pound test) and rolls into a compact ball. I tie one end around my waist with a bowline knot. (This is the rabbit-out-of-the-hole knot that every backpacker should practice because, unlike a slip knot, it won't tighten around your middle in a suffocating vise.) Someone in my party belays me across, that is, he pays out the rope as I need it, pulling the rope from a coil at his feet through his left hand, around behind his back, and out through his right hand. A belayer must be careful not to jerk the rope in any way that upsets the balance of the crosser. Once across, I tie the rope to a tree or, if I'm above timberline, around a boulder. If no tie points are to be found, I wrap the rope around my waist in a belay stance, and the rope man across the stream and I provide a fixed rope for the remaining crossers. The next crosser can tie into the fixed line in this way: Loop a short section of rope several times around the waist and tie it with a bowline-on-a-coil knot. Then snap a hinged carabiner around the waist coil and into the fixed line. Should the crosser fall, this will prevent him from being washed downstream. At the same time, his hands are free to probe the river bottom with a hiking pole. Belayers must take care to keep the rope taut, because if the crosser slips and grabs the line for balance, he could fall if the rope is too slack.

Another method of stream crossing is the continuous loop system. The rope ends are tied together and three persons holding the rope form a triangle with the first crosser forming the apex of the triangle and the other two on shore forming the base. The first crosser ties a loop in the rope, steps into it, and pulls it to his armpits. He supports himself on the upstream rope held by his upstream friend while his downstream friends pays out rope. Once across, the lead crosser pays the rope back until the loop reaches his downstream friend. This person then steps into the loop and crosses diagonally from the upstream person. The last man crosses supported by the two men already over in the same upstream-downstream triangular fashion as the original crossing. The advantage of this "upstream-downstream" method is that should a person fall while crossing, the downstream

159

In the belay method, the first crosser ties the rope around his waist, leaving his hands free to use a hiking pole as a probe and for balance. The belayer on shore pays out rope, always alert to arrest a fall by the crosser.

Once on the other side, the first crosser ties the rope around his waist (or to a tree or boulder, if available) to provide a fixed line for succeeding crossers. They tie short ropes around their waists, then clip into the fixed line with a carabiner. Thus, their hands also are free to use a hiking pole. (*Photo by Paula Gifford.*)

person can pull him in. If you tried to pull him in while upstream of him, he would likely be dragged under. The one disadvantage of this continuous loop method is that a lot of rope may be required for wide streams. You can solve this problem by gathering ropes from several members of the party and tying them together. Again, be sure you use a good knot to tie the ropes together.

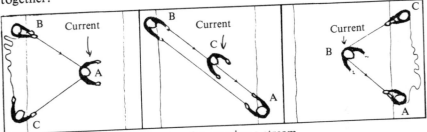

Diagram of continuous loop system for crossing a stream.

■ Footwear for Crossing Streams

I am a strong proponent of removing boots before crossing water. Some old-timers will say that the best way to maintain footing on rocky bottoms is to remove your socks, put on your boots, and cross in them. I've tried this method and stumbled lead-footed with water-filled boots, wondering how I ever let anyone talk me into it. When getting ready to cross a stream, my first instructions to every member of my party are remove your boots, stuff your socks deep into the toes, tie the laces together, and hang the boots around your neck. Another reason for removing boots is that once wet they rarely dry again during a trip, and wearing damp boots greatly increases the risk of hypothermia. Also, fine sand seeps under inner soles and then later works through socks, causing irritation to the skin.

The tenderfooted, who wince just looking at the pebbles on a shoreline, can wear canvas shoes while crossing streams. Rather than canvas shoes, I wear coral boots, which are the brown rubber boots with the big toe worn by coral divers to protect their feet. Coral boots have a corrugated bottom for traction on slippery rock, and the ankle fits tightly enough to provide a wet-suit effect, i.e., water enters and is warmed and the tight, stretch rubber ankle seals off further water. They have the added advantage of drying almost instantly and compressing easily into a side pocket of the pack. These boots are hard to find in the continental United States, and I browsed through numerous native stores in Hawaii before I found my pair. Many hikers use regular wet-suit diving boots for stream crossings. These are the foam neoprene booties worn by divers with wet suits. They, too, have a corrugated bottom and stretch to form a tight barrier around the ankle, but not before a small amount of water enters the boot and warms to body tempera-

161

ture. Most alpine water is icy and bare feet lose sensation in minutes. So, although I recommend that you remove your hiking boots, I also recommend that you put on some sort of footwear—tennis shoes, coral boots, diver's boots—before hitting that cold water and sometimes rocky bottom.

When a rope is used merely as a hand line, it is held high and taut. Note that hiker is carrying her boots around her neck. (*Photo by Chuck Heath.*)

■ Getting Across

After you've prepared your feet and rolled up your pants legs (or completely removed your pants if the water is deep), then what? Find a good third leg. If you're in birch or aspen country, there are usually sturdy branches lying near a stream. But be careful that the pole is not so dead that it breaks midway in your crossing. For years I have carried a walking staff cut from a live birch sapling. A friend uses a six-foot bamboo pole, reinforced with electrical tape wound along its length, for a walking stick. Although my staff is sometimes cumbersome to carry, especially on small charter planes, its value has been immeasurable during stream crossings and traverses of steep slopes. Some died-in-the-wool mountaineers swear by the ice axe as a third leg, but I do not. It is too short and requires a bending posture, which tends to throw a person off balance in strong current.

Hikers dry their feet and re-boot after a stream crossing. The author strongly recommends that tennis shoes, coral boots, or diver's boots be worn for crossings. Wet boots are an invitation to blisters and hypothermia. *(Photo by Bill Wakeland).*

Now you're ready to conquer the unknown. Be sure your pack waist belt is unbuckled, in case you fall and have to get out of it in a hurry. Take a deep breath and promise yourself you won't panic or try to hurry across. Face slightly upstream, but do not turn your body completely in that direction. Never face downstream because the current will hit the back of your knees and buckle them. Stand upright. Lift only one foot at a time but don't lift it high or you're liable to find it taking off with you attached. Remem-

163

ber that rocks tip easily, so be sure your lead foot is on firm footing before lifting your anchor foot. Use your pole to probe the rocks ahead to find a stepping place. This may be slow going: I remember one stream in the Wrangell Mountains where each step was into the V between two slippery rocks, and it seemed an eternity before I completed the crossing. At a time like that you must discipline yourself not to panic or to hurry. If the swirling water makes you dizzy, look ahead at the opposite shore and work by feel. Naturally, you'll have to swipe a few quick looks at the torrent around you, but you'll be surprised how much can be done by feel alone.

If you do fall, try to regain your footing before your pack submerges, either by pulling yourself out using the rope or, if you're not roped, by sheer adrenalin. If you can't regain your footing quickly, get out of your pack. If the current already has you, drift downstream feet first, if possible. When the current brings you near the bank, grab anything in sight to pull yourself out of the water. Then get out of those clothes and into dry ones as fast as you can, even if it's ninety degrees in the shade. Hopefully, your friends will be around to loan you dry clothes, or they may even have retrieved your pack.

I have recently read about a backpacking boat. It's an inflatable raft that weighs around twenty pounds and can be lashed to your pack frame where your sleeping bag usually goes. The bag then goes into the lower half of the pack and everything else in the top. When you carry a raft you may have to forgo a tent to keep the pack weight under fifty pounds, and this

An inflatable raft can be used to cross streams too deep to wade. This photo shows how the raft is retrieved by others waiting to cross. (*Photo by Bill Wakeland.*)

would probably limit a trip to three or four days. *Backpacker* (October/ November 1980) has a good article by William Sanders on backpack inflatables.

In winter and late spring, you may be able to take advantage of ice bridges to cross streams. If possible, walk downstream and look back up at the understructure before walking on an ice bridge. Then poke ahead with a ski pole or branch and walk slowly, one person at a time. Skiing across ice bridges in winter is preferable to walking because your weight is spread over a larger surface and the chances of breaking through are slimmer. Usually a side view of the bridge will tell you how thick it is.

Although you can't use them to get across a river, ice shelves running along the river edge can save you a lot of travel time in winter and early spring. Before venturing on these, check your map to be sure you aren't heading into a canyon from which you might have to backtrack. These ice shelves are usually rock solid, but use caution when the stream is rolling fast underneath.

Another stream phenomenon encountered in winter, and sometimes in summer in the Arctic, is called aufeis, or overflow. This occurs when ice forms tightly against the river bed, forcing the running water to the top and over the ice. It's scary, but usually safe, to walk in this few inches of water because it wouldn't be there if the river wasn't frozen solid. But spread out and proceed slowly.

CHAPTER SEVENTEEN

THINGS THAT GO BUMP
IN THE NIGHT

High-country is home for an assortment of wild creatures, which have various means for coping with the sometimes inhospitable climate. Some of these creatures occasionally find their way into more settled environs, for example, the moose who was caught watching television through the picture window of a house on the outskirts of Anchorage. But the wild animals that concern backpackers are the ones encountered along the trail, where they have to be dealt with on their terms. When this happens, it's best not to have a four-legged domestic animal at your side. Not only is a dog absolutely unreliable when you come up against a wolf, cat, bear, moose, etc., it may even provoke an attack. So unless you plan to leash your dog all the way, leave him at home.

Let's start with the wild ones of least interest to man with pack. Snakes were mentioned in previous chapters, and as I observed, none venture into the far north. Beavers present no great problem except when they build a dam and flood the trail you're trying to follow. On the other hand, their dams sometimes make good bridges. Don't let the slap of a beaver's tail psych you even if it sounds like a gunfight on a quiet night. As you move ever upward, you will talk indulgently to squirrels, marmots, gulls, and magpies; you may converse with a raccoon, pika, or shrew.

You may grin the first time a camp robber swoops in and snatches a week's ration of sausage. I have noted a decided mood change, however, when, upon awakening, one finds the rollicking rodents have gnawed through a pack and polished off half the freeze-dried dinners. The no-more-nice-guy plan goes into immediate effect. How do you handle these pack robbers? Obviously, you can't hang your food in a tree if you're above timberline. I once tried spreading mothballs around my pack in the Brooks Range. I first tied the pack tightly, then slipped it into a heavy-duty garbage

THINGS THAT GO BUMP IN THE NIGHT

The above-timberline camper must be on the lookout for a small army of camp robbers, including the pika, also known as rock rabbit. *(Photo by Bill Wakeland.)*

bag, set it about fifty yards from my tent, and piled rocks around it. I have no idea whether there were any night visitors, but the pack showed no signs of break and entry the next morning. If you are certain that you are not in bear country, the pack can be stored in your tent. Now I suppose someone will tell me he knows a rodent that chewed through the wall of his tent.

If you're winter camping, there is a very real threat from ravens who sometimes look big enough to carry off the whole pack. I say winter, because they always seem to be more threatening when prey is scarce or burrowed in for the winter. But you'll see ravens around in the summer also. One way to beat them in winter is to dig a small snow cave for your pack. McKinley climbers must be wary of these alpine robbers or suffer some hungry days on the mountain. According to Superintendent Bob Gerhardt, ravens have been seen as high as eighteen thousand feet on Mt. McKinley and have invaded food caches at fourteen thousand feet.

Moving right along, we come into wolf, coyote, fox, moose, elk, deer, goat, sheep, and, oh yes, bear country. I'm not dumb enough to get into the wolf hassle, except to say that, yes, they do attack the young and healthy of anything that makes good eating and, yes, they have been known to attack man. I once had fun calling to a wolf in the Peters Hills of interior Alaska and he had fun answering, but that's as far as I'll go towards humanizing an animal that lives in the wild, acts wild, and survives by the rules of the wild.

Coyotes don't bother me except when they howl all night, but that may be music to some ears. Elk, deer, sheep, and goats usually spook too fast to

Ravens have been sighted at high altitudes on Mt. McKinley and are known to scavenge food from camps.

be photographed. So too, the mountain cats, or so I've read. I used to think the same of moose, who sometimes wander through town in the winter, dodging cars and dogs and generally avoiding humans. Then I took up backpacking and began encountering them in their home country. Somehow I lost the upper hand and discovered they had a bit of an aggressive streak, especially moose moms with kids. But I didn't consider that the bulls were anything but full of bull until two good friends, Emile and her husband, were challenged and chased on a ski tour. Emile can make a good, fifteen-minute story out of that incident, and she credits her husband with saving her life because he distracted the charger while she skied off behind a

If you hope to photograph Dall sheep, you must move cautiously because they have acute hearing and eyesight. (*Photo by Bill Wakeland.*)

168

tree. Since then I, too, have encountered macho male moose and I give them wide berth. Real wide.

And then there are bears. Ten years ago, after only a few hundred miles of packing and a couple of bear sightings, I agreed with Goldilocks: If they wanted a bowl of porridge, let 'em eat. But the bears I'd seen were intimidated by a whistle and getting out of the way seemed uppermost in their minds. Now, alas, Alaska has campground bears. Kenai Peninsula blackies used to confine their marauding to the dark hours when campers were asleep; now they brazenly wander in broad daylight sending people in all directions. McKinley grizzlies nonchalantly give their best side to photographers in the park. Katmai browns insist upon their share of every fisherman's catch. My husband didn't argue, but he had to be rescued by a ranger when Ma Brown chased him right into the drink. But the wild ones in the wilderness still maintain their distance.

That is not to say that I encourage chance meetings with bears. Mine is the busiest whistle on the mountain after the first scat sighting. A bear-sized

Though wary, Alaska lynx are not considered dangerous. (*Photo by Bill Wakeland.*)

bed of matted grass will cause the hills to be alive with the sound of music. Under stress, I can even remember all the words to the national anthem. If you are an experienced shooter, a holstered 44 Magnum, weighing about three pounds, is added insurance. In the earlier years of hiking, I carried a 30–06 rifle, but nine pounds of rifle can get wearying when you are also carrying a fifty-pound pack. When the rifle-club graduates in my family no longer accompanied me, I set the gun away and hung a police whistle around my neck. Now, ten sightings later, I can say the whistle detoured all but two bears. One exception was a Kobuk-Jade Mountain griz who had to be tone deaf, but it didn't take him-her too long to get the message sent out over two frying pans. The other exception was a monster grizzly who advanced within two hundred yards of our Chitistone Pass camp in the Wrangell Mountains, casually listened to the whistles, yells, and clanging pots of ten people, then nonchalantly detoured to another section of *his* south forty.

I am even more cautious in the springtime. Most bears are not true hibernators. The blacks do drowse and do not eat for a while in winter. Their body temperature drops five to ten degrees, but their respiration and heartbeat remain about the same. Once the cubs are born, a female sleeps while the cubs help themselves to an ample supply of milk. However, it doesn't take much to rouse the female if you have the misfortune to step into her house. I have spotted black bears as early as March while skiing in the mountains. They lope along like one of my groggy teenagers, but in no way

Nowadays, even Alaska has campground bears. This brown bear came calling in Katmai National Monument. (*Photo by Chuck Heath.*)

do I test their temperament. Until I am well out of the way, I keep a keen eye out for climbable trees. But blacks sometimes climb trees. Grizzlies don't. Though I've hiked the mountains of Kodiak Island, I have yet to meet up with that giant of the bear world. I intend to keep it that way.

Once in camp, how do you discourage nocturnal visits? I won't even attempt to answer that question for national park visitors who travel bear freeways and measure their trips by the number of bears per night. Nor will I try to minimize the horrible grizzly gobblings that have occurred in Alaska the past several years. But there are some dos and don'ts for avoiding in-

The wise backpacker will be extremely cautious if confronted by a bear and cubs. The author's primary defenses against bears are distance and a loud whistle. (*Photo by Leonard Lee Rue III.*)

camp confrontations. First, keep a clean camp because bears have a sharp sense of smell. If you're still enroute to timberline and can find a tall tree with extended branch, hang your food high. Tie a rope to a rock, throw it over the branch, and pulley your food up. (I carry my food in a heavy plastic, drawstring bag or a drawstring nylon bag, both of which tie easily into a rope.) Then, anchor the rope to the tree trunk. Hang the food bag high—bears can jump—but let it hang at least two feet below the limb to discourage squirrels or any other high-wire artists. If you're above timberline, look for crevices high up on rock walls and stuff your food sack into the crack. If it's hard for you to get to it, it will be just as difficult for a burglar. Just be sure there are no rodent walkways to the niche. Be especially careful to get rid of fish smells or other smelly bear bait. If you're a menstruating female, you shouldn't be in bear country.

But what if you surprise a bear and an encounter is imminent? If you're carrying a holstered gun, you should aim for the most visible vital area, such as the head. Be sure the shot is low enough to kill, not just glance off

To discourage camp visits from bears, keep your camp clean and hang your food bag in a tree. Suspend the bag two feet or more below the limb so that squirrels can't get to it. (*Photo by Emile McIntosh.*)

the scalp. A wounded bear is a great menace to you and everyone else within miles.

One of my friends, a veteran hiker in the mountains above Anchorage, effectively scared off a grizzly bear by shooting off a Penguin flare right over the bear's head. He said the flare sounds like a rifle, and that, plus the swishing sound, scared the bear. I have learned from experience that the noise must be really loud or piercing. Bells on a pack just don't do it. Recently, I read that a researcher got good results with a boat horn. If I can find a boat horn as lightweight as a whistle that can be worn on a string around my neck, I may add it to my bear-proofing gear. But my police whistle will be right beside it.

CHAPTER EIGHTEEN

SETTING UP CAMP, FINALLY

In much-peopled areas the choice of a campsite often is quick and easy; you pitch your tent where the regulators decree. But where the choice isn't so straightforward, picking a campsite sometimes causes a larger brouhaha than the mini-war that breaks out between two siblings arguing over the last cup cake. Then is when the leader must be his firmest, inviting input, but making the ultimate decision before things get out of hand. Even then, some independents will insist on pitching exactly where they wish.

Wherever you camp, be a good neighbor. Don't hog the overlook but back up so others may enjoy the view, too. Camp away from a stream or lake, but close enough to get your water supply. Above timberline, you usually won't need to worry about crushing ground cover, but that certainly doesn't apply to a field of alpine flowers. Large rocks can be moved, but it might be considerate to move them back when you leave. One way to judge your impact on the wilderness is to ask if those coming after you will know you've been there.

If insects are bugging you, pitch into the wind, and stay away from waterfalls. If the wind is bothersome or promises to be so, find the protected lee side of a boulder or even a scrub pine patch. Then pitch your tent in the direction of the wind and open the door; the wind will blow through and billow the tent out. If a thunder-lightning storm is brewing, stay off of prominent outcroppings and also out of gullies and off of sandbars, which might be in the path of rising water. Flash floods are serious business, as is rapidly rising water caused by a night of steady rain. I woke one morning with my tent stakes in the stream. Because it was a broad valley stream with many braids, I thought a streamside location would be safe when I set up my tent the night before. Wrong again.

173

You've picked a site and are ready to set up your home. Prop your pack against a rock; if you carry an ice axe or hiking stick, you can use it as a pack prop. Get out your tent and spread it out. Lie down on it to see if you've removed all the roots, rocks, or other deterrents to a restful sleep. Pitch your tent, spread out your ground pad, and fluff up your sleeping bag. Change clothes. Set up your kitchen. If firewood is available and the ground safe, you may want a fire. Remember that alpine tundra is prone to underground smoldering, so try to find a rocky area for your fire, or line the fire pit with rocks. (Before you leave, be sure the ashes are cold to the touch, all pieces of foil or other evidence are removed, the rocks spread about, and the pit covered with ground cover. In other words, no one should know you were there.) When packing or unpacking items from your pack, follow a system. When you use a utensil, put it back where it belongs. When fueling mountain stoves, tighten the stoppers on both the fuel container and the stove, then set the fuel far away, before lighting the stove.

Pitch your tent with the door open and into the wind to prevent the sides from being blown inward. Prop your pack against your walking stick for easy access.

Next, locate the women's and men's rooms. In much of the wilderness area of Alaska, this can be done with cat-like precision and without a degree in architecture. I usually yell to the crowd that the women can go this way over the cliff or behind that rock, and the men can go that way. I never really gave much thought to the subject except that when you had to go you went. That was before I began leading groups and was startled when one woman confided to me that wilderness modesty was a real problem for her. Some even confessed that they had avoided hiking in mixed groups because they didn't know how to tackle this problem of elimination. So, first rid

Use biodegradable soap to wash your hair. If your water source is a mountain lake, rinse your hair away from the lake shore.

175

yourself of the puritan notion that the bodily function of elimination is somehow an unnatural subject. Private, yes; but unnatural, no. Then exercise the common sense to not follow a male who steps off the trail for obvious reasons and to tell the other hikers that you will catch up shortly when you need a little private space.

With larger groups that are staying in one location for several days, somewhat more elaborate provisions are required to accommodate the call of nature. Then, set up a latrine. Above timberline, it may be as easy as digging a hole behind a boulder, burning the toilet paper in the campfire, and covering up the hole with a rock or soil or moss. There's a lot to said for a comfortable log to sit on, if one is available. Some ingenious campers sink forked stakes several feet apart and place a small pole or log across that—voila, a seat of sorts. The even more ingenious sink three forked stakes to make a triangular seat. Regulations are getting tougher and tougher, but I do stop short of carrying out feces and toilet paper in a plastic bag. Next thing, they'll be diapering the wildlife. I will emphasize that anyone with a grain of sense knows better than to perform this ritual in a location that drains into the water supply. And ladies, take your mosquito lotion with you.

I've already expounded on the need to use biodegradable soap and to bathe and dispose of wastewater away from streams. If you simply must wash your hair every day, have a friend pour water over your head as needed, but not right beside a stream or lake. Use good judgment about where you swim: There's a world of difference between a million-gallon-a-minute stream and a mountain tarn.

By the way, if you melt snow for drinking, make sure it is clean. If the snow has a pink-red cast, avoid it like the plague because it might contain harmful fungus. Boil snow water for ten minutes. Do the same with any other water of questionable origin.

Now, with all these chores out of the way, sit down and relax with your favorite beverage. This bit of relaxation will tend to erase the nausea and lack of appetite associated with fatigue or strenuous climbing. It will also do wonders for your state of mind. Then, when your appetite has returned, dine leisurely and enjoy the nicest part of the day.

Before bedding down, stash your food away from your tent if you're in bear country, or simply cover your pack with a plastic bag if there are no nocturnal visitors about. If the night promises to be chilly, wear a hat and put on an extra layer over your socks and underwear. If aches and pains threaten to keep you awake, take a couple of aspirin. Stash your water and flashlight near your head. Use your stuff bag filled with clothes as a pillow. Then, sleep, sleep.

Breaking camp requires a more disciplined regimen if you expect to be

If you lose your appetite after a hard day of hiking, relax before dinner with your favorite beverage, or even take a nap, as these hikers are doing in the Arctic National Wildlife Range. (*Photo by Chuck Heath.*)

ready to leave with the others. I allow one and a half hours for preparation. I dress in the tent, set up and start my stove, put water on to boil, and then attend to personal hygiene before breakfast. If there is a particularly beautiful view or it's an unusually lovely morning, I allow an extra fifteen minutes for coffee and musing. Next, I stuff my sleeping bag, which was airing while I had breakfast, into the stuff bag. If it's raining, I do all this in the tent.

The next order of business is dismantling the tent and packing my pack. Here is where one must exercise discipline to be sure every item is put in its proper pocket and nothing is left behind. Search the rocks and landscape for wet socks, jackknives, sunglasses, watch—everything you may have set down in a weaker moment. Be especially sure that you pulled up all the tent stakes. Walk the area to be sure that not even a gum wrapper remains. Then go forth with clear conscience and light heart.

177

WINTER HIGH

Alpine ski touring is an antidote for winter blahs. Bears are asleep; insects are in hiding; summer types are at home in front of the television; and the alder and brush have disappeared under a white carpet. The streams that were impassable in summer are now a winding highway through canyon or valley. As quiet as it is, though, you are not alone: Hundreds of tracks, tiny and huge, tell you who's in the neighborhood. On a glistening day, you can see forever, but it's best to avoid taking forever to get there because the days are short and temperatures low. The predeparture agenda is a bit more complicated in winter than in summer. But with the proper equipment and skill, you will enjoy a whole new world on a winter outing.

While cross-country skiing is almost as easy as they say (just put them on and walk), a few lessons and some short day tours will ease beginner's pains. Alpine skiers should practice how to get up and down a hill. Falling and getting up in deep snow has abruptly ended some ski-touring careers. Carrying a full pack on skis is a mite different than toting one with two feet planted firmly on the trail. At times, markers will be buried and trails obliterated, so always carry maps and compass, no matter how well you think you know the trail.

Check and re-check your predeparture list of gear. It should include boots, skis and poles (or snowshoes) to suit your size and intended use; a daypack or internal-frame pack for longer tours; special winter equipment such as ice axe, crampons, goggles, headlamps, warm winter clothing, and double sleeping bag; and tent, ground pad, sunscreen, flashlight, cooking gear, and food. The list is somewhat similar to your summer list, but there are some winter modications, which I'll discuss in the coming chapters.

CHAPTER NINETEEN

GEAR FOR WINTER TRAVEL

Some winter outdoor types prefer snowshoes to skis, especially in deep powder snow. Much can be said for the better balance possible on snowshoes, especially when you're carrying a pack. Because I knew nothing about skis and skiing, and had not the wherewithal to buy a pair, my first winter trip was on rented snowshoes. I lagged miles behind the group. Finally, because of intense fatigue and deteriorating weather, I stopped in a drafty mining shack. The group leader came back and coaxed me to join the rest of the group in a cozy mining shaft further up the mountain. Blizzard conditions were developing, but once more I shouldered my pack, put on my snowshoes, and attempted to follow him. He was on skis and raced ahead of me. My snowshoes were so cumbersome and unwieldy on the ice-glazed slope that I fell far behind. Suddenly, I slipped and plunged headfirst down the slope. When I finally extricated myself from my pack, I pointed the snowshoes back to the cabin and stayed there despite the pleadings of the patient leader who rejoined the group. That night the temperature fell to zero and the winds howled at thirty miles per hour, which calculates to a chill factor of around minus fifty-five degrees Fahrenheit. I lived through the night, but since then I've advocated skis over snowshoes. For me, skies are far easier to control both in deep, flatland snow and in alpine areas, where you work hard to get up but have so much fun coming down.

■ Snowshoes and Crampons

It would be unfair, however, not to mention some new innovations in snowshoe design. For centuries, man made his way through snow on shoes of wood and leather; now we hear about Sherpa Snow-claws and Tubbs Alum-a-Shoe, both constructed of aluminum. Sherpa describes their featherweight version as 8 inches wide, 25 inches long, with anodized aluminum frames and a claw-like traction device. Cost is around $100. Tubbs says their Alum-a-Shoe has a one-piece aircraft aluminum I-beam construction, is four ounces lighter than "a competitor's shoe," and is engineered with stainless steel crampons. They are 10 inches wide, 36 inches long, and cost $125, plus $62 for claw and bindings.

These short, narrow snowshoes are best for narrow trails and are easy to lift over and around logs and brush. Longer and wider snowshoes, however, are less likely to sink into soft, deep snow.

Both companies claim that their shoes have greater stability than skis, especially when the wearer is carrying a heavy pack. Sherpa claims that you can walk naturally, not waddle as seemed to be necessary with old-style snowshoes. It may be that these new snowshoes are more maneuverable on high-angle slopes and in dense timber than were older styles.

Neither snowshoes nor skis are very helpful for getting up a steep, icy slope of, say, thirty-five or more degrees. Crampons, which require some getting used to, are the solution. They are hinged, toothed devices that are clamped and strapped to footwear to provide traction on ice or packed snow. Because of their sharp points, crampons should always be carried outside the pack with rubber tips covering the points. They should also be adjusted and fitted before you leave home. Most have a center adjustment bar and neoprene straps which fit over almost any winter boot. I wear vapor barrier boots in winter and it's not easy to attach crampons to these monsters. Double mountain boots, however, have a deep indentation between the sole and upper boot, making it easy to attach crampons. So too, Sorel and ski boots.

Use crampons to get traction on ice and hard-packed snow, especially on slopes. The points are very sharp, so take care not to snag clothing or jab your legs.

Crampons avoid the necessity for cutting steps in hard snow or ice. Every step should be taken carefully to avoid snagging trousers or gashing the opposite leg. Remember also to step flat footed. The neoprene straps must be tightly wound and buckled securely, since neoprene stretches even in cold. During a climbing school, I was embarrassed when, trying to make my way up an ice cliff while on belay, one crampon fell off. I dangled in midair and tried to get it back on while my belayer gallantly gritted his teeth and hung on. I wouldn't have blamed him if he'd decided to chuck the whole thing and let me seek my own level.

■ Cross-Country Skis and Poles

The Nordic boom is on and we of the barrel-stave generation are awed. Ten years ago, I bought a pair of metal-edged, wood touring skis and wore them for ten seasons. To intelligently replace them, it was necessary for me to wade through innumerable options: touring or racing style, made from wood, plastic, metal or combinations; edgings of lignostone, plastic, aluminum, or steel; single or double camber; wax or no-wax; scales or mica; scales in or out of the kicking area; and would you believe, five or six patterns of scales. Part of the decision was made for me by the substantially higher cost of wood skis. Longing for the security of my ancient metal-edged skis, I finally settled for fiberglass with inlaid steel edges. The new, narrow width is yet to be mastered.

Ski length is still determined in the ancient manner: When you stand with an arm upraised, the ski tip should come to your wrist. Don't buy them even a centimeter too long, especially if you intend to bushwack. Lifting a ski over, out from under, or around a log or tree can become a Houdini operation.

Bindings come in two general categories, pin-type toe or cable. Some cross-country skiers wouldn't be caught dead with anything but toe bindings, but I prefer cable bindings. I've extricated myself from many snowbanks on many cold, wet days and found it helpful to have a ski that stayed on, at least until I found it somewhere in the jumble of legs and body and snow. I am also impatient with toe binding holes that ice up so much that putting them back on after a trail stop requires fifteen minutes lead time. I also feel more secure on a downhill run with heels securely attached to the binding. As always, personal preference and expertise dictate the choice.

Backpacker published several detailed articles on how to buy cross-country skis for backpacking in the October/November 1978 and October/November 1979 issues. A more recent article by Wayne Merry (*Backpacker,* October/November 1980) contains up-to-the-minute information on skis. If you want to delve even further, read the equipment catalogs or chat with your local backpacking and ski equipment dealers.

You might even become a connoisseur like my friend Emile who maintains a stable of skis: no-wax mountain touring for uphill wet snow in early winter or late spring; wax mountain for cold snow touring; narrow wood for track skiing; and heavy, wide wood for deep, fresh snow. Emile must choose her friends carefully on no-wax days, because the constant whistling of no-wax skis does test friendships. But probably no more than the breed known as The Waxers.

Some types play the wax scene to a fare-thee-well, others run on bare wood. If you have purchased wood or fiberglass skis you will need to learn a few things about waxing for alpine skiing but not to the point where it's all wax and no ski. First, there is base wax. If you can't stand the smell or goo of pine tar, have the first coat put on your wood skis at the shop. It shouldn't cost over ten dollars. If you purchased fiberglass base skis, use a plain paraffin base wax and heat it, either over several burners of an electric stove or with a hot iron or blow torch. I don't need to emphasize that the

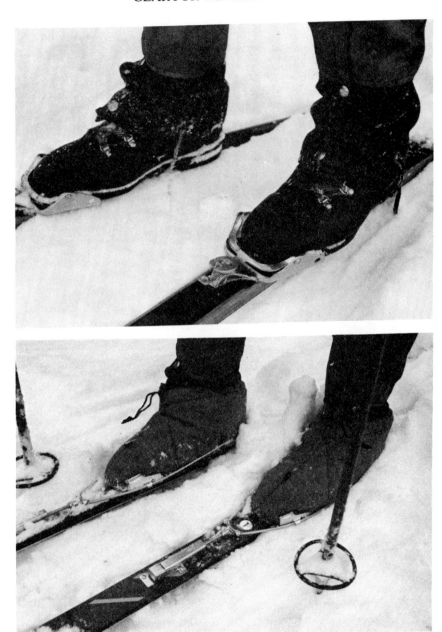

Toe bindings (*top*) have pins on the skis which fit into holes in the boot sole and are secured by a clamp. The author prefers cable bindings (*bottom*), which have a cable running behind the heel, because they seem to stay on better in deep snow.

heat should be limited to merely melting the wax, not burning up the ski. With a small piece of cork spread the wax smoothly and then apply running wax. Use a hard wax (blue or green) for dry snow; a soft one (red, yellow, or purple) for wet. I always wax my skis at home because I detest standing around at the trailhead. If you find that the skis slip backwards, you can correct by adding a rougher layer of wax in the kicker area, that is, the eighteen inches or so on the bottom of the ski under the binding. I advise against using klister except on extremely wet, slippery uphill climbs. For real mountain climbing you may need mohair skins that slide over your skis; or you can use poly rope, twisting it around and around your ski at five-inch intervals and securing it near the tip of the ski. Modern mountaineers may opt for scale bottom skis.

The author's friend Emile is shown with skis for different snow conditions and terrain. *Left,* no-wax fiberglass mountain touring skis with scales; *center,* waxable mountain skis; *right,* narrow wood skis for track skiing. (*Courtesy Emile McIntosh.*)

There's more. You need two ski poles. They come in bamboo, fiberglass, or metal with baskets to meet the most professional requirements. They should fit comfortably under the armpits. I have sometimes resembled the eye of a cyclone as I descended a slope, dragging my poles behind me. Until recently, I thought only chickens indulged in this braking procedure; now I learn from Kelley Weaverling, an expert skier, that it is a perfectly honest way to slow down. So poles are used for more than bolstering the confidence of a beginning skier.

Here is a good place to mention that efficient backpackers carry an extra ski tip, duct tape to patch it, an extra basket for the ski pole, and an avalanche cord.

First step in waxing hickory base skis is to apply the wax, usually blue or green, concentrating on the kicker area under the foot. Some say this is the only area that should be waxed, others prefer to cover the entire ski.

After the wax is applied, warm it over two burners of an electric stove, being careful not to burn the ski.

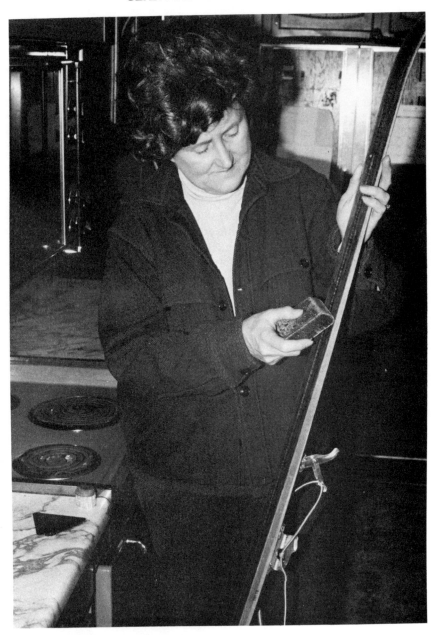

Finally, spread the softened wax with a cork until it's smooth.

■ Ski Boots

Once you have assembled your skis and poles, you think about boots. Track skiers, flatlanders, and racers tend to choose low-cut, lightweight shoes that resemble tennis shoes. New on the market is a Gore-Tex cross-country ski boot. It is an oxford with a nylon outer layer bonded to an inner Gore-Tex film layer. Next is an insulating layer of foam, finally a nylon tricot or other smooth liner. There's also a high-cut model.

Alpine skiers opt for the support and warmth of a high-cut, lined boot and usually buy it large enough to accommodate several pairs of socks. For extreme conditions and longer trips, the ski mountaineer may prefer double boots. The price range in the current REI catalog runs from $38 for the low-cut trail boot to $153 for the double boot. Because of the high cost of double boots, I have experimented with overboots. These are a PolarGuard, down, foam, or Thinsulate insulator that slides over the boot, leaving the bottom open for binding contact. I tested Lowe's foam overboots at twenty degrees Fahrenheit on a February overnight and had warm feet.

Another must for ski tourers are gaiters, which protect the lower pants legs and prevent snow from entering the top of the boot. The knicker crowd will snicker at that. I think knickers are great for track skiing, but they are too tight, and cut off leg circulation too much, to be practical for backcountry deep snow. There is a problem in stretching gaiters over bulky overboots, but the extra warmth is worth the inconvenience. A new product

All-in-one gaiter and Thinsulate overboot shown on the right is a new product that solves the problem of trying to stretch gaiters over bulky overboots.

190

from Outdoor Research—an all-in-one gaiter and Thinsulate overboot—has recently appeared in sporting stores and should make things easier for cold-weather ski tourers.

Leather ski boots require protection. The Bee Seal Plus folks say their wax lubricates without breaking down the leather. It's available from Sierra West (6 East Yanonali Street, Santa Barbara, California 93101) and some other stores. One liter costs about ten dollars.

There is much to be said for having confidence in your equipment. It gives a psychological edge when you're new to the upland ski scene. So don't skimp; outfit yourself with good, properly fitting skis, poles, and boots. And now, let's go cross-country skiing.

CHAPTER TWENTY

CROSS-COUNTRY SKIING

Some say cross-country skiing involves nothing more than donning skis and walking forward. Still, the following tips contributed by ski instructor Kelley Weaverling may help you when you first try to move across snow on slats with pack on back.*

■ On the Flat

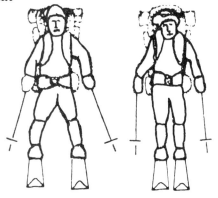

Keep a wide stance. In normally spaced tracks, a person skiing with a pack becomes a top-heavy, inverted cone. Spread your skis to roughly shoulder-width, and your balance and control will improve. Glide when you can. Shift your weight cleanly and positively to the forward-moving ski as

---

*These suggestions and illustrations are taken, with slight modifications, from an article by Kelley Weaverling in *The Anchorage Daily News,* November 8, 1979. Weaverling is a cross-country ski instructor and vice-president of Bear Bros. Wilderness Guides, Instructors, and Outfitters, located in Anchorage, Alaska.

you drive your knee forward. This will improve your body position, increase your glide, and help prevent your skis from wandering off in different directions.

Stay loose. Tension is an energy drain and you should seek ways to relax wherever possible. Adjust the pole straps so that your wrists and arms can control your poles. Grip your pole only for the initial pole plant, then relax and transfer the load to your straps. Use the weight of your pack and your weight shift to aid your pole push, then relax again and let your arm swing forward naturally.

Use the angles. Keep the poles close to your body and be sure you plant them at a favorable angle. If you don't do this, your poles will push you right, left, or even backwards.

Use your pack. Find ways to make your heavy pack actually work for you. When double-poling, plant your poles and, rather than pushing, bend at the waist and let your weight and the weight of your pack sink onto your straps to push you forward.

Keep a level head. When single poling, keep your knees slightly flexed and avoid bobbing up and down with each stride. Every time you lift your head, you also lift your pack.

Get the rhythm. Find a tempo that you can comfortably maintain and then stay with it. Synchronize your gait with your respiration and you will travel farther and easier. Remember the old story about the tortoise and the hare.

Keep your head up. Take your eyes off your ski tips and look around you. You can use the knowledge gained to modify your route; you'll also see many beautiful things you might otherwise miss. Take advantage of slight irregularities in the terrain (kick off the bumps, not off the dips). Vary your poling technique and stride while maintaining your tempo.

■ Uphill

Slide up small hills. Glide up small hills as far as you can. On small bumps, you can often double-pole at the base and with this momentum glide close to the top so that a quick step or two will carry you up and over with little effort.

Contour up long hills. Take an oblique angle that is not as steep as a direct assault when going up long hills. If the slope is not wide enough to climb in a single traverse, do a kick turn and traverse off in the opposite direction. A combined traverse and side step is also good on long hills.

Herringbone, if it isn't too steep. If the slope is too narrow to contour and if it is not too steep, just herringbone away and you'll get there. The farther you lean forward, the less likely you'll slip backward.

Sidestep steep and narrow slopes. If the slope is too narrow to contour and too steep to herringbone, you'll have to sidestep up it. About all you can do here is to make big steps and solid platforms to stand on. Take your time, breathe deeply, and do everything possible to ensure that your progress is uphill. It's hard enough to step up once, and doubly hard to do it twice.

194

■ Downhill

Take it easy. Save the Franz Klammer downhill moves for those areas with ski patrolmen and first-aid stations. A head first crash with a heavy pack can put a big dent in your wilderness experience.

Downhill turns, if you can do them. Nothing is more pleasant or beautiful than a long series of linked telemark or downhill turns, but only if the turns are within the limits of the terrain and your skiing technique. Practice these turns on the rope tows at home before attempting them in the wilderness.

Hunker down. Lower your weight and brace your forearms just above your knees. Adopt a wider-than-normal stance and possibly even a snow-plow position. This is a very stable position with a low center of gravity and it is useful for descending moderately steep slopes with a pack.

Drag your poles. While in the hunkered-down position, grasp the handles of both poles in one hand and as close to the baskets of the poles as possible with the other hand. Lean back and apply pressure to lever the poles into the snow and slow your descent. This technique gives you three points of contact with the snow and is a super stable system for descending steeper slopes.

Lower your angle of descent. If the slope is too steep to schuss and you can't make turns, then hunker down, drag your poles, and traverse. Step uphill to stop, then do a kick turn and traverse off in the opposite direction.

Sidestep steep and narrow hills. If the hill is too steep and narrow to ski down or even to traverse, then you should sidestep down, making solid platforms for your skis.

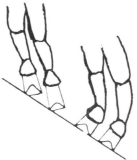

Sideslip hardpacked snow and ice. If the snow is too hard or icy to make sidestep platforms, you'll have to sideslip down it. With your skis flat on the snow and perpendicular to the fall line, you will slide sideways down the slope. If you angle your uphill edges into the slope, you will slow your descent.

■ Transitions

As you approach the bottom of the hill, anticipate the change from downhill to the flat and modify your stance. Step forward with one ski and hold your poles ready to catch your balance through the transition. Leading with one ski in this fashion will improve both your forward and aft stability. This telemark position is the same one that ski-jumpers use when they make the transition from air to snow. It provides the maximum amount of stability on landing.

196

■ Falling Down and Getting Up

Sooner or later, you'll find yourself out of control or balance, heading for a fall. Often it's better to take the fall, relatively gracefully, than to unsuccessfully fight it. Wild maneuvers designed to regain your equilibrium may simply cause you to fall in a very unfavorable position. Get as low as you can before you fall, and avoid falling on your knee joints, elbow joints, and head. Fall backward if possible, and sit down and drag your hands. Watch out for your pack—it's right behind you.

Getting up will probably be easier if you first remove your pole straps and pack. If you are really tangled, you might even want to take off your skis and start all over from the beginning. Put your skis on first, and then hoist up your pack. Then give it another try.

CHAPTER TWENTY-ONE

OVERNIGHTING IN WINTER

Treating the symptoms of winter touritis is not unlike curing an attack of summer backpackitis, except that you *must* avoid chilling, take lots of fluids, eat properly, and get your rest.

Avoiding chill requires the addition of such pieces of winter gear as a double down jacket, a PolarGuard jacket, or other outer garments that can beat the thermometer down to zero or lower. Underwear is a must for winter. Choose one of the types mentioned in Chapter 7 that matches your perspiration level. Don't wear tight stretch pants. Loose-fitting, ankle-length trousers of tightly woven wool are best. Knickers and thigh-high socks are too tight to permit entrapment of warm air. Carry extra wool socks, double wool mittens, and a pair of wool gloves to use while cooking. Adding felt insoles to your boots may help. Layer, layer, layer. Then remove a layer as you begin to sweat. Re-read the section on hypothermia in Chapter 14. Wear a balaclava, which can be pushed up when you're active and pulled down for rest stops and camp. Or if it's too restrictive and the day is mild, wear a headband that covers your ears and forehead. Wear vapor barrier boots or mukluks in camp; down booties in your sleeping bag. Don't put on your ski boots until just before departure in the morning. Wrap them in a stuff bag or piece of clothing and place them in the bottom of your sleeping bag overnight—not outside the tent.

After you've assembled the chill chasers, pack your pack. I said in Chapter 8 that I preferred a framepack over an internal-frame pack. I will now hedge and admit that there are downhill moments on skis when I wish I had a pack that hugged my back more securely than does an external-frame pack, which tends to throw a skier off balance. I do dislike the weight of a softpack on my hips, and I am also very compulsive about locating each item of gear at the zip of a zipper. But REI, Jansport, Kelty, and Lowe now sell softpacks with some outside pockets. Kelty features a touring pack with four outside pockets and a bottom panel section that zips open. The welded aluminum frame is removable, and the padded waist belt and shoulder straps can be zipped inside the back panel. A two-inch strap attaches to the side for carrying like a suitcase, which might be handy for those who must travel to the trailhead via train or plane or car. The Kelty pack also has leather accessory patches for holding winter items such as ice axe, crampons, skis, and snowshoes. The REI softpack has two side pockets with slots for skis. If you've ever carried skis for any distance, you know the value of this feature.

Maintaining water in a fluid state can be difficult during winter. This insulated cover fits a quart-sized widemouth plastic bottle.

You should drink from 2½ to 4 quarts of water per day during a winter trip. But maintaining water in a fluid state on a winter's day can be a problem. If you can stand the extra weight, carry a thermos, or wrap your plastic water bottle in an insulated cover or a wool sock and carry it inside your coat. Take a bottle of warm water into your sleeping bag at night and it doubles as a hot water bottle. You'll also have liquid refreshment during the night and liquid for coffee in the morning. You can also try burying a pot of water in the snow. (Since snow is a good insulator, this trick usually keeps water liquid.) If you are lucky enough to be near an open stream, getting liquid water is easier. Be careful, though, because most snowbanks along streams are high and precarious. To avoid an icy dunking, tie a piece of rope around the neck of your bottle and lower it to water level from the top of the bank.

In a pinch, you can eat snow to meet the need for water. However, melted snow is preferable to the frozen form: After eating snow itself, you generally feel thirstier than before, and the chill inside makes you feel miserable. Even when melted and boiled, snow alone often produces gas and diarrhea, very likely because of its lack of minerals. If you boil it with tea, coffee, or soup cubes, this doesn't seem to happen. Don't ask me for a scientific explanation of that.

Unstable slush or ice near a stream edge may require unusual procedures to get water. One way is to tie a rope around a widemouth bottle and toss it into the open water; getting it back full takes a little practice.

■ Cooking in Winter

Because it's cold outside, most winter tourers prefer to cook inside their tents. White gas and kerosene work best in winter because butane does not vaporize easily at below freezing temperatures. Hand pumps are helpful to build up pressure. Stoves must be warmed and setting them on an Ensolite pad or other insulation speeds up the warming. If you're cooking outside the tent, a windscreen is essential. As stated before, firestarter paste is another aid especially helpful in winter. *Backpacking Equipment Buyer's Guide* gives a five-star rating for winter use to five stoves: the Coleman Peak 1, the MSR 9-A and MSR-MF (called MSR G and MSR GK in recent catalogs), the Optimus 111B, and the Phoebus 725 (later modified). My "former" Svea 123R gets only a four-star rating because of its starting problems in cold weather, which I discussed in Chapter 11.

OVERNIGHTING IN WINTER

No matter what stove you use, if you intend to cook in your tent, the hazards of carbon monoxide poisoning are ever present. How does this happen in a tent with supposedly breathable walls? First, several bodies in a tent, together with the heat of a gas stove, can cause the interior walls to glaze over in cold weather. Then, with steady use of the stove, usually to melt snow, the oxygen in the tent is rapidly depleted. Finally, continuous use of a stove prevents the burner flame from firing hot enough to burn the fuel efficiently, and instead of throwing off harmless carbon dioxide, the stove pumps out deadly carbon monoxide gas.

Carbon monoxide is dangerous because it combines with hemoglobin in the blood and reduces the ability of the blood to transport oxygen to the body tissues. (The condition of reduced oxygen flow to the tissues is called hypoxia.) When the hemoglobin is only 90 percent saturated with oxygen, an individual may experience drowsiness, lassitude, and mental fatigue. At 85 percent saturation, headache, occasional nausea, and euphoria may be experienced. Symptoms intensify and a throbbing headache occurs at 80 percent saturation; vomiting and collapse occur at 70 percent saturation; coma at 60 percent, and death at 40 percent.

The effects of breathing carbon monoxide increase dramatically at higher altitudes because, as altitude increases, atmospheric pressure decreases. Because of this, the oxygen saturation of the blood decreases from its normal 97 percent saturation at sea level to 90 percent at 10,000

Cooking in winter can be done on a snow bench or, if wind is a problem, behind snow windbreaks. If you must cook in your tent, be very careful to avoid flare-ups and carbon monoxide poisoning. (*Photo by Mike Goodwin.*)

feet, to only 70 percent at 20,000 feet. (The reduction in oxygen flow to the body tissues that occurs at higher altitudes causes many of the problems associated with acclimatization.) Thus, *both* altitude and carbon monoxide reduce the oxygen saturation of the blood, and their effects are approximately additive.

As you can surmise from this discussion, high-altitude winter backpackers run a substantially greater risk than others of carbon monoxide poisoning. You might want to consult *Backpacking Equipment Buyer's Guide* for the results of tests on carbon monoxide production by different stoves before deciding on which one to take on a winter outing. But no matter which stove you use, or at what altitude, if you are cooking in a tent, ventilate adequately and watch for symptoms of carbon monoxide poisoning.

Food for winter touring should be of the high-energy variety. Raisins, candy, peanuts, cheese, hot chocolate, hot cider, and salami in addition to your freeze-dried fare will help to produce those five thousand calories needed to keep your inner core and extremities warm. By the way, leave your metal cup and silverware at home. Using an insulated plastic cup and the new Lexan dinnerware will save your lips from an instant freeze.

Before moving on from your campsite, you must burn all garbage. A brochure from Mt. McKinley National Park suggests a good method for doing this under cold-country conditions. Pour a small amount of gas into the bags of garbage and shake so that the garbage gets wet. Dig a snow hole and line it with foil wrappers from freeze-dried food. Start a fire in the snow hole and add the garbage one handful at a time until it is all burned. After all the garbage is burned, remove the residue from the hole, and pack it out with you.

■ Wintertime Sleeping

Getting proper rest on a winter overnight requires a proper tent, good ground pad (or two), and a warm sleeping bag. *Backpacking Equipment Buyer's Guide* features the results of a test done in 1977. A selection of tents were pitched on a frozen lake in northern British Columbia and left there for two weeks in March. Winds gusted, heavy wet snow piled up, and winter prevailed. The tents were checked daily for their performance on twenty-two test criteria from sag to seams, to flapping and weatherproofness. If you plan to add winter to your camping experience, check out the *Guide,* which gives a thorough analysis of the wintertime abilities of one heap of tents.

Manufacturers say a geodesic structure, which has the greatest strength to weight ratio of known structural systems, provides greater resistance to wind and snow loads than conventional designs. Poles for some geodesic tents are made from tubular aluminum and are shock-corded, so pitching

202

time is about five minutes. Most geodesics have a rainfly and the door can be kept partially open (the flap falls forward rather than to the side). This is a real aid to ventilation when cooking in the tent. Some dome tents have fiberglass poles, which decreases their weight even more.

Staking a tent in snow can be a little tricky, but using anchors makes the process easier. Early Winters sells a stake called the Lucky Fluke for five dollars. (It better be lucky at that price.) It is an angular stake, six by eight inches, fabricated from heavy-gauge aluminum alloy with a webbing harness attached. Because of its shape and design, the Lucky Fluke holds extremely well in snow, sand, or loose soil. A less costly way to anchor a tent in winter wind and snow is to bury heavy plastic stakes in holes dug in the snow, then pour a bit of water over them. Some veterans pull the tent guy lines through aluminum pie plates and bury the plates. As previously warned, you might have to leave the frozen-in stakes (or pie plates) beind when you depart.

Ice axes, skis, or ski poles can be used to stake tents in snow. (*Photo by Mike Goodwin.*)

When selecting a tent site, it's wise to stay out of basins where cold air settles. On the other hand, mountain tops are windy. A level area half way between seems your warmest bet. Stamp down a level space with your skis. Pitch away from the wind but not sideways to it. Use a whisk broom and sponge to get snow out of the tent. Don't use your skis to anchor your tent, then discover that you need them to go after water.

If it's warm enough to cook outside, construct a snow table by scraping

203

out and leveling a snowbank. A snow sitting bench can be made more comfortable by sitting on your ground pad. My favorite ground pad, as mentioned in an earlier chapter, is the Therm-A-Rest, a self-inflating, open-cell foam and air mattress. If you want to double your winter comfort, carry a pad of Ensolite in addition to the mattress. You'll be amazed at how little ground cold seeps through this double barrier. Blue Foam, another inexpensive closed-cell ground pad, also provides good insulation on snow. Both Ensolite and Blue Foam do become brittle at very low temperatures. One Alaskan backpacker discovered that his foam pad broke at minus fifty-eight degrees Fahrenheit. With any kind of luck, you can manage to be at home when temperatures reach that low.

Sleeping bags for winter camping should be temperature rated as low as you can afford, like about minus thirty. Down is great, but what if it gets wet? PolarGuard solves the wetness problem, but isn't all that warm. Some of my friends use a down liner in their PolarGuard or Hollofill II bags and, for even more warmth, an overbag of Gore-Tex or other breathable fabric.

A few of my more daring friends swear by the vapor barrier concept for wintertime sleeping, thereby reducing the bulk of their nightly attire. In this method, a waterproof material such as coated nylon is used to lock in body moisture, so you bask in your own sweat (or so the theory goes). This sauna arrangement can increase the temperature by fifteen to twenty degrees. Because the coated fabric prevents warm humid air from evaporating, your body doesn't have to work as hard to keep warm.

If you are a dry heat advocate, like myself, change to dry clothes before bedding down for the night, even if it means some temporary discomfort. I wear Duofold underwear (cotton and wool) or Thermolactyl (acrylic and vinyon). Then, depending on the temperature forecast, I layer with a wool shirt or sweater and wool pants, cotton and wool socks, down booties, wool balaclava, and gloves. If the temperature hits the sub-zero range, I add a down jacket and anything else I can find in my pack. Snuggle up to your tent partner and conserve even more heat.

■ Snow Shelters

There is yet another way to beat the weather if large drifts are available: Dig a snow cave. If large drifts are not available, or if there is only powder snow, try piling a mound of snow using a collapsible pack shovel. Let the mound age for an hour or two and then hollow out your home for the night. Dig your entrance lower than your sleeping bench so cold air will move out. Punch an air hole through the top. Take your tools in with you just in case snow drifts in during the night and you have to dig out.

Even better, but a lot more work than a snow cave, is an igloo. I have watched rangers and instructors build one in about four hours. If you plan

to set up a base camp for several days or weeks of outdoor activity, an igloo gives good protection against the elements. The inside of a well-constructed igloo will always be calm, quiet, and a comfortable few degrees below freezing even when the cold outside is fierce and the wind is raging.

Kelley Weaverling offers some tips on building an igloo that will keep you warm and dry.* The only tools needed are a lightweight aluminum folding snow shovel and a snow saw. Weaverling suggests that the igloo be located in an open area to avoid overhangs, cornices, and possible avalanche. Do not build it beneath trees, as snow-laden branches may break and fall, collapsing your shelter. Wind-packed snow that has accumulated on the lee side of a large rock above timberline is a good site to quarry your snow blocks. The blocks should be about 30 inches long, 18 inches high, and 6 inches wide. After cutting a dozen or so blocks, begin your house. Mark out a circle in the snow, about 8 to 9 feet in diameter for an igloo big enough to house one or two people. An easy way to make this circle is to tie a piece of rope to a center stake and walk about it, holding the rope taut at the desired radius and stomping out the circumference in the snow. Place the first row of blocks around the circle you have marked, making sure that they are tilted slightly inward from the vertical and that all the end joints radiate toward the center (Figure A, next page).

After the first row of blocks is in place, cut away the top edge on three or four blocks to form an inclined plane. This is the start of the spiral construction that will finish with the fitting of the king block at the very top of the dome. Each additional block must be cut so that only three corners on its lower edge rest on the blocks already in place. This will hold them in place even with huge gaps of daylight in the middles. As the spiral construction continues, the walls lean in more and more, and the blocks, now resembling trapezoids more than rectangles, actually become more secure and easier to fit (Figure B). As the walls get higher, it is necessary to pass blocks inside through a small hole and trench that is cut and dug through the bottom of the igloo. When the walls become the roof, and the hole in the roof is small enough, you are ready to fit the king block. The hole should be longer than it is wide to allow this last block to slide through easily. Hold the king block aloft with one hand and shape it to fit with the other, then lower it lightly into place (Figure C).

After the basic structure is completed, dig a tunnel entrance and cover it with blocks. Inside the igloo, build a sleeping platform higher than the entrance and fashion a cooking platform and shelves (Figure D). (Some folks do this in the beginning.) Chink all gaps both inside and outside and cut a vent in the top and in your snow block door. If there is a lot of windblown

---

* Kelley Weaverling's secrets of snow masonry and the accompanying illustrations are taken from an article in *The Anchorage Daily News,* January 31, 1980.

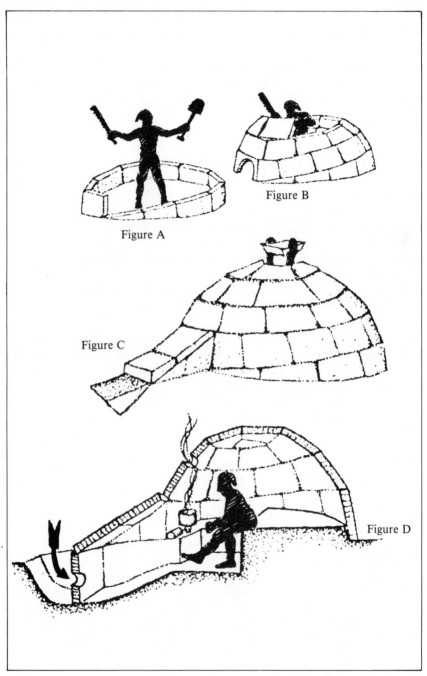

Making an igloo. (*Courtesy Kelley Weaverling and* Anchorage Daily News.)

snow, you will want to build a wall of snow blocks to windward to keep the base of the igloo from eroding. Always have your entry start low and rise up into the interior to allow cold air to drain downward and out and not in. The sleeping area should always be higher than the top of the entrance for the same reason. And, the ceiling should always be a dome, since a dome will support more weight and ventilate better than a horizontal or pointed ceiling.

The major hazard of igloo living is overheating: At about 33 degrees Fahrenheit the walls will begin to drip and clothing and sleeping bags will absorb moisture. If this happens, turn off the stoves, blow out the candles, and let your igloo cool for a while. You must be sure of good ventilation for the reasons mentioned before (low level of oxygen and high level of carbon monoxide), but with proper ventilation at the dome and in the door, the moisture can work for you. Snow walls suck vapor out of the air so fast that boiling water hardly forms a visible vapor. Then, after a few hours of soaking up vapor, the walls bind themselves together and become harder and stronger.

Building a snow block wall around a good winter tent is one way to enjoy some of the advantages of a snow shelter, while avoiding the disad-

Should darkness or fatigue catch you unprepared, the well around a tree can provide protection from the wind.

vantage of dripping walls. The snow wall will protect the tent from wind and drifting snow.

One last idea for winter shelter is a tree well. These are the sometimes deep indentations you see around the base of spruce, fir, and other mountain trees. Be sure to knock the snow off the branches (carefully, to avoid breaking) before bedding down in a tree well. This is a quick way to have outdoor protection if you've been caught on the short end of daylight and don't have time to pitch a tent or are just too tired to bother or, worse yet, did not bring a tent.

CHAPTER TWENTY-TWO

MOVING MOUNTAINS

I find it difficult to write this chapter because it necessitates having to recall circumstances surrounding the deaths of friends who perished in avalanches. All, save one, were experienced mountaineers. One young friend perished while crossing a snow gully at four thousand feet in January. The slab snow fractured and buried him.

Several years later, five ski-touring friends climbed to an upland valley and continued to ski towards a pass. Snow had fallen early in the previous fall, and was followed by a very cold November. Then January had been unseasonably warm and rain had fallen continuously during the previous week. The ski party heard hollow cracking sounds beneath the snow, so stopped to put on avalanche cords. They spread out and skied on towards the pass. A short time later, the entire mountainside of snow slabbed off and carried each of them with it. One skier, apparently in the center position, was swept down to a stream bed, then up the opposite slope where he recalls popping out of the moving snow. After searching in vain for his four fellow skiers, he managed alternately to crawl and walk through hip-deep snow to the highway where he hailed a passing motorist. The avalanche snow was so hard-packed that it was nine months before the first body was found and twenty one months later when two friends and I located the last body.

Up to the time of these tragic incidents involving personal friends, I had subconsciously thought that avalanche deaths happened mostly to Everest or Annapurna or McKinley climbers. My memory is now etched with the knowledge that avalanches occur wherever mountains and snow exist. If you plan to combine mountains and snow, read the following paragraphs carefully. Avalanches *can* happen to you.

Unless you are a snow hydrologist or someone intimately associated with avalanche control, it is difficult to remember the technical factors of avalanche detection. Therefore I suggest you purchase *Avalanche Handbook* by Pete Martinelli and Ron Perla to read at home and *ABC of Avalanche Safety* by Edward R. LaChapelle to carry in your pack. The first one is available (for $6) from the U.S. Government Printing Office as Agricultural Handbook No. 489, c/o Supt. of Documents, USGPO, Washington, DC 20402. The second is small enough to carry in your pack and can be referred to when it becomes necessary to read snow. It includes sections on technical factors, general safety rules, and rescue. This pamphlet costs only $1.50 and is available at many outdoor equipment shops and bookstores or can be ordered directly from the publishers, The Mountaineers, 719 Pike Street, Seattle, Washington 98101. The following information about avalanches is taken, in part, from LaChapelle's booklet with permission of the publisher.

Two main types of avalanches are recognized: loose-snow avalanches and the more dreaded slab avalanches. A loose-snow avalanche usually involves a top layer of snow which originates at a point and billows downhill. A slab avalanche occurs when a strata of snow fractures its bond with a lower layer, resulting in the entire mountainside breaking away.

What causes a fracture? Although their causes are complex, fractures generally occur where the underlying snow layer is weakened and becomes unstable for some reason. For example, moisture may move upwards in the snowpack forming a crystal condition below known as sugar snow (dry granules with little cohesiveness). When sugar snow is the bottom layer on a thirty to forty-five degree slope, it can provide the skids on which heavy, wet snow will easily slide. Another snow condition that may contribute to

This slope is a good candidate for a slab avalanche. (*Photo by Doug Fesler.*)

Deep cracks are often the first sign of deep slab instability caused by a bonding failure within the snow pack. (*Photo by Doug Fesler.*)

slab formation is wind-drifed snow, which creates an unstable base for later-falling heavy, moist snow. Another such unstable layer is called sun crust. When anchorage of these layers is submitted to sufficient stress, the layers part company and the dreaded slab avalance is in progress.

State avalanche expert Doug Fesler adds two other types: ice avalanches and slush-flow avalanches. Fesler says that ice avalanches, which occur in glacier terrain, are becoming more of a hazard as ski backpackers head into glacier areas to explore more challenging backcountry. As the name implies, ice, rather than snow, breaks off, usually in huge chunks, and travels long distances. Here, picking a camp is important to insure that you're not in the path of a potential ice avalanche. Slush-flow avalanches, according to Fesler, occur on very shallow slope angles and could be a problem in northern latitudes in late spring, as free water percolates in the snow pack. Spring hikers should be especially cautious when traveling down snow-covered stream beds or gullies, even on very gentle slope angles.

How then to detect possible avalanche conditions? If you step out of your tent in the morning and jagged cracks run out from your ski track, this is a sign of unstable snow. If digging down a foot or so you encounter a layer of sugar snow, it could be the lubricating layer you had hoped to avoid. The same test can be made with a ski pole, pushed strap-side down into a layer of snow. If you encounter less resistance at any point, this, too, could signal a layer of unstable snow below. You may have had the wits scared out of you by a sudden "whoomp" sound beneath the snow which

211

generally signals compacting or breaking of a snow layer because of your weight. This air gap could have been caused by a deposit of wind-driven snow, and again, it is a highly unstable condition. You might also do a shovel-sheer test. Use your shovel to cut back a wall of snow; if a block of snow drops out as you're cutting down, you can bet that it's an unstable layer. But analyzing snow pack is not for amateurs. If in doubt, retreat.

Terrain has much bearing on avalanche potential. Steep gullies and open slopes are natural avalanche paths. Trees and rock outcroppings provide natural barriers, but not if the snow is moving at 225 to 250 miles per hour. (One avalanche in Switzerland is reported to have reached that velocity.) You need only look at huge spruce trees piled like matchsticks along an avalanche path to know that they offer little impediment to a high-speed avalanche. Spring skiers should be aware that wet, spring melt permeates the snow to low-lying layers of rock or ice, then drains along these furnishing an ideal lubricated runway for sliding snow. Convex slopes found at the tops of gullies and ridges are very dangerous. My young friend mentioned earlier was swept down and covered in this type of terrain.

The chances of surviving an avalanche like this one that derailed an Alaska Railroad train are small. Avoidance is the best policy. (*Photo by Doug Fesler.*)

Broad valleys are not always safe. I often ski with friends in a wide valley about sixty miles from Anchorage. We stay close to the frozen creek in the center of the valley, avoiding potential avalanche slopes. At one point, we must pass a traditional avalanche chute, but in many years of skiing this valley, I had never seen evidence of snow runout reaching the creek.

One Sunday, we followed our normal creek route, but because snow conditions were unstable, we spread out and quietly skied by this suspect point. The following Wednesday, we returned to find that the entire snow slope had slabbed off, and not only had huge chunks of snow traveled all the way to the creek, but the tremendous wind force of the slide had sheared off the upper half of all the trees in the area.

The wind generated by an avalanche near Bird Creek, Alaska, didn't leave much of this van. Avalanche winds often shear off tree tops. *(Photo by Doug Fesler.)*

Beware of slope angles between 25 and 55 degrees. Somewhere back in my youth, I got an A in geometry, but for years I wouldn't admit that I hadn't the foggiest notion how to calculate the angle of a slope. Then one day I sat down with my kid's protractor and stared at it for a long while. I imagined pushing the straight edge of that piece of plastic into the mountainside parallel to the base of the mountain and it suddenly became obvious that 20 degrees at the lower end of the arc was a less steep slope than 60 degrees at a higher point on the arc. From then on, as I climbed, I mentally jammed a protractor into the slope and calculated at what point on the arc it would emerge.

Doug Fesler suggests another way to estimate the degree of slope. Jam your boot into the slope and imagine a right angle formed by your foot and leg. By measuring the distance from the ground to your knee, then the distance from your knee to the slope, the slope angle can be determined. For instance, it is 20 inches from my foot to my knee. For me, 34.5 inches out to

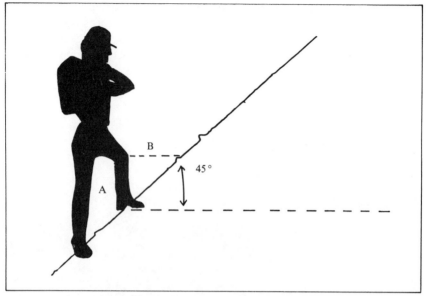

You can estimate slope angles by jamming your foot into the slope and measuring distance A, from your foot to your knee, and distance B, from your knee to the slope. For a 30-degree slope, B is twice A; for a 45-degree slope, A equals B, as diagrammed; and for a 60-degree slope, A is twice B.

the slope would calculate to a 30-degree angle; 20 inches out, to a 45-degree angle; 11.5 inches out, to a 60-degree angle. A very rough way to estimate would be to say that one part up and two parts out means a 30-degree slope; one part up and one part out would be 45 degrees; and two parts up and one part out would correspond to 60 degrees. You must memorize your own measurements to calculate your "rise and run equation." (That's trig talk according to my kids.)

Now you ask, what if you were debating crossing a snow-covered slope some distance ahead and wanted to calculate if it fell in the avalanche-prone 25- to 55-degree category. Doug Fesler suggests that you raise your left or right hand to eye level and make a right angle of your thumb and forefinger. Move your hand until the thumb "bumps into" the slope. Then estimate where in that 90-degree angle the slope measures.

If you don't trust your knees or your fingers, you can always ram a ski pole or ice axe or hiking staff into the slope to form your right angle. Just remember that the right angle is the starting point. Why all this obsession with slope angle? Because on snow-covered slopes, (or even loose rock slopes for that matter), it is part of the decision-making process when considering whether to turn back or go ahead.

214

Don't make the mistake of thinking that by skiing straight up to the top of a ridge, you lessen your chances of causing a fracture line. The danger is still there if the underlying snow conditions are tenuous.

Be careful, too, of a ridge that slopes gently on one side and breaks into an abrupt cliff on the other because it's likely that giant cornices will have formed on the steep side. A cornice is caused by prevailing winds that pull the snow over the top of a ridge and pack it in a concave lip, like a wave of frozen surf at the moment of breaking. Don't walk on cornices even if there is no visible fracture line. Sometimes they are not detectable when you are walking a ridge, but expect to find them in the terrain described above and proceed cautiously.

Cornices form along ridge tops. Fracture lines often occur a considerable distance back from the lip, so beware when walking on a snow-covered ridge. (*Photo by Doug Fesler.*)

If, after testing for unstable snow bonding and estimating the slope angle, the signs indicate that an avalanche might, *just might,* be possible, then do not proceed. Turn around and go some place where no sign indicates avalanche potential. Avalanche cords, pieps (radio transmitting devices), probes, and other such devices do not prevent avalanches. The best prevention is avoidance of danger.

Despite dramatic case histories of victims being found hours after burial in snow, I have become skeptical about the advice often reiterated in manuals and books as to what to do if you are caught in an avalanche.

These all say to throw away your poles, release your bindings, get out of your equipment, use a swimming motion, keep your head down and hands in front of your face. I simply do not believe I would have the presence of mind to remember any of these rules if I were caught in avalanching snow. Victims have been found lying on their backs or on their faces, skis ripped off, packs thrown over the head, avalanche cords either looped many times around the body or yards away. Then there are those survivors who were located because their transmitters were in the on position and rescuers picked up the signal within minutes after the disaster; others whose cords miraculously trailed above the snow surface; others whose arms near the face provided breathing space until rescuers found them with probes. Some were located by D.O.G.S. (Dogs Organized for Ground Search). They were the lucky ones.

But I have known the unlucky ones.

A LITTLE BIT
OF PHILOSOPHY

New acquaintances ask why a woman my age enjoys challenging nature when I could relax at home on my laurels after raising a family of seven kids and one husband. My flippant reply: I needed therapy. There is of course a reply of greater substance, and it can only be described as spiritual. Who can stand on a mountain top surveying the grandeur of valleys and peaks for as far as the eye can see and not recognize a Master Builder. Backpacking supplies a magnificent supplement to my go-to-church-on-Sunday life, much like a visit to the Holy Land enhances one's understanding of the Old and New Testament readings. But as Colin Fletcher said, ''I do not want to suggest that out in the wilderness my mind is always soaring. Sometimes it operates on a mundanely down-to-earth level. Sometimes it dives into the depths.''

It is probably the unpredictable nature of the backpacking game that fascinates me most. I find fording a fast stream, outfoxing a bear, or finding a route much more stimulating than cocktail conversation. It must have something to do with the basic instinct for survival. I only know I love it.

Way back when I started this book, I knew I could not conclude until I had aired my views concerning preservation versus conservation of the wilderness. Then I read Jim Whittaker's parting remarks in the Viewpoint pages of the REI catalog on the occasion of his retirement after twenty-four years with REI. They so beautifully expressed my feelings that I quote them here:

> Climbers, backpackers, skiers are an elite corps, you might say, in preserving values of the environment. Who better knows that we need the wilderness to bring people closer to their origi-

nal nature, that we need a place to be alone, where nature can bring us its good tidings. But we outdoor people know full well that we also need, for survival, the raw materials found in nature. Our backpacks of aluminum, our pitons of steel. We need synthetic fabrics and insulation—the products of petroleum. Even as we stand alone on some outcrop of rock looking at a landscape few may have ever seen, we know we are very much a part of the world of men and women, of industry and energy, of expanding demands on the fragile environment of the planet . . . There must be a balance. To find it is an awesome challenge.

My sentiments exactly, Jim.

APPENDIX I

TECHNICAL MOUNTAINEERING FOR THE NOVICE
Jack Duggan

British mountaineer George-Leigh Mallory, of Mt. Everest fame, is best remembered for answering the popular question, "Why do you climb?" with the brief response, "Because it's there." I much prefer the more literal reply by one of Mallory's less well-known contemporaries, "Because it's *steep.*"

That's what this chapter is about: What to do when the going get's steep. Technical mountaineering, whether on rock, snow, or ice, requires personal commitment and a period of apprenticeship for the beginner to achieve journeyman status, just as do more mundane crafts like carpentry or cooking. Mountain sense and judgment are the seasoned climber's principal tools. These don't come from simply reading a book like this, however, but rather from combining what you read here and elsewhere with practical field experience in the company of a safe and skillful climber.

The rewards of mountaineering are great as are the risks, so a beginning climber must proceed with caution and patience, learn the fundamentals, select good equipment, and always remember that sport and pleasure are why we go to the mountains in the first place.

■ Rock Climbing

Technical climbing usually starts when the decision is made to "rope up" or "tie in." The rope, more than any other item of equipment, symbolizes mountaineering and is literally the climber's lifeline. Accepted practice and etiquette require that when any member of the climbing party is uncomfortable about a dangerous drop below or the difficulties ahead, he requests a rope. No discussion is usually necessary, nor criticism condoned, and the whole group promptly ropes up.

Ropes and Knots

Experienced climbers are often distinguishable by the careful (almost reverent) way they care for and handle their climbing ropes. One globe-trotting mountaineer I know even carries his ropes on his lap when he travels by airplane from expedition to expedition rather than entrust them to baggage handlers. Walt Wheelock in his *Ropes, Knots and Slings for Climbers,* says it well: "The climber's rope is a precision tool, used for a skilled occupation. It should be treated with the same care and respect as any other fine instrument. When your life may literally 'hang by a thread,' too much care cannot be given for its preservation."

Nylon ropes of kernmantel (core and sheath) construction are the preferred type for climbing because of their superior handling qualities. The most popular size for all-around climbing is 150 feet in length with a diameter of 11 millimeters. When selecting a mountaineering rope, make sure it has a UIAA tag, which means it has been tested and approved by the Union Internationale des Association d'Alpinisme.

One of the cautions you can expect to hear in your early mountaineering instruction is to never step on the rope. Few things are more unnerving than dangling precariously in the fresh air on a rope that's been stomped, abraded, or cut. Always check the condition of the rope, as well as all other climbing gear, before and after each use. A climbing rope should be used for no other purpose.

A half-dozen or so knots will see you through almost every climbing situation. These basic knots have become accepted for their dependability and ease of manipulation when conditions are particularly adverse. It is far better to learn a few knots really well than to be intimidated by, and to only partially master, the wide array of knots available. So practice the following knots until you can tie them with ease and confidence.

The *bowline knot* is commonly used to tie the climber into the end of the rope. To tie it, pass the rope behind your back, form a loop in the running end and pass the tail end up through the loop, saying to yourself, "the rabbit comes out of the hole, goes around the tree and back into the hole." Tighten the knot around your waist and that's it. Very basic!

Because knots tied in nylon rope tend to slip before they tighten under shock loading, most climbers back knots up, especially the bowline knot, with a half-hitch wrap or two. The half-hitch will secure the main knot and prevent its loosening.

The *figure-eight knot* is a very simple loop or stopper knot. It is frequently used to clip the climbing rope by the middle man on a three-man rope, tied at the ends of a rappel rope, or to attach a fixed point on the rope to an anchor.

The *double fisherman's knot,* which is borrowed, obviously, from fishermen who used it years ago to tie slippery leaders together, is a strong and

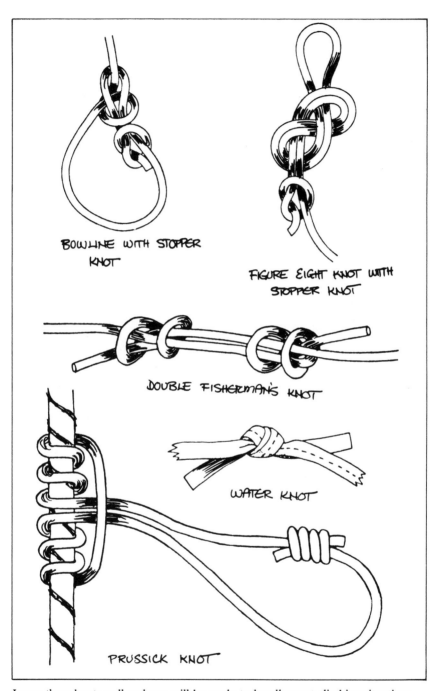

BOWLINE WITH STOPPER KNOT

FIGURE EIGHT KNOT WITH STOPPER KNOT

DOUBLE FISHERMAN'S KNOT

WATER KNOT

PRUSSICK KNOT

Learn these knots well and you will be ready to handle most climbing situations.

reliable knot most often used by mountaineers to tie the ends of a rope or sling together. Many beginning climbers find it the hardest of the basic knots to learn; most experienced climbers think it is indispensable.

The *water knot* is also used to join two ropes or, more commonly, the two ends of a length of nylon webbing to make a continuous loop "runner." It is most easily completed by tying an overhand knot in one end of the rope and reversing the order of that knot with the other rope end back through the first overhand knot. Tug both lengths to snug the knot and secure it. This knot tends to loosen and should be backed up by a half-hitch or two on each side.

The *prussick knot* is used to attach a smaller-diameter loop to a larger-diameter rope. When tension is applied, the knot tightens, and the loop will not slide along the larger-diameter rope. The prussick knot can be alternately tensioned and slid to climb a vertically hanging rope, or it can be used as a rappelling safety device.

Hardware

The types and specialized applications of mountain equipment are so numerous that technical mountaineering is a haven for the gadgeteer. Although knowledge about all the variations available comes only with experience, the beginner must be familiar with the basic hardware, in addition to climbing rope, in order to get started as a mountaineer.

Stiff-soled climbing boots, and sometimes even the more sophisticated *rock shoes* with their smooth rubber soles, are essential for solid footing on more challenging climbs.

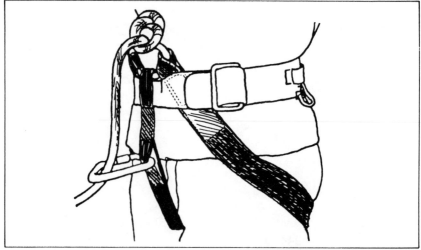

A sit-harness is more comfortable and safer than a simple rope tie-in in some climbing situations.

APPENDIX I

A *helmet* is recommended on almost all climbs to protect the climber's head if he falls or if stones or ice fall from above.

A *sit-harness* is an efficient device for attaching a rope to the body. It's more comfortable than a simple rope tie-in when the climber dangles on the rope unsupported. Also, a sit-harness insures against suffocation caused by restriction of the diaphragm, which can happen after a fall with a loose waist loop tie-in.

Carabiners are oblong metal snap-links fitted with a spring-loaded gate. The screw-lock model is preferred for snapping the climber into the rope. Carabiners are extremely useful and often seem to hold the climber's whole security system together. A dozen is definitely not too few to start with.

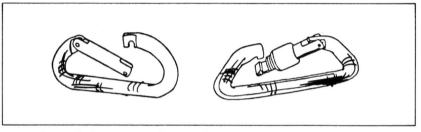

Mountaineers find many uses for carabiners. Take a dozen or so on any climb. A locking carabiner is shown on the right.

Slings, or *runners,* are continuous loops of nylon rope or webbing tied in various lengths with a water knot. They can be placed around spikes of rock or clipped to anchors to protect the leader as he climbs. Slings, like carabiners, are useful in a variety of situations. One-inch tubular webbing is the most popular sling construction material.

Climbers use artificial anchors to attach themselves to the mountain when no natural anchor, such as a rock or a tree, is available. Artificial anchors include pitons and artificial chock stones, often referred to as nuts or chocks.

Pitons are metal wedges that are driven into cracks in the rock. Their holding power comes from the force exerted on the sides of the crack. They have an eye near the head into which a carabiner is clipped. Like everything else in climbing gear, pitons come in many shapes and sizes to fit the varying mountain terrain that climbers encounter.

Nuts and *chocks* can be placed and removed more easily than pitons; they are wedged between, rather than driven into, cracks in the rock. They are attached to a wire loop or a nylon sling through which a carabiner can be clipped. "Clean climbing" with nuts and slings is preferable to piton-craft in popular climbing areas because the use of such undriven hardware avoids the destructive effect of repeatedly hammering pitons into relatively fragile rock cracks.

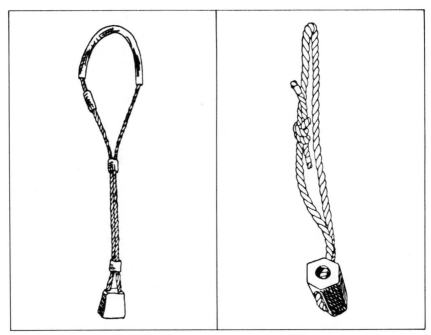

Left, chock on wire sling; *right,* chock on nylon rope sling. Chock is wedged between the cracks in rocks and then a carabiner is clipped to the sling.

Using pitons requires that the climber carry a *hammer.* Climbing hammers should be attached with a shoulder sling and length of cord to avoid loss at an untimely moment.

Climbing Techniques on Rocks

With a workable understanding of the special gear used in mountaineering, the beginning climber can concentrate on the techniques of climbing on steep mountain slopes. Stated most simply, the act of climbing combines physical balance and mental control to overcome an obstacle. The skill of a top-notch climber comes only with considerable practice and experience, of course, so don't be discouraged if it doesn't come readily. Just remember that a hard-won victory is all the sweeter for the effort and that climbing—even the most arduous kind—is a joyous activity.

Ideally, the climbing mountaineer stands straight, poising his weight over his feet. He uses his hands to simply maintain balance as he steps comfortably upward from equidistant foothold to foothold. Real life is a different story, however. Holds are never where you need them and your flailing charge up the cliff ends in the desperate contortion of an impossible stance with arms and legs trembling with fatigue. You fall as you make a frustrated lunge for that "just-out-of-reach bomber" and bounce like a puppet on the end of the climbing rope.

But don't let such common, beginning experiences deter you. And do be sure to savor each modest success, and well-executed manuever, for awhile afterward. Don't become discouraged, for once you have mastered the fundamental "dos" and "don'ts" listed below you will improve quickly:

DO hold yourself out from the rock and avoid the instinctive tendency to lean in so that you won't lose foot traction.

DO try to keep three points of balance at all times (that is, two hands and one foot, or vice versa). Avoid kneeholds—they are unreliable.

DO scan and study the pitch and line of ascent looking for specific holds and rest spots. Use your imagination.

DO test hand and footholds before you trust your weight to them.

DO try different types of practice pieces, such as jam cracks, friction slabs, and laybacks.

DO wear your helmet at all times, even when belaying.

DON'T try for too much distance on each move.

DON'T rely on your arms too much. It's more efficient to push with your legs than to pull with your arms because the leg muscles are stronger.

DON'T get spread-eagled. Maintain your balance and try to look three holds ahead.

DON'T be afraid to fall. Use top ropes at practice areas and don't back off until you fall or make the top. Challenge yourself.

Rock climbing follows relatively rigid, standardized procedures that allow climbers to pursue their goals in reasonable safety. The fun of climbing must always be enjoyed within the limits of well-understood safety rules. The serious consequences of not following safe climbing techniques are recorded annually in *Accidents in North American Mountaineering,* compiled by the American Alpine Club (113 90th Street, New York, New York 10028). This publication is recommended reading for the beginner.

When a climbing team has gained some altitude and reaches the foot of a steep pitch, some method must be used to protect the lead climber as he ascends to a safe ledge, perhaps seventy-five to a hundred feet up. Belaying is the rope technique used to prevent a long fall and injury to the lead climber in such a situation. (*Belay* is an old mariner's term that means something has been secured or tied down; it retains about the same meaning in mountaineering. Belaying also is used when crossing streams; see Chapter 16.)

The most experienced member of a climbing team takes the lead on a technical pitch, and another member belays him. After the leader is tied into the rope and has organized the hardware he will need for the climb, the belayer secures himself to a very good anchor at the base of the climb. The belayer must be aware of the direction of pull that would be exerted if the leader fell, and he must position himself so that he would not be tugged from his stand in such an event.

Friction is what belaying is all about, and there are several different techniques to achieve it. The hip belay and use of a friction device such as a figure-eight are two popular methods. The idea is that only enough rope is payed out by the belayer to allow the leader to proceed slowly. The inactive portion of the climbing rope is held back and must pass through a braking or friction point (for example, a figure-eight device or around the belayer's hips) that will brake a sharp pull on the active side of the rope if the leader "comes off," or loses his grip. The braking action is controlled by the "braking hand," which is the one on the inactive rope side of the friction point. As the leader moves up, slack is fed out by the "feeling hand," pulling rope through the friction point and braking hand. The braking hand must never leave its grip on the rope.

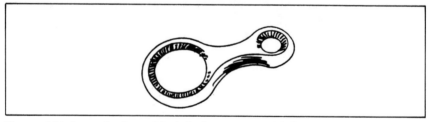

Figure-eight descender is used in belaying to create friction on the rope and help maintain control.

The belayer pays rope out slowly until the lead climber is securely anchored on top of the pitch. Then the process is reversed with the second climber belayed by the leader from his secure perch above. He slowly pulls in the rope through a braking point anchored above as the second man follows his route upward. The leader does not pull the second climber, but merely keeps the rope taut to protect him against a long fall. Slack in the active end of the rope is the worst enemy of a good belay. Slack means that any fall will be longer, harder to check, and cause a greater shock to both the climber and the belayer.

Of course, it is necessary to have some communication between climber and belayer to keep things running smoothly throughout. The following

226

standardized call system has evolved so the team can pass information back and forth by brief, easily understood instructions:

BELAYER (when he is solidly anchored and ready to start): "On Belay!"

CLIMBER (acknowledging that he has heard his belayer and is prepared to climb): "Climbing!"

CLIMBER (to request the belayer to take in excessive slack): "Up rope!"

CLIMBER (if tension on the rope is restricting the climber in his maneuvering): "Slack!"

CLIMBER (if the leader dislodges a rock or drops an object): "Rock!"

CLIMBER (to alert his belayer that he is about to come off or fall): "Falling!"

CLIMBER (after he has reached a safe spot and anchored himself): "Off Belay!"

BELAYER (confirming he has heard the climber's last call and released the rope): "Belay Off!"

A tight belay is not the only security system relied on by the lead climber. As he negotiates his way upward, the leader will place protection along the way. Following climbers trust to a snug overhead belay for safety and can climb with little fear of a serious fall. The leader, however, will fall *twice* the vertical distance between himself and his belayer below unless he secures the climbing rope to various intermediate anchors as he goes along.

The leader can "take his belay with him" by clipping the rope with carabiners to slings, chocks, pitons, or other hardware set as he goes. All the specifics of how, when, and where to place an anchor would fill this book and are best learned through on-the-job training, anyway. A couple of good things to remember about securing anchors are to try to place intermediate protection *before* it is needed for (for example, at the start of a particularly difficult passage) so that if you fall you won't have far to go, and to pay attention to the direction of pull on the anchor so you won't pull it out unintentionally when the tension on the rope increases as you go higher.

Once the team has regrouped at the top of a steep section, the belayer sets up his stance and the leader moves out again. Oftentimes, team members will rotate positions to give everyone a chance at the lead.

Belaying is a technique more easily demonstrated than described. The beginner should practice belaying with an experienced climber until the technique is mastered, as it is one of the most basic and important maneuvers in mountaineering. You can't get by without it.

The basic technique for descending steep terrain is rappelling, which is a controlled slide down an anchored and doubled rope. The control is achieved by friction on the rope, applied by the hands and body or by a mechanical braking device.

Beginning climbers, particularly, are enamored by rappelling, which is often a pleasantly exhilarating maneuver and looks great in photos.

Experienced climbers aren't as naive, however. They know that rappels are dangerous because they usually occur on exposed and steep terrain with the climber having only the rope for protection rather than the carefully chosen holds and stances used during accents. A safe rappel requires a bombproof anchor, sound equipment, and practiced technique.

To lower yourself on rappel safely, first review the chain of security, checking the rappel anchor and knots used. Make sure that both ends of the rope reach the base of the pitch or the next anchor position, and that each rope end is tied off in a figure-eight knot so you won't accidentally slide off the end of the rope.

Rappels are commonly set up by doubling the rope through a sling attached to an anchor located near the edge of the steep section. The climber clips himself into the two ends of the rope by running them through a figure-eight, carabiner brake, or other braking device and then attaching that to his sit-harness or waist loop. Going over the edge at the start of the actual rappel is often a tricky maneuver. As you back off the edge, keep your weight back and spread your feet at least shoulder width apart for added stability. Move down the face in a controlled and steady manner. The jumping and jerking rappel motion seen in movies and television is unnecessary and places undue strain on the anchor. The upper hand is placed on the rope for balance, while the lower, or braking, hand is held back on the hip to control the amount of friction and the speed of descent.

One good way to belay yourself on rappel is to tie a prussick loop around the rappel line above the friction point and clip it into your sit-harness. The prussick knot is slid lightly down the rope by the balance hand unless there is a sudden slip or fall which will cause the knot to lock and hold the climber.

■ Snow and Ice Climbing

Although some writers have claimed that snow and ice climbing is a higher craft than rock climbing, the basic climbing technology is the same for both types of mountaineering. No mountaineer worth his salt is likely to pursue one to the exclusion of the other. In fact, the world's great mountains offer challenges on both rock and ice, often on the same route.

Equipment

There has been such a revolution in recent years in snow and ice climbing equipment that today's novice is faced with a staggering assortment of gear. Probably the best advice is to use what you already have or can borrow until you are ready to make an informed choice.

The indispensable *ice axe* is a good place to start. In buying an ice axe, its length and shaft material are the principal consideration. The recommended length for general snow and ice climbing is 70 centimeters; for use on steep ice, the 55-centimeter length is more popular. Wood shafts were the standard a few years ago, but fiberglass or metal versions are the principal choices today. The Forrest Verglas or Chouinard Piolet are both high-quality tools.

At the bottom of the axe shaft is the spike. The wide blade on the axe's head is the adze; the narrow one, the pick. Always keep the spike, pick, and adze edges sharp using a fine mill file. Using a grinding wheel is risky because the metal may heat up and lose its temper.

On steep slopes of snow and glaciers, you will need *crampons* (see Chapter 19). These are steel frames that fit on the bottom of climbing boots. The popular 12-point adjustable models by SMC or Chouinard have ten spikes pointing downward and two spikes that curve out from beneath the toe of the boot. Crampons should fit snugly and be outfitted with neoprene-covered nylon straps. Rigid-frame crampons have appeared on the scene in recent years and are particularly useful for steep ice climbs because they penetrate better and seem to make it easier to keep your heel low and in the right position. Each kind has its proper application.

Anchors for snow and ice climbing differ radically from the pitons and chocks commonly used on rock ascents. Anchors include *snow pickets,* which are three- to four-feet-long aluminum tubes or T-sections that are

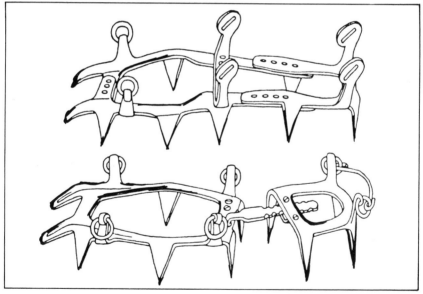

Two types of 12-point crampons: *top,* rigid adjustable type; *bottom,* hinged semi-adjustable type. Crampons are attached to the bottom of the climber's boots with neoprene-covered nylon straps.

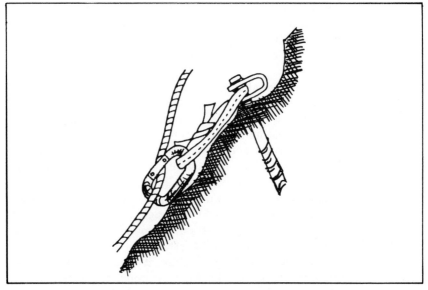

Ice screws are used to provide secure anchors in hard ice. Sling is looped through the eye and around the screw shaft, and a carabiner then attached.

driven into the snow as an anchor. The rope is attached to the protruding end by a carabiner.

Snow flukes are also used as anchors in snow. These basically triangular metal plates are attached to a properly angled wire sling and planted firmly in the snow. The climbing rope is clipped into the end of the wire sling so that if a fall occurs, the force exerted on the fluke will tend to make it dig deeper in the snow and hold the fall. Some practice is definitely needed before trusting your life to these temperamental little devils.

Neither flukes nor pickets are practical on hard ice, so the tubular *ice piton* or *ice screw* has evolved to protect ice climbers. To place a tubular screw, start a hole in the ice with the pick of your hammer or axe. Insert the screw and turn it until the threads catch and the eye is all the way in. Frequently, you must put the pick of your axe or ice hammer through the eye of the screw and use it as a lever to get the screw all the way in. Ice screws are most solid when inserted at a 45-degree angle to the slope.

As a last resort, if you find yourself lacking any of these anchor devices, you can simply chop a *bollard* with your ice axe. A bollard is created by chopping a trench in the ice so that a mushroom-shaped protrusion with a notch on the uphill side remains. The mushroom must be slanted at least ten degrees towards the hill and must be deep enough so that a rope can be hooked behind this homemade but effective anchor.

Climbing Techniques on Snow and Ice

Step-kicking is the most efficient way to move on most snow-covered slopes. A pair of stiff-soled and vibram lugged boots is necessary to do the job right. On steep slopes, a climber may climb straight up facing the slope. As he goes, he drives his ice axe directly into the snow to provide a quick self-belay in case he slips. If the snow is soft, it is important to come down onto the surface from directly above. This motion will leave a step which the next climber in line can improve on. On harder snow, one swift kick straight in should carve a satisfactory platform. One strength-saving approach on hard snow is to climb diagonally to the fall line in a series of switch-backs. Step-kicking in this mode involves using the inside and outside serrated edges of the climber's vibram-soled boots as saw teeth. The climber stands upright, using his axe in the uphill hand for balance and kicks the hard snow horizontally with the edge and tips of his boot sole. This is actually a form of step-cutting, but not nearly as time-consuming or difficult as the sort described next.

True step-cutting with an ice axe is almost a forgotten art in many climbing areas where crampon front points are the preferred and expedient method. Step-cutting is, nevertheless, one of those special skills that are worth having in your repertoire of mountaineering techniques.

Steps are normally chopped in a diagonal zig-zag up the slope. It is a slow and tiring process, so the experienced climber does everything he can to minimize the number of strokes necessary. Hold your body steady and swing the axe powerfully from the shoulder. Aim for a specific point and don't stretch off balance. One glancing blow will usually cut a slash a few inches long. Keep the angle of penetration steep so the adze won't stick in the hard snow. Nothing throws your rhythm off quicker. The leader moves up when he is satisfied with the new step, and other members of the party often wield their own axes to improve the holds as they follow. If you plan to descend by the same route, don't chop the steps so far apart that you'll throw yourself off balance using them on the way down.

Talking about descending, one of the really enjoyable maneuvers in mountaineering is glissading down open snow slopes. Skiers usually pick up the technique quickly, but with practice and some precautions, even non-skiers can learn it. For the standing glissade, start in a semi-crouched position with the knees bent. Hold the ice axe out and away from the body and begin ski-sliding downhill on your feet. Turn the toes to one side or the other to change course and link turns to control speed. Stop by digging in your heels and throwing your weight back on the spike of the axe. A sitting glissade is also useful on some slopes, but has the drawback of obstructing your view of the slope below. Speed is decreased by dragging the ice axe spike and once you have slowed enough you can stop by digging in your boot heels. Glissading should only be done where there is a safe route to the base of the slope and after all extraneous climbing equipment—especially crampons—is stowed or adjusted.

Climbers who set out across snow and ice must be skilled in self-arrest techniques for stopping a slip on snow. If a climber feels himself slipping on a snow slope, he should immediately slide one hand over the head of his axe with the thumb locked underneath; the other hand is moved down the shaft of the axe to a spot near the spike and even with the hip. Both hand grips must be solid and, above all else, must be maintained. The ice axe pick is stabbed into the snow at the climber's shoulder on the same side as the hand holding onto the axe. The shaft usually runs diagonally across the climber's chest and the spike is held close to the opposite hip. The climber uses his toes, or knees if he is wearing crampons, in conjunction with the pick to quickly slow and stop his descent. It's important to keep the spike of the axe and crampons off the snow.

When you are practicing self-arrest don't just slide on your stomach down a gentle slope of soft snow. Practice self-arrest with an ice axe for every conceivable type of fall—on your back, on your face, on hard snow as well as soft. The main points are to get onto your stomach quickly and roll toward the pick, not the spike, end of your axe.

Belaying on snow or ice is not as popular as it is in rock climbing. Anchors don't usually seem as solid and the belayer can't help but get cold as he stands and stoically feeds out rope to the leader. Despite these few negative points, a belay should be set up whenever reasonably necessary. The most popular belay technique on snow is the sitting hip belay backed up by a picket or fluke. It is set up by stamping out a firm seating platform in the snow. The belayer then braces his outstretched legs against the berm formed at the edge of the seating hole. Friction is applied by passing the rope around his lower back and hips.

The French, or Eckenstein, method is a flat-footed anchor technique used on slopes that are too steep for other techniques but aren't so steep as to require the difficult front-pointing method. Although less tiring and more efficient than front-pointing, the French method does require considerable concentration to maintain balance and firm planting of the crampon points to be effective.

In the French method, the mountaineer plants all the vertical points of his crampon and his axe as anchors while moving on fairly steep ground. As the terrain steepens, the climber turns obliquely to the slope with his feet pointing down and his face and body outward. He reaches over his shoulder and plants the pick of his axe in the snow or ice. Next, he grabs the head of the axe, pushes up on his legs and steps up one foot behind the other until the handle of the axe is almost too low for good balance. The axe is planted again higher up, and the process repeated as many times as necessary or until balance becomes so precarious that front-pointing is preferable. Body weight should be kept over the feet and movement should be as smooth as possible to lessen strain on thighs and ankles.

Front-pointing is the ice and frozen waterfall climbing technique in which only the front two points of each of the climber's crampons are in contact with the ice. Cramponing up nearly vertical, hard ice requires stiff-soled boots and well-fitted crampons, as well as sharp tools and crampons.

In this method, the climber faces the slope, reaches up, and then swings the axe or ice hammer to set the pick as high as possible. One tool is held in each hand and alternately placed overhead as the climber progresses upward. After the hand tool is set, the climber steps up, setting the front points of his crampons solidly. The heels are kept low so the front points don't shear out. Long reaches between steps should be avoided because they tend to push the climber off balance and force the front points to shear out. The climber places ice screws as intermediate anchors and clips into the rope as he moves higher, choosing screw placements as he would in rock climbing. The interval between protection points should be no longer than the climber is willing to fall; it's always a good idea to place a screw just before trying a difficult move or bulge.

Front-pointing is a fairly straightforward technique, but there are numerous tricks, which come with experience, that are applicable to various conditions. Again, nothing written here can compare with well-coached on-the-ice practice. Front-pointing on steep ice is great fun and not nearly as difficult or dangerous as it first appears. Some aficionados fondly refer to it as ice dancing!

The techniques described above permit climbers to cope with and successfully negotiate the various snow and ice conditions they are likely to encounter. There is one snow condition, however, that it is best to avoid entirely—avalanche. I can't emphasize too much the need for climbers to be well schooled in the principles of avalanche awareness. Start by reading *Avalanche Handbook,* by Pete Martinelli and Ron Perla, and don't stop until you acquire a wary respect for any wide-open, snow-covered mountain slope of 25 to 55 degrees, especially one on the lee side of a ridge after a snowstorm. (See Chapter 22 for more on detecting avalanche hazards.)

■ Glacier Travel

As many mountains are covered all year with snow and ice, traveling through icefalls and on glaciers is something a mountaineer must be prepared to do.

The first rule of glacier touring is to always travel roped up. A hidden crevasse (deep split in the ice) is a serious and ever-present glacier hazard. Three persons to a rope is the recommended minimum for safety on glaciers, and two rope teams are better than one in case additional manpower is needed to rescue a teammate who drops into a hole.

Almost every mountaineer who has spent time in the high mountains has found himself at least once suddenly dangling from a rope in the icy blackness of an unseen crevasse. As unpleasant and startling as the experience may be, it is a fairly common one and not dangerous in itself if the unlucky climber and his teammates are prepared and familiar with the basics of crevasse rescue.

Each glacier traveler should clip into the climbing rope immediately in front of him two prussick loops or mechanical ascenders with loops attached that he can step into after a fall. Packs and sleds should also be secured with a sling and carabiner so they can be removed and clipped in to hang by their own weight if the climber makes an unexpected descent through a snow-covered hole.

As this climber is doing, you should practice climbing out of crevasses so you will be prepared to handle the occasional fall.

Everyone fears he will be pulled into the crevasse if someone else on the rope falls, but that very rarely happens if the team members are careful to keep the rope stretched out between them. As soon as the fall occurs, the remaining two members drop into a self-arrest position and anchor the rope to a securely placed snow fluke or ice screw. At least one member of the party should cautiously approach the edge of the crevasse to make contact with and check on the condition of the dangling team member. An ice axe or pack should be placed under the rope at the lip of the crevasse so the rope will not cut a trench into the snow hindering extrication.

If the climber who has fallen is able, he should step into his prussick loops and secure his pack, skis, and ice axe to the rope below him or send them up on a hauling line lowered from above. He can then prussick out himself or be hauled out by his teammates. Speedy hauling is, of course, required if the victim is unconscious or otherwise injured.

Pulley system for raising someone from a crevasse.

To raise a crevasse victim easily, a pulley system can be rigged to gain some mechanical advantage in lifting the load (see accompanying diagram). Here's where the extra rope comes in most handy. The pulley system is set up by placing an anchor about fifteen feet back from the lip (1). The climbing rope runs from the man in the crevasse through a pulley attached by a sling to the main anchor (2). The climbing rope runs from the pulley back to another floating pulley attached to a short sling fastened by prussick or mechanical ascenders to the climbing rope near the lip (3). As the rope is hauled on (4), the floating pulley will draw back from the edge until the two pulleys are almost touching. At this point, a safety anchor (5), holds the load while the floating pulley is moved back to the starting position near the lip. The process is continued until the incapacitated member is extricated.

This pulley system for extricating a crevasse victim, which can be easily simulated almost anywhere, should be practiced until every glacier traveler is comfortable with the technique. Remember, it's cold and dark beneath the snow surface and there is little likelihood of outside help being available. So, you've got to be self-sufficient on the ice.

Glaciers are fascinating places to travel and explore; with a mastery of the proper techniques and precautions, you will probably be as safe on a glacier as on any city sidewalk. Be careful to keep the rope stretched fairly taut when traveling, don't bunch up during lunch or while making camp without completely probing the site for holes, and don't unrope unnecessarily. Cocky is the worst thing you can be on a glacier because the dangers aren't apparent, and the guy who falls in usually is the one who isn't paying attention or disregards the few simple safety rules.

There's a lot more, of course, to learn about the technical side of mountaineering and that's true for all of us, not just the beginner. But once you have learned and practiced the basic skills until you are comfortable with them, you will be ready to go almost anywhere in the mountains, taking pride in your knowledge and ability and enjoying the true freedom of the hills.

Edward Whymper in *Scrambles Amongst the Alps* offered the aspiring mountaineer of 1871 the following caution which can hardly be improved upon today:

> There have been joys too great to be described in words, and there have been griefs upon which I have not dared to dwell; and with these in mind I say, climb if you will but remember that courage and strength are naught without prudence, and that momentary negligence may destroy the happiness of a lifetime. Do nothing in haste; look well to each step; and from the beginning think what may be the end.

APPENDIX II

SOURCES OF MAPS, TRAIL GUIDES, EQUIPMENT, AND SUPPLIES

Topographical Maps

The following offices handle mail requests for topographical maps. If you are uncertain about the designation of the map(s) you need, first write for a free index map of the state or province where you will be hiking.

Distribution Section
USGS
1200 Eads Street
Arlington, VA 22202

Maps of areas east of the Mississippi River

Distribution Section
USGS
Box 25286, Federal Center
Denver, CO 80225

Maps of areas west of the Mississippi River

Alaska Distribution Section
USGS
Box 12, Federal Building
101 12th Avenue
Fairbanks, AK 99701

Alaskan maps

Map Distribution Office
Department of Mines and
  Technical Surveys
Ottawa
Ontario, Canada K1A OH3

Canadian maps

Topographical maps may be obtained in person from the USGS Public Inquiries Offices whose addresses are listed below. These offices do not handle mail requests.

508 West Second Avenue
Anchorage, AK 99501

7638 Federal Building
300 North Los Angeles Street
Los Angeles, CA 90012

Room 122, Building 3 (MS 33)
345 Middlefield Road
Menlo Park, CA 94205

504 Custom House
555 Battery Street
San Francisco, CA 94111

169 Federal Building
1961 Stout Street
Denver, CO 80294

1028 General Services Building
19th and F Streets, N.W.
Washington, DC 20244

1C-45 Federal Building
1100 Commerce Street
Dallas, TX 75242

8105 Federal Building
125 South State Street
Salt Lake City, UT 84138

302 National Center
Room 1C 402
Reston, VA 22092

678 U.S. Court House
920 West Riverside Avenue
Spokane, WA 99201

Trail Guides and Information

Appalachian Trail Conference
  System
1718 N Street, N.W.
Washington, DC 20036

Guides to 2,000-mile Appalachian Trail running from Maine to Georgia

Backpacker Books
Wilderness Bookstore
Bedford Hills, NY 10507

Catalog of books and hiking guides

Colorado Mountain Club
2530 W. Alameda Avenue
Denver, CO 80219

Information on 3,000-mile Rocky Mountain Route along the Continental Divide from Canada to Mexico

Keystone Trails Association
P. O. Box 144
Concordville, PA 19331

Guide to trails in Pennsylvania (Enclose $0.25)

Pacific Crest Trail System
   Conference
Hotel Green
Pasadena, CA 91109

Guides to 2,300-mile Pacific
Crest Trail from Cascades
to Mexico

Signpost Books
8912 192nd Street, SW
Edmonds, WA 98020

Guides to many areas

Wilderness Press
2400 Bancroft Way
Berkeley, CA 94704

Guides to many areas

Equipment and Supplies
   The following stores and manufacturers will send catalogs upon request. Those marked with an * have additional retail stores; write for a list of their locations.

L. L. Bean
Freeport, ME 04033

General outdoors gear and
clothing

Because It's There
Whittaker / O'Malley, Inc.
1000 1st Ave., South
Seattle, WA 98134

General camping gear and
clothing

Coleman Company, Inc.
250 North St. Francis
Wichita, KS 67201

Stoves and other gear

Damart
1811 Woodbury Avenue
Portsmouth, NH 03805

Thermolactyl underwear and other
cold-weather clothes

Early Winter, Ltd.
110 Prefontaine Place South
Seattle, WA 98104

General backpacking gear

*Eastern Mountain Sports
Vose Farm Road
Peterborough, NH 03458

General backpacking gear (most
stores also rent skis, tents,
backpacks, and other gear)

*Eddie Bauer
Fifth & Union
Seattle, WA 98101

*General outdoors gear
and clothing*

Granite Stairway Mountaineering
120 Woodland Avenue
Reno, NV 89523

*Natural food dinners and
camping gear*

Mountain House
Oregon Freeze Dry Foods, Inc.
P. O. Box 1048
Albany, OR 97321

Freeze-dried foods

The North Face
1234 Fifth Street
Berkeley, CA 94710

Tents and outdoor wear

*Recreational Equipment, Inc.
P.O. Box C-88125
Seattle, WA 98188

*General backpacking and
expedition gear*

BIBLIOGRAPHY

Acerrano, Anthony. *The Outdoorsman's Emergency Manual.* Tulsa: Winchester Press, 1976.

Aleith, R.C. *Basic Rock Climbing.* Rev. ed. New York: Charles Scribner's Sons, 1975.

Backpacker Magazine. For subscription information write, P.O. Box 2784, Boulder, CO 80321.

Banks, Mike. *Mountain Climbing for Beginners.* New York: Stein & Day, 1978.

Bridge, Raymond. *America's Backpacking Book.* New York: Charles Scribner's Sons, 1973.

Chouinard, Yvon. *Climbing Ice.* San Francisco: Sierra Club Books, 1978.

Darvill, Fred T. *Mountaineering Medicine: A Wilderness Medical Guide.* 9th ed. Mt. Vernon, WA: Darvill Outdoor Pubns., 1979.

Emergency Family First Aid Guide. New York: Simon & Schuster, 1972.

Ferber, Peggy, ed. *Mountaineering, The Freedom of the Hills.* 3rd ed. Seattle: Mountaineers Books, 1976.

Fletcher, Colin. *The New Complete Walker.* New York: Alfred A. Knopf, 1978.

Footnotes Newsletter. For subscription information write, P.O. Box 2784, Boulder, CO 80321.

Gebhardt, Dennis. *A Backpacking Guide to the Weminuche Wilderness.* Durango, CO: Basin Reproduction & Printing, 1978.

Hackett, Peter H. *Mountain Sickness: Prevention, Recognition and Treatment.* Available from American Alpine Club, 113 90th St., New York, NY 10028.

Jensen, Clayne R. *Winter Touring: Cross-Country Skiing & Snowshoeing*. Minneapolis: Burgess Publishing, 1977.

Jerome, John. *On Mountains: Thinking About Terrain*. New York: McGraw-Hill, 1979.

Kemsley, William, and Backpacker Magazine Editors. *Backpacking Equipment Buyer's Guide*. New York: Macmillan, 1978.

Kjellstrom, Bjorn. *Be Expert With Map & Compass: The Orienteering Handbook*. New York: Charles Scribner's Sons, 1976.

LaChapelle, Edward R. *ABC of Avalanche Safety*. Seattle: Mountaineers Books, 1978.

Landi, Val. *Great Outdoors Guide*. New York: Bantam Books, 1979.

Lyman, Tom, with Riviere, Bill. *The Field Book of Mountaineering and Rock Climbing*. Tulsa: Winchester Press, 1975.

Manning, Harvey. *Backpacking, One Step at a Time*. New York: Random House, 1980.

Martinelli, Pete, and Perla, Ron. *Avalance Handbook*. Agricultural Handbook No. 489. Available from U. S. Government Printing Office, Washington, DC 20402.

Nienhueser, Helen. *55 Ways to the Wilderness in Southcentral Alaska*. Rev. ed. Seattle: Mountaineers and Mountaineering Club of Alaska, 1978.

Petzoldt, Paul. *The Wilderness Handbook*. New York: W.W. Norton, 1974.

Riley, Michael J. *Mountain Camping*. Chicago: Contemporary Books, 1979.

Riviere, Bill, with the staff of L.L. Bean. *The L.L. Bean Guide to the Outdoors*. New York: Random House, 1981.

Robbins, Royal. *Basic Rockcraft and Advanced Rockcraft*. Glendale, CA: La Siesta Press, 1973.

Sax, Joseph L. *Mountains Without Handrails: Reflections on the National Parks*. Ann Arbor, MI: Univ. of Michigan Press, 1980.

Schipf, Robert G. *Outdoor Recreation*. Littleton, CO: Libraries Unlimited, 1976.

Schreiber, Lee, and Backpacking Journal Editors. *Backpacking*. New York: Stein & Day, 1978.

Schuh, Dwight R. *Modern Survival*. New York: David McKay, 1979.

Smith, Howard E., Jr. *The Complete Beginner's Guide to Mountain Climbing*. Garden City, NY: Doubleday, 1977.

Stebbins, Ray. *Cold-Weather Camping*. Rev. ed. Chicago: Contemporary Books, 1979.

Thomas, Lynn. *The Backpacking Woman*. Garden City, NY: Doubleday, 1980.

BIBLIOGRAPHY

Wheelock, Walt. *Ropes, Knots and Slings for Climbers.* Glendale, CA: La Siesta Press, 1967.

Wilkerson, James A., ed. *Medicine for Mountaineering.* Rev. ed. Seattle: Mountaineers Books, 1975.

INDEX

A

Acclimatization, 138–140, 202
Acute mountain sickness,
 symptoms, treatment, and
 prevention of, 118, 138–139,
 140
Adirondack Mountain Club,
 The, 6
Air masses
 effects of, on weather, 124–125
 in United States, 125
Airlines, commercial, 13
 traveling on, with equipment,
 17–18, 98
Airplanes, chartered, 13–17
 capacity and weight limits, 15
 costs of, 14–15
Alaska
 climate of, 125
 geographic features in, 7
 thunderstorms in, 125–126, 130
Altitude
 and blood oxygen, 201
 and carbon monoxide
  poisoning, 201–202
 and hiking time, 32, 33
Altitude sickness, symptoms,
 treatment, and prevention of,
 118, 138–140
Alum-a-Shoe, 181–182
Animals, wild, 166–172. *See also*

Bears; Moose. keeping out of
 camp, 166–167, 171–172
Anorak, 73
Appalachian Mountain Club, 6
Appalachian Trail, 5
Arctic National Wildlife Range
 permits and regulations for, 9
 photo, 177
Aufeis, traveling on, 165
Avalanches, 209–216
 accidents in, 209
 detecting, 210, 211–213, 233
 slope angle and, 213–214, 233
 surviving, 215–216
 terrain prone to, 212–213, 215
 types of, 210–211

B

Backpack(s), 77–82. *See also*
 Softpack(s)
 attaching pack to frame, 78, 80
 design of, 77–78, 79
 external vs. internal frame,
  77–78
 keeping dry, 78–79
 lifting, 122
 packing, 78, 79–81
 weight of, loaded, 81–82
 for winter use, 198–199

INDEX

Backpacking
  alone, dangers of, 46–47
  alpine, attractions of, xiii–xv,
    217
  beginner's problems, 21
  children and, 25
  in groups, 43–46
  older persons and, 24
  physical conditioning for,
    21–25
Balaclava, 75
Batteries, comparisons of, 110
Baxter State Park, regulations
  in, 10
Bears
  deterring with whistle, 109–110,
    169–170
  encounters with, 44, 169–170,
    172
  keeping out of camp, 171–172
  prevalence of, 169
  in springtime, 170–171
Belaying
  in rock climbing, 225–227
  on snow and ice, 232
  during stream crossings, 159
Blisters
  causes of, 64
  preventing, 64, 117
Bollard, 230
Bones, broken, first aid for, 145
Boots, 61–66
  care of 56, 57, 58, 63, 191
  construction of, 61–62
  cross-country skiing, 65, 190
  fitting, 63–64
  mountaineering, 222
  types of, 62, 63, 64–66, 222
  vapor barrier, 65–66, 143
  waterproofing of, 63
  for winter, 65–66, 143
Boulders, traveling on, 150–151

Bowline knot, 159, 220, 221
Brooks Range
  photo, 84
  vegetation in, 3–4
Burns, first aid for, 144
Bush pilots, locating, 13, 14

C

Cagoules, 72
Calories
  in different foods, 105
  required while hiking, 106
Camp
  breaking, 176–177
  setting up, 174–176
  sites for, 10, 173, 203
Campfire, location of, 174
Campgrounds, near cities in
  mountains, 19–20
Campsites
  locations for, 10, 173
  locations for, in winter, 203,
    208
Carabiners, 159, 160, 223
Carbon monoxide poisoning
  altitude and, 201–202
  prevention of, 102, 140
  symptoms of, 102, 140, 201
  treatment of, 140–141
  in winter, dangers of, 201
Cerebral edema, symptoms,
  treatment, and prevention
  of, 140
Children, backpacking with, 25
Chilkoot Pass, photo, 129
Chinooks, 126
Chitistone Glacier, photo, 78
Chitistone Goat Trail, photo,
  88, 151
Chocks, 223, 224
Chugach Mountains, photo, 157

sources of information about,
54–55, 239–240
variety of, 53–54
Eureka Sentinel tent, 86
Eyes, protection of, 111–112, 135

F

Fatigue, avoiding, 136
Figure-eight knot, 220, 221
First aid
for altitude sickness, 138–140
for broken bones, 145
for burns, 144
for carbon monoxide
poisoning, 140–141
courses and books about, 117,
146
for dehydration, 136
for frostbite, 144
for heat exhaustion, 137
for heatstroke, 134
for hypothermia, 142–143
kit, contents of, 117–118
for lightning victim, 145–146
for snakebite, 146–147
for sprains, 145
Flash floods, 132–133
Flashlight, 110
Fog, traveling in, 128
Food, 104–108
airdropping, 16, 82
calories in, 105
checklist of, 59
daily requirements for, 106,
136
problem of carrying enough,
16, 81–82, 104–105
selection of, 106–108
storage of, in camp, 166–167,
171–172, 176
for winter backpacking, 202
French method, 232-233

Front-pointing, 233
Frostbite
and dehydration, 143
symptoms, treatment, and
prevention of, 143–144
Fuel. *See* Stove fuel(s)

G

Gaiters, 65, 190
Garbage, disposal of, 49, 202
Glaciers
crevasses in, escaping from,
234–236
terminology of, 154, 155
traveling on, 154, 233–234, 236
Glissading, techniques of, 153,
231–232
Globetrotter stove, 97
Gloves, 74
Gore-Tex
development of, 70
pros and cons of, 70–71, 87
Greasewool, 71
Great Smoky Mountain National
Park, permits and regulations
for, 8–9
Ground pad(s)
effect of cold on, 95, 204
size of, 95
types of, 94–95
for winter use, 204
Groundcover, alpine, traveling
on, 148–149

H

Head gear, 75–76
Headlamp, 110–111
Heartburn, 137
Heat exhaustion, symptoms,
treatment, and prevention of,
75, 137, 138